The Rise of the National Basketball Association

The Rise
of the
National
Basketball
Association

DAVID GEORGE SURDAM

UNIVERSITY OF ILLINOIS PRESS

Urbana, Chicago, and Springfield

Library of Congress Cataloging-in-Publication Data
Surdam, David G. (David George)
The rise of the National Basketball Association /
David G. Surdam.
p.   cm.
Includes bibliographical references and index.
ISBN 978-0-252-03713-9 (hardcover : alk. paper) —
ISBN 978-0-252-07866-8 (pbk. : alk. paper) —
ISBN 978-0-252-09424-8 (e-book)
1. National Basketball Association—History. I. Title.
GV885.515.N37S87   2012
796.323'64—dc23   2012009723

Contents

Acknowledgments

A large number of people provided help along the way in completing this manuscript. As always, few authors work in isolation.

Several curators and research librarians provided crucial material. Thanks to Matt L. Zeysing, historian and archivist, and Kip Fonsh, curatorial assistant, of the Joseph M. O'Brien Historical Resource Center, Naismith Memorial Basketball Hall of Fame for their help in unearthing BAA and NBA financial data. George Rugg, curator of the Joyce Sports Collection at Notre Dame University, once again supplied access and guidance to sports periodicals and team programs.

Librarians at the Multnomah County Library, Gregory Heights Branch; University of Oregon; and University of Chicago helped me in tracking down articles and sources. Robert W. Fogel's office staff graciously provided me computer access while editing a previous rendition of this book. Mark Watson of the University of Oregon Knight Library provided some computer and printing resources during a research visit there.

Graduate research assistant Ling Ling Cao printed articles from the *New York Times*. Economics department student assistant Gabe Kalkbrenner helped with formatting the citations, saving me a great deal of time and effort. University of Northern Iowa Professor Ken Brown ran the fixed-effects panel regression equation discussed in appendix A.

As I was polishing the arguments and contents of this book, participants at the Illinois Economic Association and University of Northern Iowa College of Business Administration Friday seminar series provided helpful remarks. Professor Michael Haupert of the University of Wisconsin at LaCrosse provided detailed comments on an earlier draft of the manuscript. Two anonymous referees suggested significant changes to the manuscript that strengthened it.

The University of Northern Iowa's College of Business Administration funded research trips to Springfield, Massachusetts, and South Bend, Indiana.

Farzad Moussavi, dean of the University of Northern Iowa's College of Business Administration, and Fred Abraham, head of the Economics Department, generously provided encouragement and financial help throughout the process, including funding for the index.

A professor receives inspiration from a parade of good students. University of Northern Iowa students Trevor Boeckmann, Emily Goranson, Eric Sauser, and Jessica Kunzelmann were energetic and enthusiastic students both within and outside the classroom. Mr. Boeckmann compiled an interesting research paper on wagering in the television game show *Jeopardy!* Mr. Sauser and Ms. Kunzelmann were able officers for Beta Gamma Sigma, the collegiate business honor society. Ms. Goranson was one of the only students to get perfect exam scores in Introduction to Decision Techniques.

I had some excellent teachers along the way. Nobel-Prize winner Robert W. Fogel, David Galenson, and the late D. Gale Johnson taught me a great deal about research methods. My high school teachers Bert Kronmiller and Bette Hack imbued me with an enthusiasm for business methods. Ms. Hack transformed me from a "hunt and peck" typist into a competent typist, which has been a true blessing in my academic career.

Janine Goodwin edited some text early on in the process; Jill R. Hughes did a thorough job editing the manuscript and was a pleasure to work with. Kudos to Tad Ringo for uncovering a Sheboygan Red Skins program that resolved that the nickname was two words instead of one word (as previous historians have indicated). Sarah Statz Cords compiled yet another wonderful index.

My brother, Stanley Surdam, introduced me to basketball many years ago. His enthusiasm for basketball has enriched my life greatly. In addition, he urged me to become ambidextrous, a blessing for a short player.

The Rise of the National
Basketball Association

Introduction

The National Basketball Association (NBA) is a successful professional sports league that has either absorbed or thwarted at least three rival leagues. Its athletes are among the most recognized and highest paid on the planet. However, the league and its players were not always so highly acclaimed.

The Basketball Association of America (BAA), the NBA's precursor, struggled to gain credibility and popularity among the country's sports fans. While basketball was quite popular in the 1940s, and college basketball had shown promise as a spectator attraction, professional basketball still had an air of disrepute: barnstorming, uncouth players, and poorly lit (and often poorly ventilated) gyms or dance halls.

The BAA/NBA exhibited such "bush league" characteristics during its early seasons as relying on exhibition games featuring the Harlem Globetrotters; playing doubleheaders; using territorial draft picks of stars from local colleges; playing regular-season games out of town; and having teams fold mid-season. Some teams continued to play league games in high school gymnasiums well into the 1950s.[1] Even the fabled Madison Square Garden had its primitive aspects. Sportswriter James Murray depicted a situation not much improved since the Roman Coliseum's heyday: "Dressing Room 34 at Madison Square Garden was a dingy, bare place with peeling plaster walls, a row of coat hooks above a line of splintery benches and a bath and shower room that afforded no privacy. A bare-bulb overhead light shone down."[2]

Johnny "Big Red" Kerr remembered winning the NBA championship his rookie season. His Syracuse team beat the Fort Wayne Pistons. Because of a bowling tournament in Fort Wayne, the Pistons' home games were played in

Indianapolis. After Kerr's team won, they received some money and a plaque from the Optimists Club that read, "Congratulations, World Champions."[3] Players in today's NBA may well view the money from winning the playoffs as so much pocket change, but they do at least get a gaudy ring.

The league's greatest star, George Mikan, dominated the league in a way few players, aside from Bill Russell and Michael Jordan, have. His Minneapolis Lakers won five titles in the team's first six years in the BAA/NBA, as well as National Basketball League titles earlier. Mikan led the league in scoring three years in a row and finished second the next two years. Some observers believe the rule changing the width of the free-throw lane from six to twelve feet was in reaction to his dominance. While the lane-widening rule contributed to his drop-off in scoring, Mikan continued to dominate.[4] In today's media-driven market, he might have fared poorly with his glasses and bow ties. However, despite his mild appearance, Mikan was frequently hailed as the league's best drawing card.[5]

While shoe contracts may be de rigueur for today's basketball players, poor George had to wait until he retired to be featured in a Pro Keds advertisement. The yearly periodical *Basketball's Best: A Pictorial Review of the NBA* often had a full-page advertisement for the shoe company on its inside front cover during the mid-1950s. The Harlem Globetrotters held the spot for the 1955–56 issue, while the advertisement proclaimed the company's shoes were "tested by World's Champion Minneapolis Lakers" in its 1956–57 issue. Mikan appeared alone in the advertisements for the next three years before being displaced by top high school coaches and eventually no endorsements at all. The advertisement didn't even use a photo of Mikan in action; it just showed him wearing a jacket and bow tie. Be like Mik(an), indeed. By this time, Elgin Baylor and his high-flying acrobatics were available to tout the attributes of Pro Keds, but the company did not use the exciting new star.

Although the league survived Mikan's retirement and stabilized by the mid-1950s, vestiges of the bush league remained. Wilt Chamberlain's famous one-hundred-point game occurred on March 2, 1962, when the Philadelphia Warriors played the New York Knicks in Hershey, Pennsylvania. After the game, a photographer snapped the famous photo of Wilt holding a pen-scrawled "100" on a piece of paper.[6]

Historians of the NBA claim that college basketball's gambling scandals helped the professionals gain favor with fans. Associations with gamblers aside, professional basketball players appear to have been more innocent and less flamboyant during the postwar period than in our time. They seemed immune to the self-promotion that arose in the 1960s with the likes of Cassius

Clay (Muhammad Ali) and Reggie Jackson. Many of today's players would find 1950s NBA players to be stuffy and dull. The fans, too, appeared more naïve than fans of a later generation.[7]

How did the NBA transform from a tawdry collection of owners and players to America's third most popular professional team sport by the early 1960s, thereby laying the foundation for the high-flying league-to-be? What factors triggered the transformation: the twenty-four-second shot clock; the introduction of superstars in the late 1950s; or the movement of franchises to larger cities? The 1954–55 season looms as a pivotal one in the league's development.

The league's owners made a series of decisions that proved crucial in transforming the league. This book details these decisions. This is not a general history of the NBA. The book opens with a general overview of economic aspects of professional team sports leagues and the American economy before focusing on these decisions.

Economic analysis helps explain the rise of the NBA. Professional team sports are prime candidates for applying economic analysis. Owners and players were pursuing goals with scarce resources, whether of capital, labor, entrepreneurship, or time, for example. The ways in which they allocated their scarce resources among alternative uses determined their success or failure to a large degree. While owners tried to improve their bottom lines, players sought to maximize the gains from their NBA careers through better play and improved working conditions. The owners' and players' actions can therefore be viewed as the actions of people attempting to do the best for themselves, given their scarce resources. Participants in the early days of the NBA would certainly have subscribed to the reality of scarcity in professional basketball.

The subsequent chapters proceed in a roughly chronological order, focusing on the owners' key decisions during each period. The owners spent most of the first decade simply trying to remain solvent. They grappled with how to create sufficient customer demand to generate sufficient revenues and profits. Not until the late 1950s did the league's survival seem assured. Getting from its precarious beginning to a measure of prosperity was a harrowing ride for the owners and players and forms a cautionary tale on the hazards of launching a professional team sports league.

1

Economics of Sports Leagues

Owners in professional team sports leagues enjoy advantages that other business owners do not. The league owners are, in a sense, a cartel. Cartels are usually against U.S. antitrust laws. All professional team sports leagues have partial or full antitrust exemptions, thanks to the courts and to congressional legislation.

Not all cooperation between firms violates antitrust laws. The league owners must have a minimal amount of cooperation in setting schedules, arranging playing rules, and determining champions. These minimal activities, denoted by economists as single-entity cooperation, are permissible because they make competition possible and therefore benefit fans.

The owners are not content with minimal cooperation, however; they also seek actions that boost collective profits. These actions include granting territorial rights, fixing minimum prices, establishing a reserve clause and a player draft, and negotiating national TV contracts; economists call these actions joint-venture cooperation. Antitrust authorities would usually consider such activities to be beyond the pale of acceptable behavior. Thus, the owners and their appointed commissioners must persuade legislators and antitrust authorities to countenance such blatant violations. Sports league officials have generally relied upon an argument that such actions prevent ruinous competition and foster competitive balance, the latter being beneficial for fans.

In the early days of the NBA, owners' joint-venture cooperation manifested itself in two primary ways. Because leagues conferred territorial rights that limited direct competition from other teams, or franchises, in the same region, owners had greater discretion over prices they set for their product;

this price-setting power often generated greater profits than owners would have earned under more competitive conditions. Owners often stipulated minimum ticket prices as a backstop, lest some desperate owner slash prices unilaterally. The reserve clause and player draft bound a player to a single team. Under the reserve clause, the owner could trade, sell, or release a player at will. This power gave owners disproportionate bargaining leverage over players and generally suppressed salaries relative to what employers facing a more competitive labor market would pay. But there were limits to how far owners could slash salaries.

The distinction between single-entity cooperation and joint-venture activities is not without ambiguity. Tampering with schedules and playing rules were not always single-entity activities, as they both could be manipulated to generate additional revenue and profits. However, these manipulations were not necessarily joint-venture cooperation either, in the sense that, say, controlling players was. The manipulations of the schedule and playing rules often benefited the owners only by pleasing fans, whereas the reserve clause primarily benefited just the owners.

The NBA's turbulent birth as the BAA demonstrated that professional sports team owners' twin advantages of price-setting power over ticket prices and enhanced bargaining power over players were not sufficient conditions to ensure profitability. Price-setting power without sufficient demand could still lead to losses. The challenge was to increase demand, which would have led to higher ticket prices, more attendance, and greater revenues and profits. Greater profits would have enabled owners to pay higher salaries and to improve conditions, helping to erase any fly-by-night image.

To generate sufficient revenue, owners might have tried to create greater demand for their product by avoiding that bête noire of professional team sports: competitive imbalance. Some observers argued that basketball owners should have promoted competitive parity, not only through their draft of college players, but by using gate sharing (the sharing of only gate receipts) to shift badly needed revenue from the New York Knicks to owners of teams in smaller cities. Then again, as in many new industries, pro basketball owners may have decided upon a rugged individualist approach of winnowing weak teams. The basketball owners, similar to their brethren in Major League Baseball and the National Football League, found that relocating moribund franchises to cities with stronger demand for their product was a better tactic than sharing revenue from various sources.

The owners could have tried to create more demand by improving their product through innovations in rules, or by tapping a new pool of talent, such as African American players. Owners might have hoped that a new technology—television—might expand their market and fan base.

Profits

Similar to their peers in baseball and football, pro basketball owners are loath to reveal profits and losses. They are more likely to divulge losses, though, when they want the public to ante up funds for new stadiums. The pioneering NBA owners had yet to aspire to such bold actions as agitating for new stadiums, but their losses were real enough.

A congressional committee studying antitrust issues in 1957 requested owners of all professional sports teams to supply financial data for the mid-1950s. While all profit and revenue figures provided by owners should be viewed with skepticism, in this case there were some built-in checks. First, the owners may not have wanted to supply falsified information to a congressional investigation, especially since they hoped to gain approval of antitrust exemption. Second, the NBA owners lacked some of their owner peers' ability to camouflage profits. The original owners had not paid anything but a nominal membership fee when the league was formed. This meant they could not "depreciate" the value of their player contracts, a tactic pioneered by baseball's New York Yankees (although Bill Veeck of the Cleveland Indians took credit for figuring out the tax loophole). Subsequent owners of existing franchises could depreciate the value of the player contracts they obtained from purchasing their franchise. Given the relatively small franchise values of the early 1950s, this depreciation allowance would have been minimal. It was not until the later 1950s and early 1960s that franchise values appear to have reached the level of hundreds of thousands of dollars, much less than the millions of today. Even accurately reported financial data was not definitive evidence of profitability or of losses. Owners who had other business ventures could often decide to which venture to charge some expenses (and sometimes revenues). These owners had additional discretion over how much profit or loss to report.

The question of whether owners of professional sports teams are "profit maximizers" is an intriguing one. Owners often portray themselves as "sportsmen" (being, with rare exceptions, men) or "civic-minded." Undoubtedly the owners receive some satisfaction from fielding a championship team and may be willing to jettison some profits in order to do so. Owners might also accrue benefits for their other business ventures by creating goodwill via providing a city with professional basketball. League president Maurice Podoloff tried to allay congressional concerns that the owners were strict profit maximizers:

> Professional sports is not a business; professional sports is not a business, because if you look at these—if you look at these gate receipt reports and see the money they have lost, you must be an addict and a bit of a lunatic to stay in professional sports. It is something unusual. . . . And if we produce sports, we want to have an audience, and the receipts are a measure of our success. But I will tell you one thing; I have seen more than one team owner and manager come off the floor on the verge of tears. He didn't moan and groan because he had lost money. He moaned and groaned because he lost the game.[1]

Some basketball owners probably shed real tears over the losses they incurred.

Since many of the early NBA owners were poorly capitalized, even if they were not profit maximizers, they were undoubtedly forced to pay close attention to their ledgers. Owning a professional basketball team was not for the faint of heart.

Franchise values provide another clue regarding profitability. When an owner sold his team, the prospective buyer weighed the team's past profitability and its expected future profitability. If owners chronically experienced losses, they could either get out entirely or sell their team, possibly at a loss. If franchise values were rising, though, then the owners were probably making or increasing their profits.

Player Salaries

When businesspeople are losing money, they often look to trim costs. Like owners of other professional sports teams, basketball owners tried to keep player costs low. BAA/NBA owners held a major advantage versus their Major League Baseball and National Football League peers. They employed only ten to twelve players, a coach, and perhaps an assistant coach or trainer. Their entourages, therefore, were much smaller than those of baseball or football (which had thirty or more players and coaches). Even with the smaller rosters, BAA/NBA owners experienced difficulties in meeting the payroll for their twelve to fifteen employees. Unlike Major League Baseball, however, with its salaries in the tens of thousands of dollars, pro basketball owners were severely limited in how much they could reduce team payrolls, which had never been munificent.

In a competitive market for labor, employers must pay their employees "what they are worth." In economic terms, an owner estimates how much additional revenue a player will bring to the team, which, in turn, depends on the demand for the team's games. Such calculations, of course, are at best impressionistic. However, market forces tend to compel owners to comply roughly with this concept of paying market value.

Fans think high salaries drive higher ticket prices, but in reality it is higher demand that tends to lead to higher ticket prices. Salaries in basketball generally followed demand for the final product. If the league prospered, then player salaries would rise, even under the reserve clause.

Because of the reserve clause and the player draft, owners had salary-setting power over their players and could exercise discretion in how much they paid the players. Fans and envious sportswriters, though, often saw athletes as overpaid. Many pro basketball players earned more than the average American. Then again, pro basketball players were not average Americans. Few people would pay money to watch the best plumber at work, but thousands, and eventually millions and billions, would pay to see a top basketball player.

Basketball owners, though, were unable to reduce salaries too much, even with the reserve clause. All workers have a reservation salary, the minimum necessary to induce them to work at a particular job (or for a particular employer), so if an owner cut salaries too deeply, his players might opt for their best alternatives.

If owners were constrained in trimming salaries, they could have limited the number of players permissible on a roster. This tactic, of course, was restricted by the necessity of fielding five starters and at least a handful of substitutes, lest quality of play suffer. In addition, a tight limit on roster size typically meant cutting lower-paid players, resulting in minimal savings. Having a limit on the number of players, however, not only prevented owners of wealthy teams from stockpiling too many players; it also helped owners resolve the problem of being the first to trim a roster in times of financial duress and suffer from a competitive disadvantage from having done so.

Players generally benefited when there were rival leagues, such as baseball's Mexican League and football's All-America Football Conference (AAFC) during the late 1940s. Just a little competition could spur owners to suddenly find the means to significantly boost salaries even with a reserve clause. I discuss later how competition from non-NBA teams affected salaries.

Players could respond to the owners' actions by forming a union. While players clearly differed in productivity and popularity with fans, precluding the desirability and the feasibility of a uniform salary, they could create a monopoly of labor by uniting. By doing so, their negotiating strength would increase. When owners possessing monopsony power confronted a monopoly of players, the outcome would be indeterminable and would depend upon the bargaining strength of the opposing entities. This indeterminacy is one of the reasons negotiations between players and owners are often protracted and acrimonious.

Despite low pay relative to other professional athletes and a grueling travel regime, BAA/NBA players were hesitant to make significant demands until the mid-1950s.

Competitive Balance

Today's NBA fans take the league's superiority for granted. America's "Dream Team" of 1992, comprised of NBA stars, destroyed international competition in the Olympics. Although subsequent U.S. Olympic teams have suffered misadventures in international competition, no one seriously doubts the superiority of the NBA's best teams (in part, because they are comprised of the world's best players and not just the best American players). But the league's superiority wasn't always so pronounced.

In addition to establishing a reputation for having the highest-quality teams, sports leagues also battle the scourge of competitive imbalance. Did the NBA suffer from competitive imbalance, which might have adversely affected profits, as did many professional sports leagues? While sports economists have difficulty estimating the cost from competitive imbalance, the New York Yankees' penchant for running away with pennants during the late 1930s provides an example. The Yankees tended to squelch gate receipts by clinching the pennant early. After the pennant was decided, gate receipts fell for the remaining games.[2]

Although people discuss competitive imbalance, few have a precise definition of the concept. If the New York Yankees were not so successful, then much of the interest in the issue would vanish. People often dislike the Yankees' dominance of baseball, even though such dominance has waned somewhat despite the largest payrolls in the game, because it exemplifies the advantage a team playing in a large market has over, say, the Kansas City Royals. Indeed, the Yankees became the "gold standard" and the reference point for dominance in professional sports.

Sports fans can think of competitive imbalance by looking at the standings at any given time. What is the gap in winning percentages between the top and bottom teams? How many games back are the second-place or the last-place teams? In this era of many divisions with a handful of teams, these numbers are becoming less useful.

Sports economists use the statistical concept of standard deviation to measure competitive imbalance. The idea is simple enough. Suppose you invited some friends over for an exciting evening of flipping coins ("heads you win; tails I win"). You play an eighty-two-game schedule. On any given toss of the coin, you would have a 50 percent likelihood of winning, assuming you are tossing a fair coin and ignoring the highly unlikely event of the coin landing on its side. Over eighty-two tosses you probably would not win exactly forty-one games, but you would have a strong likelihood of winning "around" forty-one games. The standard deviation is a way of measuring the spread around the expected number of wins.[3] For the NBA's current eighty-two-game schedule, the expected standard deviation would be about 4.5. In other words, a range covering one standard deviation would be 36.5 to 45.5 wins (or .445 to .555 in terms of win-loss percentage). Two-thirds of the teams in your coin-flipping league should have records within this range. About 95 percent of the teams would be within two standard deviations of the mean: .390 to .610. This is not too far from actual league standings, so a coin-flipping league approximates a real league.

Not all sports teams are, of course, created equal. When the Los Angeles Lakers play the Toronto Raptors, the odds are rarely even. By comparing the actual standard deviation with the coin-flipping standard deviation (which I will denote as the "idealized standard deviation"), economists can measure the imbalance both within the NBA and across professional sports leagues by calculating the ratio of actual standard deviation to idealized standard deviation.

Economists James Quirk and Rodney Fort examined the competitive balance in the NBA, National Football League, National Hockey League, and Major League Baseball using the ratio of actual standard deviation to idealized standard deviation by decades.[4] They concluded that the NBA was frequently the most imbalanced of the four sports leagues, although they showed that the league was not particularly imbalanced during the 1950s. The NBA's ratio rose during the 1960s and was even higher in the 1980s.

What institutional factors affect competitive balance? The NBA had a reverse-order player draft of amateur (primarily collegiate) players (where teams select players in reverse order of their previous season's win-loss record), albeit with the territorial pick rule (where teams select players from local colleges ahead of the reverse-order selections), but no gate sharing. The NFL had both gate sharing and a reverse-order draft of amateur players. Major League Baseball also had gate-sharing rules but did not implement a draft of amateur players until 1965, although teams had control of many minor league players. Owners justified their blatant disregard of a player's right to sell his labor by claiming the reserve clause promoted competitive balance. They made a similar claim regarding the draft of college players, invoking the specter of a New York team getting all the best players because it had more revenues. Economists are dubious about the effectiveness of the reserve clause and reverse-order draft in promoting competitive parity, for reasons I will discuss. Scheduling, too, affected competitive balance.

During the 1940s and 1950s player movement was primarily at an owner's behest. Only if a player was released from his contract would he become a free agent. Ronald Coase won a Nobel Prize based largely on his work studying the effects of property rights in his paper, "The Problem of Social Cost." Economists have applied the Coase Theorem to player movement and talent distribution in professional sports leagues. Economist Simon Rottenberg anticipated Coase's more general theory with his 1956 paper "The Baseball Players' Labor Market."[5] His basic insight was that who owns the property rights to a resource does not affect the ultimate distribution of that resource. As applied to professional sports, the resource was a player's ability. The property rights could be assigned to the owner (reserve clause), the player (free agency), or a combination (owner has the initial rights to a player's talent but with potential free agency after so many years of service).

To see how the Coase/Rottenberg idea applies to professional sports, consider a hypothetical player: George Jordan (GJ). George combines the inside dominance of Mr. Mikan and the outside dominance of Mr. Jordan. He aspires, as fictional character Roy Hobbs did in *The Natural*, to be the best there ever was. Suppose the Sheboygan (Wisconsin) Red Skins have the rights to George Jordan. He obviously boosts both the team's record and home attendance. Suppose he increases Sheboygan's home gate receipts by $100,000 over the course of a season. The covetous owner of the New York franchise figures GJ could boost the Knicks' gate receipts by $200,000 per season. GJ is more valuable to the Knicks than to the Sheboygan team. There is an impetus for the Knicks' owner to offer enough money (perhaps camouflaged with the addition of a few throw-in players) to persuade the owner of the Red Skins to part with GJ. All things equal, GJ will be transferred to the Knicks. If GJ possesses the property rights to his talent, he can sell himself to any NBA team. The Knicks can acquire him by offering more money than the Red Skins or any other team. In either event, GJ ends up in New York.

There are two considerations in this type of situation. First, the cost of exercising these property rights must not be too high. Otherwise a friction of sorts deters moving players to where they are most valuable. One potential source of friction is fan antipathy to an owner of a team in a small city who frequently trades or sells his star players. While a team would usually lose attendance with the accompanying drop in its win-loss record, fans might further punish an owner by boycotting the team altogether. Second, if a team becomes too good, its gate appeal may begin to wane, and adding an additional star player would not be worthwhile. No team is likely to corner the market on all the best talent, because the incremental gain to its win-loss record would become smaller, and the impact upon gate receipts would begin to dwindle if not fall into the red. Even baseball's New York Yankees will not obtain the best player at every position.

As mentioned earlier, owners defended the reserve clause by saying it promoted stability and competitive balance. Economists see the reserve clause as not promoting competitive balance in most cases, but instead as giving the owner enhanced bargaining power in determining player salaries. Major League Baseball owners left one gaping loophole in dominating the property rights to a player's talent: until the advent of the reverse-order amateur draft, a talented high school or college player could sign with any team. The NFL and the NBA sealed this loophole early on in their experiences with their drafts (the NFL in 1936; the BAA/NBA in 1947).

Smaller rosters in basketball might mean that an individual star would have a greater effect on a team's win-loss record than in other sports (with the possible exception of quarterbacks in football), which might propel his salary above that of an NFL star—depending, of course, on the demands for professional football and basketball.

Aside from the Green Bay Packers, who were within easy driving distance of Milwaukee, every Major League Baseball and National Football League team played in a large city, while the NBA still maintained teams in smaller cities such as Syracuse and Rochester, New York, and Fort Wayne, Indiana. The New York Knicks did not share the city with another NBA team, unlike the three Major League Baseball teams that shared the city until 1958. The disparity between the Knicks' and the Fort Wayne Pistons' population bases might have triggered a larger disparity in win-loss records than those in Major League Baseball or the National Football League.

There are several factors, then, that affect competitive balance. Owners frequently considered the effects of their rules upon competitive balance.

Revenue Sharing

Many observers of professional sports think that revenue sharing promotes better competitive balance. Major League Baseball was often chided for its "stingy" revenue-sharing rules compared with the "enlightened" National

Football League's policy. Compared with Major League Baseball, though, the NBA was rugged individualism personified.

Sports fans and pundits believe revenue sharing would be the cure for professional team sports' woes. It seemingly makes sense to redress differences in teams' revenue streams, which are primarily made up of gate receipts and television revenue, that give teams such as those in New York City an edge in acquiring top talent. This Robin Hood effect of taking from the rich and giving to the poor, though, is neither straightforward nor necessarily effective in promoting competitive parity. The NFL, paragon of revenue sharing, has had its perennial losers, such as the Detroit Lions and the heretofore inept New Orleans Saints. Modern-day baseball, too, suffers from the existence of chronic losers, such as the Kansas City Royals and the Pittsburgh Pirates, despite an array of palliatives ostensibly designed to promote parity.

Economists studying revenue sharing have developed some insights into such plans' likely effects. They believe that gate sharing might indeed shift revenues from teams with strong demand to those with weak demand, possibly ensuring the survival of some weak franchise. However, they have doubts about such plans' effects upon parity.

In the simplest story, gate sharing lowers the benefit (marginal revenue product) of signing a talented player, since what gains in revenue he brings to a team are *shared* with visiting clubs. The end result may be that gate sharing suppresses the benefit, and hence the demand for and the accompanying salaries, of star players without having much effect upon parity. This may help ensure that owners of wealthy teams do not overload their teams with too many stars, but it does little to boost weak-drawing teams in the standings. In most cases, competitive balance is unchanged. This depends, in part, on an assumption that the ability to draw attendance on the road is negatively related to the visitors' win-loss record.

Owners, though, cite an earthier fear of a too generous revenue-sharing plan. As with the disputed concept of demoralization arising from welfare payments to indigent Americans (such as during the Reagan administration), owners of well-heeled teams worried that their less-fortunate fellow owners might be tempted to pocket their share of the gate while doing little to improve their team, a situation economists dub as "moral hazard." Major League Baseball implemented a more generous revenue-sharing plan in the 1990s, but in return the owners of wealthier teams insisted on a minimum payroll. Setting a minimum salary for players also presses owners to field minimally competitive teams.

The Robin Hood aspect of most gate-sharing plans, however, depends on having "rich" parties to transfer revenues from. In a league where there are differences in gate potential but all teams are incurring losses (that is, there are big losers and small losers), revenue sharing may seem futile, and perhaps detrimental, if it threatens the viability of even the teams that are losing only small amounts.

Revenue sharing, then, is not a guaranteed means for promoting competitive parity. How any such hypothetical BAA/NBA plan might have worked will be discussed later, as well as why the owners did not implement any such plan.

Relocation and Expansion

Gate sharing was not likely to narrow differences in drawing power among cities. Teams moving to larger cities had the potential of creating larger crowds and of bestowing a "major league" cachet upon the NBA. In addition, the league needed teams only in large cities, which, in turn, would attract the best national television contract. Relocating franchises might have improved both of these aspects, but sports league owners were constrained by geographic reality. Due to the lack of gate sharing, though, owners might have fixated on transportation costs, because they would not have shared in any gate bonanza that could have been achieved by a fellow owner who moved his team to a more lucrative market (such as baseball's Boston Braves' shift to Milwaukee) if this market was remote from the other teams. NBA owners were always concerned about transportation costs during the post–World War II period: at least they expressed concerns in their public pronouncements.

Los Angeles and San Francisco were shimmering locations that tempted baseball and basketball owners. Their NFL peers had quickly established teams on the West Coast after the war. Football, though, had a schedule of one game per week, while the other two sports featured multiple games each week, making traveling and scheduling more difficult. After the NBA shrank from seventeen to eight teams, most of the surviving teams moved to larger cities as the 1950s waned, but the teams frequently remained in the northeast quadrant of the United States.

Once the NBA achieved a measure of prosperity, prospective owners lobbied for teams. The incumbent owners worried that expansion to other cities might reduce the number of traditional rivalry games while forcing their teams to play unattractive expansion teams. Expansion also meant that incumbent owners would face more competition for players, reap a smaller piece of the national-television pie, and experience diluted voting power. Despite these potential disadvantages, incumbent owners knew that judicious expansion might forestall the entry of a rival league.

Increasing Demand by Innovating

Owners (and players), of course, are keenly interested in developing more demand for their product or service. Owners of firms generally try to avoid being perceived by customers as "perfect substitutes" for (and thus as interchangeable with) another firm's product or service. If two or more firms are perceived as producing perfect substitutes, none of them has the ability to increase its price without losing all of its patrons. Firms producing perfect substitutes are called price takers, because they have to accept the market prices determined by the forces of supply and demand; these firms lack the ability to set prices.

Avoiding the unenviable situation of being perceived as perfect substitutes induces owners of many products to create positive differentiability in their products. For instance, Coca-Cola and Pepsi have battled for decades trying to persuade consumers that their products are different from (and better than) each other. By creating brand loyalty, the two beverage giants can raise their prices and still retain some or most of their clientele. College students spend much of their time creating impressive résumés with the hope of convincing prospective employers that they are not cookie-cutter versions of other college graduates; they are trying to create positive differentiability by achieving high grades, taking difficult classes, volunteering for extracurricular activities, and making other efforts. Athletes, too, work hard at developing a unique set of skills. These efforts, if successful, can give the owner, student, or athlete a measure of price-setting power.

Throughout the 1940s and 1950s the NBA faced competition from college basketball and the Harlem Globetrotters. The NBA owners worked hard to convince basketball fans that their brand of basketball was superior, whether because it boasted the best players or because the league implemented rules that made the game faster and pleased the fans. Although basketball had been around for more than fifty years, when the NBA's immediate predecessor, the Basketball Association of America, debuted, the game had not matured into the high-speed acrobatics that fans enjoy today. Fortunately, BAA/NBA owners were not purists and proved willing to tinker with the rules to develop a more appealing game.

NBA owners, then, hoped to distinguish their games by introducing a host of new rules designed to create excitement and crowd-pleasing scoring. The owners would gain by increasing their price-setting power (by making the demand for their product less sensitive to price increases) if their innovations proved successful. As with any change, owners had to weigh the potential benefits versus potential costs from an innovation. Implementation of the NBA's twenty-four-second rule, under which a team had to attempt a shot within twenty-four seconds of gaining possession of the ball, meant buying specialized timepieces, which raised costs. Intangible costs could arise, too; if scoring proved too easy, fans might get bored or the games might lose credibility.

Discrimination

The NBA did not evolve in isolation, and the league was swept along by integration as were all Americans. Americans today may fondly remember the 1950s as a quiet, conservative decade, but social ferment was rampant.

Many Americans revised their attitudes about race after World War II. While the NBA lagged behind Major League Baseball and the National Football League in introducing African American players, the story was not one of simple racism. Today, of course, many of the NBA's best players are African American.

There are many forms of discrimination. Economists describe "statistical discrimination" as a case where decision makers rely on group averages when assessing individuals. Sight unseen, a basketball coach's first question regarding a player may be "How tall is he?" based on the obvious truism "You can't coach height." Early basketball owners might have believed and relied upon a perception that African American players were not good enough for their teams, but the evidence from serious competition belied the reality of any such notion.

Discrimination in sports can emanate from three sources, which are not necessarily mutually exclusive. Owners, players, and fans can be the starting point for discrimination that precluded African American players from participating in the BAA. Owners might have preferred not to hire African American players, whether out of ignorance of these players' abilities, personal aversion, or a fear that fans and white players would rebel. Under typical assumptions, economists (such as Nobel Prize winner Gary Becker, a pioneer in the subject of the economics of discrimination) predict that discriminating owners pay a premium to indulge their preferences, individuals in the favored group receive higher wages, and individuals not in the favored group receive lower wages.

This simple result leaves unanswered one crucial question: why did *none* of the BAA owners break the color bar until 1950? An owner without a strong preference for white versus black players could have hired black talent in 1947 or 1948, for instance. If his basketball judgment was sound, he could have fielded a competitive team at lower cost than his rival owners. To avoid such an unpleasant possibility, owners with a preference for white players could either get an outside authority (such as a government) to enforce a ban on hiring black players, or they could resort to an informal agreement not to hire black players. Although so-called gentleman's agreements have existed in American businesses, the BAA/NBA owners' later actions suggest they never held such an agreement.

If teammates exhibited prejudice, then teams of all-white players might compete against integrated or all-black teams. If black players were superior, then the all-white teams and their fans would experience reduced success on the court (but at least they would get to exercise their preference).

If fans rejected African American players, and if owners of teams patronized by such fans placated them, all-white teams would persist. Again, if African American players were superior or simply equal to white players, these owners would have paid more and put a less-endowed team on the court if they hired only from the diminished pool of white players. Fans of these teams might have watched their teams languish for years. Because Abe Saperstein's Harlem Globetrotters were so popular, and because talented all-black teams had played in tournaments and drew large crowds of spectators, fan discrimination might not have been a compelling explanation for the BAA's color bar.

Increasing Demand by Using Technology

Television revolutionized American patterns of leisure and culture during the 1950s. World War II delayed the diffusion of the new medium. The NBA warily embraced television. Television's great potential for businesspeople was its ability to eventually generate a wide, shallow demand for a product—that is, many people willing to pay a small amount of money for the product. In the past, artists and musicians who gained favor with a royal court during medieval times faced a narrow but deep demand: a few people willing to pay a considerable amount for their services. With radio and television, hundreds of thousands, millions, or even billions of marginally interested people could now be tapped. Even if these lukewarm fans were willing to pay just twenty-five cents each to watch a game on television in 1950s purchasing power, an owner could reap a handsome amount. Players, too, would ultimately benefit as the wide, shallow demand boosted revenues and raised a player's benefit to an owner, and, hence, the player's salary.

American Economy

Table 1 (see Appendix B for all tables) shows the relevant national economic indicators for 1945–61. While the American economy was generally growing during the postwar years, the first few years witnessed a bout of inflation, a rise in the general price level. America also experienced a baby boom as greater numbers and proportion of young males married and started families. If young single males were the best patrons of professional team sports leagues, then the shifting demographics might have affected attendance and demand as the 1950s dawned.

Conclusion

While economic analysis does not entirely explain an owner's or a player's actions, it provides a useful framework in examining the development of the NBA. In what follows, readers are advised to presume that owners, players, officials, sportswriters, and fans were acting in a self-interested manner then, as always. Individuals seeking their self-interest did not necessarily collide. Self-interest spurred the owners to institute both the twenty-four-second rule and integration. Owners, players, and fans benefited by these changes that made the game on the court more attractive; even sportswriters benefited. More attractive games and players increased fans' demand for games, raising attendance and ticket prices. The increased revenue enabled owners to pay players more, even under the reserve clause and reverse-order draft. All parties could benefit from improving conditions in the stadiums, assuming such infrastructure improvements were not too costly relative to the benefits.

Of course, there were issues of conflicts, such as player salaries and rights; owner competition for players; owner disagreements over schedules; and conflicts between owners and fans over relocation. The challenge for the owners and their league president was to adjudicate the competition and conflict in a manner that did not leave lasting enmity.

2

The Beginnings (1946–48)

The popularity of college basketball implied a potentially strong demand for a chance to watch well-known college stars continue their playing careers. Why not professional basketball? Major League Baseball, the National Hockey League, and professional football were enjoying the effects of pent-up wartime craving for leisure. Surely the time was propitious for big-time basketball.

The nascent BAA sought the two advantages of territorial rights and the reserve clause that other professional team sports league owners possessed, but the league faced competition from an incumbent league. The two basketball leagues contested just one or two cities and were largely able to avoid a ruinous bidding war for players, including graduating college talent. The low level of strife was unique to professional basketball and may have contributed to the eventual success of those teams that survived.

The BAA owners made crucial decisions regarding revenue sharing, team salary caps, and differentiating their product from the college game.

Conflicting Visions

The original owners of teams in the Basketball Association of America were primarily operators of large arenas in big cities looking for events. Most were associated with hockey, whether in the National Hockey League or a hockey minor league. Few, if any, had experience with basketball, with the exception of New York Knickerbockers representative Ned Irish, who had built his fame and fortune by promoting college basketball doubleheaders at Madison Square Garden.

The BAA owners faced a major obstacle: the rival National Basketball League (NBL), which predated World War II. The BAA and NBL would compete directly only in Chicago and, briefly, Detroit. The league was initially comprised of teams located primarily in smaller midwestern cities, although Chicago and Minneapolis eventually joined. Many of the teams were locally owned. In a sense, these teams' owners were similar to owners of Minor League Baseball teams: civic-minded, small-town businessmen who wanted to provide a leisure-time activity and possibly make some money.[1] Some of the owners were former players or managers of barnstorming professional basketball teams.

If they had so chosen, BAA owners could have studied the histories of Major League Baseball (MLB) and the National Football League (NFL). The BAA and NBL mimicked baseball's National League and the NFL respectively. These established leagues had different antecedents. William Hulbert proposed baseball's National League after a disastrous 1875 season for the National Association. Teams paid a nominal fee to be in the older league. Haphazard scheduling and large disparities in talent and population bases created chaos. Hulbert wanted a baseball league comprised of teams in large cities only (of over 75,000 in population). He also wanted owners to control players. His vision proved durable.[2] The American League would eventually mimic the National League by placing teams in large cities only.

The National Football League's immediate antecedent, the American Professional Football Association (APFA) was similar to the NBL, as it was concentrated in smaller cities, albeit in Ohio (Akron, Canton, Columbus, and Dayton), and larger cities such as Chicago, Cleveland, and Detroit, while basketball's hotbeds were mostly in Iowa, Indiana, Illinois, and Minnesota. While the teams in Chicago would anchor the NFL through its tumultuous formative years, it wasn't until 1926, when New York, Philadelphia, Brooklyn, and Boston acquired franchises, that the league began its transformation into "major league" status. The league eliminated most of the smaller towns, although Green Bay remains a relic of the league's early days.[3] The APFA also had haphazard scheduling. Since the schedules were haphazard for several seasons, owners voted at the end of the season to determine league champions.

Baseball's National League at the time more closely resembled what modern fans consider a major league, with its franchises only in the largest cities and playing a formal schedule. This was the model the BAA owners wanted to emulate. The BAA owners were concentrated in larger American (and Canadian) cities. The early NFL and NBL more closely resembled each other.

Minutes from the BAA's organizational meeting held on June 6, 1946, recount the BAA's requirements for its members: a franchise fee of $1,000; team salary limit of $40,000 (quickly revised to $55,000); ten players (revised to twelve and then back to ten); territorial protection for a radius of fifty miles (Boston/Providence being an exception); and an insistence on naming teams after cities instead of industrial companies.[4] While it may have been impractical, the BAA owners might have chosen to institute a minimum capital requirement. Years later, league president Maurice Podoloff testified before a congressional hearing that four or five of the eleven owners were well capitalized and could absorb losses. In his estimation, the remaining teams had a combined capital equal to the fourth- or fifth-best-capitalized team.[5] The severely limited capital of these teams placed their long-term viability at risk.

Sportswriter Leonard Koppett detailed the BAA owners' advantages over their NBL rivals. The BAA owners had established ties with big-city newspapers that would ensure publicity. The owners also had experience operating sports franchises. By focusing on recruiting college players, the owners hoped to avoid the ill repute associated with old-style, barnstorming professional players.[6]

As I will discuss in greater detail, the BAA had some disadvantages. While the teams in the BAA played in much larger cities with bigger arenas than did their counterparts in the NBL, BAA teams faced competition from existing MLB, NFL, and National Hockey League teams, along with a myriad of cultural venues such as live theater and music halls (see table 2). Would New York fans, accustomed to the likes of the New York Yankees, New York Giants (football and baseball), Brooklyn Dodgers, New York Rangers, and college basketball doubleheaders care to see players in a fledgling professional basketball league? Leonard Koppett also suggested that the owners, used to violence in hockey that excited fans and perhaps increased the crowds, proved too lenient in allowing rowdy behavior in basketball.[7]

The BAA's biggest disadvantage, though, was that the NBL had the best-known players, including recently signed college luminary George Mikan. Trying to consistently attract large crowds to New York's Madison Square Garden, where fans were savvy about top collegiate players, without possessing even a majority of the nation's best post-collegiate players was a challenge. In a way, perhaps it was best that Ned Irish had already booked Madison Square Garden with college basketball, hockey, ice shows, and other events during the inaugural 1946–47 season. The Knicks would play most of their home games at the 69th Regiment Armory, thereby avoiding the potential embarrassment of Knicks games being played in a near-empty Madison Square Garden.[8]

At least initially the BAA owners included a clause prohibiting non-league exhibition games. They hoped to avoid the bush-league barnstorming nature of the NBL teams, who scheduled exhibition games with all comers.[9] The BAA owners created a balanced schedule with equal numbers of home and away games for all teams, thereby avoiding the haphazard schedule endemic to the NFL's early years.

Koppett's *24 Seconds to Shoot* remains the standard history of the formation of the NBA. He relates how the hockey promoters turned basketball impresarios initially eschewed the gimmicky promotional stunts practiced by their NBL peers, such as free roses on ladies' nights and free-throw contests, although the BAA owners immediately approved such innovations as four twelve-minute quarters (to ensure that fans got a full evening's entertainment) and unlimited player substitution. The owners later considered fifteen-minute quarters but tabled the proposal.[10] The owners also relied on doubleheaders, often including a high school basketball game as the opening act. Even the New York Knicks had high school games prior to the, presumably, main event of the Knicks game. Sports historian Donald Fisher believes the BAA owners figured they were better off by concentrating on improving the quality of play in the league rather than on promotional gimmicks.[11] Besides competing against the NBL, the BAA faced the American (Basketball) League, a league with a longer history than the NBL, but one destined to fade quickly. The American League had teams in Philadelphia; Brooklyn; Baltimore; Wilmington, Delaware; and several New Jersey cities.[12]

The BAA's Debut

On the eve of the BAA's debut, Ned Irish stated confidently, "It is our belief that our efforts to introduce a fourth major sport will be stamped with success. In the past this truly American game has not been properly presented professionally, but we feel that we are ready to do the job correctly, backed by the major arenas in eleven cities."[13]

Ned Irish and the Knickerbockers worked hard to ensure a large crowd for the Knicks' home opener. The team had already won two of its first three games on the road. It took out a decent-sized advertisement in the *New York Times* sports section a few days before the game. With a headline reading "New York's Newest Major League Sport: Pro Basketball," the advertisement featured Stanley Stutz, who "Broke every existing scoring record at Rhode

Island State." The team listed ticket prices in the advertisement, ranging from $1.00 to $4.50 at Madison Square Garden. The smaller advertisement on the day of the game featured Sidney Hertzberg, saying, "This peppy performer made a good record as one of City College's top scorers."[14] The Knicks scheduled a fashion show and an exhibition contest between the Original Celtics (not related to today's Boston Celtics) and a team comprised of New York Giants football players. On the lighter side, Al Schacht, known as the Clown Prince of Baseball, refereed the exhibition game.[15]

New Yorkers had a variety of entertainment options that Monday night. The Knicks were up against stage and movie star Laurence Olivier as Henry V at the Golden Theatre. To watch Olivier perform cost between $1.80 and $2.40. Motion picture theaters were showing *The Best Years of Our Lives*, 1946's "Best Picture of the Year" in the Oscars. While the motion picture advertisements rarely listed prices, one theater boasted ticket prices of thirty cents.[16] The well-to-do could invest a considerable sum to purchase an RCA Victor television at Gimbels for $350. The cabinet measured 25.5″ × 14.5″, but the screen comprised a small fraction of the cabinet, possibly just 5″ × 4″. "Television now descends from the realm of the sweet bye and bye. It's here and now. . . . This RCA Victor television set is bristling with war-developed refinements. It's nothing like the distorted, wavering, blinking television you saw before the war. The pictures are so bright you can follow them with the living room lights on."[17]

The BAA's debut in New York City was a success, as 17,205 people attended the game, many of whom, however, may have attended on complimentary tickets. While this was less than the usual capacity crowd for a college double-header, the turnout was still encouraging. Unfortunately for the BAA, the large crowd was merely a cruelly tantalizing glimpse of a possible future. By the league's December meeting, the minutes reported that a number of the teams needed some sort of boost.[18] The league's first year was marked by small crowds and red ink, and although all eleven teams finished the season, a remarkable feat, many owners were discouraged. Three of the teams with the worst records—the Toronto Huskies, Detroit Falcons, and Pittsburgh Ironmen—and the Cleveland Rebels folded. Since this left only seven teams, the league was in trouble, although the owners might have taken solace that baseball's National League had evicted teams in New York and Philadelphia and survived as a six-team circuit in its second season.

Koppett's history details a growing rift between Ned Irish's vision of the BAA as a "class" operation and the other owners' desperate bids for survival. Although Irish was not initially keen on the league, given his success with college basketball, once in, he was determined to make the league a success. Perhaps more importantly, he and Madison Square Garden were willing to absorb losses in order to do so. Fortunately, they had sufficient capital to weather years of red ink. Koppett believed that the tension between Irish's and the other owners' outlook was ultimately beneficial, as the league eventually "succeeded out of their synthesis."[19]

The NBA's upheavals were due, of course, to a lack of revenues, which led to losses. While many new businesses may incur losses as owners introduce their new product, there was a limit to the financial patience of early BAA/NBA owners, many of whom had modest capital holdings and could not withstand prolonged losses. Owners might have chosen to sacrifice some profits or incur greater losses in order to pursue a championship, but they had to approximate profit maximization, or at least loss minimization, to stay in the game. The league's early turnover in franchises was proof of their inability to turn profits or to avoid losses. Whatever accounting methods owners might have desired to use in order to camouflage profits, the bankruptcies and exodus from the league argued against the likelihood of profits to conceal.

THE ANECDOTAL EVIDENCE PERTAINING TO LOSSES

The BAA/NBA operated on a shoestring for many of its formative years. As discussed later, the revenues were a fraction of what Major League Baseball teams earned, while some expenses, such as transportation, were comparable between basketball and baseball.

There are some almost unbelievable stories of NBA owner penury. As mentioned earlier, even as early as December 1946, owners expressed concern, as "some teams [were] doing poorly" according to the league minutes.[20] A few examples from Neil Isaacs's *Vintage NBA* give a flavor of the precarious nature of the league. Marty Glickman, play-by-play announcer for the New York Knickerbockers, recalled that Eddie Gottlieb of the Philadelphia Warriors was so cheap that visiting teams had to bring their own towels and soap. This wasn't Gottlieb's only penny-wise tactic. *New York Herald* reporter Harold Rosenthal recalled Gottlieb sending his players and himself to New York via three cars instead of by bus or train. Gottlieb would time the trip so that the team arrived at Madison Square Garden just before six o'clock so that they could park on the street. "One night they got to Eighth and 50th too early, about a quarter to six. The players said, 'Let's park in a garage,' but Gottlieb answered, 'Drive around the block a couple of times.'" Former Boston Celtics comptroller Eddie Powers related that one day, "The IRS came in. We hadn't been paying our taxes, and they said they were gonna shut us down. I said to them, 'Fine, just go ahead, shut us down, and I'd like to show you our list of assets. We have ten basketballs, twelve jocks, two sets of uniforms. If you want to go ahead and shut us down, shut us down. My advice to you is to let us keep going because I think we're gonna make it.'"[21]

Celtics owner Walter Brown hoped things would improve once his team started winning. With Bob Cousy, Ed Macauley, and Bill Sharman under coach Red Auerbach's leadership, the Celtics transformed into winners by 1950–51. Crowds remained sparse at the beginning of the 1951–52 season. Brown, known for a quick temper and rapid cool down, told reporters, "I'll throw the whole works out of the Garden [. . .] and that means all basketball, if something doesn't happen soon in the way of improved attendances. I thought that when I gave them a good club they would come out, but I guess Boston fans just don't want basketball."[22] Echoing these stories of penury, league president Maurice Podoloff chided owners for not providing paper cups for players to use instead of making them drink from a common water bottle.[23]

While today's NBA teams canvass the world looking for prospects, and college players are brought in for rigorous testing, the league's pioneer owners were too penurious to hire scouts. Sportswriter Ed Linn heaped scorn upon the owners for failing to do so.[24] As late as the 1950s, the Boston Celtics selected Sam Jones as their first-round pick based on a phone call from a friend of Red Auerbach. Auerbach had never heard of Jones, and his friend had watched the player only once. Podoloff received queries from interested players, including a University of Oregon graduate: "I am interested in playing professional basketball this coming season and if you should have a position open would like to talk or correspond with you about it." The player included a brief description of his playing career and listed some rather illustrious references, including former Oregon and current Yale coach Howard Hobson.[25]

Things were not much better at the league level. After Walter Brown persuaded his fellow owners to organize an all-star game, Maurice Podoloff and his publicist, Haskell Cohen, were discussing whether to give gifts to the participating players. Cohen said, "Maybe a pin or a ring." Podoloff responded, "Whatever it is, don't spend more than $2.25 each." The players were fortunate that the duo made a deal with a store for free television sets. For a subsequent game, the players each received a $100 savings bond.[26]

Another indication that NBA owners were telling the truth about their losses was the attrition among franchises. Suffice to say that of the original eleven BAA teams, only the Boston Celtics, Philadelphia Warriors, and New York Knicks survived. When the NBL teams joined the league, many of them succumbed, too. Joe Lapchick, coach of the New York Knicks, told reporter Al Ruck that the Knicks' owners were prepared to lose $500,000 on the venture. He claimed the team lost $100,000 in the initial season but that it was doing better for the 1947–48 season and might break even. He added that the games held at the 69th Regiment Armory were not profitable but that the team would add more games at Madison Square Garden in the future.[27]

ATTENDANCE

In the race between revenues and costs, BAA/NBA owners desperately sought revenue. BAA and NBA teams struggled to get enough revenue to defray their costs. The owners often lacked such basic team sports revenue sources as concessions and parking proceeds, while television revenues did not begin to trickle in until the 1950s. During the league's early years, gate receipts were therefore the paramount source of revenue. Gate receipts depended upon attendance and ticket prices. In several cases, owners played in such small arenas that they could not reap much additional revenue from hosting the best attractions in the league or from improving their teams. Raising ticket prices might or might not have increased revenue, depending on how many fewer fans would have chosen to attend the games. An increase in the demand for their product, though, would have enabled owners to experience increases in both prices and attendance, fueling a jump in gate receipts.

BAA and NBA attendance figures are sporadic and dubious. The BAA and NBA, as with their hockey predecessors, did not have gate-sharing plans for regular games. The home team kept all the receipts. Because the league did not force a split of the gate, it may have been less interested in official attendance figures than baseball or football. BAA owners paid money to the league; according to the league constitution, owners paid 5 percent of the gate receipts to the league, after deducting federal, state, and local taxes, with a minimum of $175.[28] The league therefore had good reason to keep accurate gate receipt information.

Researchers today are in a Wonderland world with regard to attendance figures for early BAA/NBA games, where the figures become "curiouser and curiouser." Keenly aware of the unflattering publicity surrounding the league's sparse crowds, Podoloff issued warnings to the owners even as late as 1949: "We are getting some very bad publicity due to the fact that some of our team managers are just a bit too scrupulously honest in giving attendance figures to radio and newspapers. If you can avoid giving the figures out, do so. If, however, you must announce figures, a little padding will be forgiven." A few months later, he followed with more advice: "One of the members of the Association recently released to the press the average gate receipts of all of the teams. I think it is most unwise for any team to release its own gate receipts to the press unless they are so good as to constitute good publicity."[29]

Whatever attendance records the NBA office and individual teams kept, such information rarely leaked to the public. The various sports encyclopedias often have comprehensive attendance figures for the NFL and Major League Baseball, but the NBA's are incomplete. Of course, attendance figures are just part of the story, since not all attendance figures are created equal. Teams offered different ticket prices, so a team with a slightly lower attendance figure might actually have reaped greater gate receipts, thanks to higher ticket prices or a greater proportion of higher-priced seats sold.

Major League Baseball and the National Football League owners may well have scoffed at the NBA's prospects. Certainly indoor arenas had seating capacities that were just fractions of the most spacious outdoor stadiums. When the Knicks boasted the then-record crowd of 18,255 for a doubleheader played in December 1957, this attendance paled in comparison to the ability of the New York Yankees to draw crowds of 70,000 or more.[30] The Los Angeles Rams, playing in the Los Angeles Coliseum, could boast even larger crowds. The entire eleven-team BAA's attendance in 1946–47 may well have been less than half of what the New York Yankees played to at Yankee Stadium during 1947. The immediate postwar period proved baseball's biggest boom yet, and undoubtedly encouraged the hockey-arena owners into thinking the time was ripe for a new basketball league. Although basketball's appeal increased, even by 1960 the now eight-team NBA had difficulty collectively drawing more fans than the Yankees did alone.

Since the NBL possessed the best-known pro players, the nascent BAA opted to build upon graduating college players. The best of these players would become well known to the public, or that was the theory. The theory was sorely tested, however, as BAA officials immediately bemoaned lousy attendance.[31] Even before the season started, some astute officials predicted difficulties. St. Louis Bombers official Emory Jones cited tough competition from college games and hockey, possible oversaturation of the market by the sixty-game schedule, and undesirable playing dates. He suggested a shorter, twenty-four-game schedule.[32] The BAA's early attendance figures were generally below 5,000 per game, although the handful of games held at Madison Square Garden averaged more than 15,000. The Knicks initially played most of their home games at the Armory, and the team's average attendance was around 11,500 for the first half of the 1947–48 season.

Table 3 shows the grim attendance figures for 1946–47 and 1947–48, as well as for the 1956–57 season. In the league's opening season, just over one million people attended games, but this figure included 239,000 complimentary tickets. League owners distributed the complimentary tickets to boost the crowds and to avoid the embarrassment of empty arenas. Historian Robert Peterson points out that only one team averaged more than 4,000 paying customers. The Chicago Stags were in particularly bad shape, issuing more complimentary tickets than the team sold, partly because of the competition of the NBL's playoff champion Chicago American Gears and George Mikan. The disappointing attendance spurred some owners to suggest offering doubleheaders, an idea the league would embrace years later. The net receipts amounted to just over one million dollars.[33] Compared with Major League Baseball and the National Football League, these net receipts and attendance figures were paltry. While the differences in stadium sizes between sports accounts for some of this lack of success, the overall picture was dismal for the hard-court owners.

Because most of the teams on the initial roster of BAA teams also fielded hockey teams, whether in the National Hockey League or a lesser league, the two sports might have diluted their fan bases. Sportswriter Dave Farrell attributed hockey's attendance doldrums to too many hockey games, but the possibility exists that the combination of basketball and hockey games may have exhausted winter sports fans.[34]

The NHL experienced a banner year at the gate during the 1946–47 season. A compilation of game-by-game attendance figures in the *New York Times* showed that the six NHL teams drew more than 2.5 million fans. The BAA owners, obviously, did not share in this bonanza.[35] Unfortunately for the hockey owners, the postwar boom was ephemeral. By the mid-1950s, attendance had slumped, although most of the slump was attributable to the Chicago Black Hawks. The New York Rangers, though, also slumped at the gate. Both teams were frequently mediocre at best. Ned Irish reminisced that during the postwar boom, "almost any show we presented was an automatic sell-out. . . . Money was freer and there were not as many television sets in operation. The basic interest in sports is as keen as ever but today it takes a top-grade attraction to fill the house." Irish admitted that Madison Square Garden's sports revenue had fallen by 40 percent compared to its postwar peak.[36] College basketball was rebounding from a scandal-plagued 1950–51 season while boxing attendance spiraled downward. At least Irish could take solace in the fact that the Knicks' average attendance at Madison Square Garden was beginning to rival the Rangers' average by the mid-1950s.

While New York City obviously had by far the greatest potential for draw-ing large crowds, the Gotham City also offered the widest array of entertain-ment options. Ned Irish was loath to jettison his lucrative slate of college basketball doubleheaders, as these events had made him a wealthy man, wealthy enough to absorb losses on a pro basketball sideline. Until the col-lege basketball gambling scandal of the early 1950s, in which players admitted shaving points by not playing their best, the Knickerbockers definitely played second banana to the collegians. Even with these factors, the Knicks almost always led the league in attendance. After the college basketball gambling scandal broke, the Knicks slowly gained ascendancy at the Garden. Through the 1950s, crowds at pro games there averaged well over 10,000 per date, al-though some of the dates featured pro doubleheaders. The collegiate games continued to attract decent crowds. By the 1952–53 season, though, Knicks games, especially when part of a pro doubleheader, were outdrawing col-legiate doubleheaders. Sportswriter Louis Effrat commented, "The powers-that-be are convinced that the play-for-pay game has arrived and if more of the same exciting bargain bills are presented, the NBA will be assured of continued success."[37] Sportswriter Joe King believed that "the Knicks in their tenth season, have only 20 percent of their attendance duplicated in college turnouts. They have built up their own following, with at least 25 percent of this a 'regular' fan group." King touched on a subject dear to Ned Irish's thinking: the still bush-league aspect of the NBA. By fielding teams in Fort Wayne, Rochester, and Syracuse, the NBA did not appear to be a true major league in the eyes of New York residents.[38] Knicks fans, though, did not avoid games with teams from those three cities. Indianapolis and Minneapolis also attracted some large crowds.

The Knicks' 69th Regiment Armory's capacity (5,200) was much smaller than Madison Square Garden's 18,000 (see table 4). Because Knicks execu-tive Ned Irish wasn't too confident about the league's viability, he hedged his bet by scheduling just six games at Madison Square Garden for the inaugural season. He didn't want to give up too many lucrative dates at the Garden for the uncertain prospects of pro basketball, although he had booked many of the dates previously. The Knicks would use the Armory for many seasons to come.[39]

Some of the attendance doldrums were preordained. When the BAA de-buted in 1946–47, although its teams played in large cities, some clubs played in arenas with capacities of only 6,000 or 7,000, including Philadelphia and Washington, D.C. When former NBL teams joined the NBA, many of them, such as the Syracuse Nationals (also known as the Nats), Fort Wayne Pistons, and Rochester (New York) Royals, also played in small arenas, but these teams were able to fill most of their seats. Sportswriter Bill Reddy wrote that league rivals lauded the efforts of the Syracuse Nationals' owner to promote crowds. The team built a base of season ticket holders and fought off a new professional hockey team in town. The owner set up a radio network throughout central New York. The Nats averaged audiences of more than 5,000 per game during the early 1950s, including a crowd of 8,700 in early 1950. The crowds were fiercely partisan and occasionally intimidating. Indeed, according to information the team supplied to the U.S. Congress, attendance between 1952 and 1957 peaked at 135,500 during the 1955–56 season. Then it slumped to 94,000.[40]

The Rochester Royals were another small-city team that enjoyed some success. The Royals relied upon loyal fans who bought season tickets. Owner Les Harrison had long fielded semi-pro and professional basketball teams. He was frequently able to fill Edgerton Park Sports Arena with 4,000 fans. The team later moved to a larger facility, the Rochester Community War Memorial, which seated 8,000. Throughout the mid-1950s, the Royals averaged 4,000 to 5,000 fans per home game. Researcher Donald Fisher presents attendance figures that were somewhat lower than those cited in the congressional hearings. The Royals may have included exhibition game attendance in their congressional data. Regardless of the true figures, even an average attendance figure of 4,000 to 5,000 was not capable of supporting very high salaries, unless their ticket prices were higher than what rival teams charged. If the big-city teams in New York, Boston, and Philadelphia opted to upgrade player salaries while banking on larger crowds, the Royals were ill equipped to compete. One Royals player, Bobby Wanzer, later mused that perhaps the prevalence of season ticket holders stunted efforts to increase the base of fans. As Wanzer recalled: "General admissions were eliminated in order to discontinue the long waiting lines of fans who shivered in the cold waiting for the ducats to go on sale only to have the tail enders find out that they were all gone before they reached the box office. The shortage of tickets, the long lines during the winter, and the decision to end general admissions alienated a significant portion of the Rochester sports community."[41] Harrison later attributed some of the doldrums to growing competition from television, blaming Milton Berle and Sid Caesar for dominating weeknight entertainment. He also believed that televising Royals games reduced crowds at home games.

A few teams suffered from antiquated "blue laws" that disallowed play on Sundays. Although Philadelphia's baseball and football teams won the right to play home games on Sundays, the city's basketball Warriors were not allowed to.[42] Sundays were often attractive playing dates for many but not all teams.

Ticket Prices

Attendance was just half of the gate receipt story; ticket prices were the other half. Teams with smaller stadium capacity might have compensated by charging higher ticket prices. Information on ticket prices is sparse; however, the collection of team programs held by the Joyce Sports Collection at the Notre Dame University has sporadic information regarding ticket prices.

The New York Knickerbockers advertised their games in the *New York Times*. The advertisements sometimes listed ticket prices (ranging from $1.50 to $3.50, including tax, in 1948). The newspaper also frequently provided articles detailing upcoming games.[43] The Knicks charged similar prices for games at the 69th Regiment Armory as for games at Madison Square Garden. The best seats for NBA games at Madison Square Garden were somewhat more expensive than box seats at Yankee Stadium during the 1946–61 period (see table 5).[44] The Knicks' ticket prices, even if higher than what New York baseball and football teams charged, did not generate sufficient revenue for the team.

While other teams might have charged a little less than the Knicks, some observers thought NBA ticket prices were still too high. St. Louis sportswriter Bob Broeg opined, "With the entertainment dollar more elusive these days, the BAA might do well to consider cutting prices that always seemed out of line for a new enterprise. St. Louis officials regard their scale of $1.05 to $2.55 as below average for the league. Yet the impression here is that the cheaper seats in the 14,000-seat arena aren't cheap enough considering their distance from the floor." Broeg urged formation of a "Knothole Gang" for children and instituting a Ladies Night, where women paid discounted admission prices.[45]

Table 6 shows ticket prices for three different seasons. The general admission prices were quite similar between Major League Baseball and the NBA. The NBA never had a class of tickets comparable to bleacher seats. NBA owners might have claimed, too, that they were giving more entertainment for the dollar than their baseball peers, especially since many NBA games featured doubleheaders. The table shows that most of the changes in ticket prices were, at most, similar to the change in the Consumer Price Index between 1947 and 1961, which rose during that period by one-third. Some of the teams even dropped the prices of their cheapest seats.[46] In any event, the NBA owners appeared to have maintained stable, inflation-adjusted prices throughout the 1950s.

The BAA/NBA's Non-Plan for Gate Sharing

Aside from sharing gate revenue from playoff games or doubleheaders, there is no evidence that BAA or NBA owners ever approved of gate-sharing rules in general. The BAA initially attempted to field teams only in large cities. While there were population disparities between New York and, say, Cleveland, St. Louis, or Pittsburgh, the owners of teams in these areas, many of whom were familiar with ice hockey owners' refusal to share gate receipts, probably figured these disparities were not fatal.

The New York Knickerbockers' early inability to stage more than a handful of games at Madison Square Garden certainly curbed New York City's population advantage. The 69th Regiment Armory seated only 5,200, and while Knicks ticket prices might have been higher than those in other cities, the disparity was not sufficient to give the team a large advantage. The other owners, then, may have thought the Knicks' gate potential was not much greater than theirs.

New York's Ned Irish probably figured he wouldn't come out ahead with gate sharing. However, given the number of games he staged at the small 69th Regiment Armory during the team's early years, it's possible that the Knicks might have been a net beneficiary from gate sharing, as were baseball's Yankees and Dodgers from that sport's existing gate-sharing plans.[47]

The minutes of the BAA's initial meeting in 1946 recorded that the owners "adopted [a] recommendation that each team keep its own gate." The NBA constitution that was adopted in 1951 showed no revenue-sharing rules, just a sharing of revenues with the league office (5 percent of net, after-tax gate revenue or a $175 minimum). These league fees were similar to a regressive tax. Teams that attracted small crowds and paid the $175 minimum incurred a higher percentage assessment. During the 1950–51 season, the ill-fated Washington Capitols paid 11 percent of their net receipts to the league treasury, while the New York Knicks, Minneapolis Lakers, and Syracuse Nationals sent in just 5 percent of theirs.[48] Since the referees received at least $40 each to work a game, plus expenses, much of the $175 went to pay them.

While the NBL had folded well before the congressional hearing in 1957, former NBL player Dick Triptow recalled that the league had a rule whereby the host team "was to guarantee a $400 payment to the visitors."[49] Other than this remark, there is no known evidence concerning the gate-sharing rules the NBL had included in its constitution.

The BAA/NBA had different rules for gate receipts during the playoffs. According to Podoloff:

> Each team retains 50 percent of its gate receipts, of its net gate receipts, and by that term I mean gross receipts less taxes paid to the Government or any municipal or governmental agency. The other 50 percent is sent to the league treasury. The league treasury, out of that other 50 percent, pays traveling expenses of the referees and their fees. It pays the traveling expenses of the players, their maintenance, and every possible expenditure incident to that. It pays for trophies and pays a playoff bonus to all of the contestants.[50]

Early in the BAA's history, some observers urged the owners to adopt a gate-sharing rule in order to succor weak-drawing teams. In recounting the St. Louis Bombers' difficulties in competing with teams with larger arenas, sportswriter Bob Broeg suggested the owners implement a gate-sharing rule. He had earlier urged such a policy:

> A definite weakness at present is the unwillingness of the strong to help the weak, the rich to aid the poor. Arena managements with large seating capacities and ample advertising budgets apparently will continue to resist suggestions that visiting clubs be cut in for a share of receipts in baseball fashion. The Garden, with its 18,000 seats, frowns at exchanging visitors' shares with, say, Fort Wayne and its 4,500-seat house. Baseball clubs moan, too, but it's a strength of the National Game that enabled the 1948 [St. Louis] Browns, for instance, to make more out of their 1,000,000-plus road attendance than their 345,000 at home.[51]

Revenue sharing did not save the Browns; selling the team's best players and relocating to Baltimore saved the franchise.

Certainly most sportswriters and fans seem to think the road to competitive balance is paved with gate-sharing rules, but the evidence is mixed. While sportswriter Joe Ives stated, "either you win or get out," his article showed that even a successful team like the Washington Capitols could falter at the gate and on the ledgers. Despite Red Auerbach's coaching and exemplary win-loss records during the team's first two seasons, the team went into a decline upon his departure. Ives attributed the team's failure to poor attendance and suggested that gate sharing might have saved it.[52] If basketball fans preferred to see the best teams as opponents for their home-team favorites, then Ives might have been right. The Capitols likely could have drawn enough on the road to be a net beneficiary of a gate-sharing rule.

Years later, sports economist Gerald Scully blamed the inequitable distribution of revenues as "the major source of all the problems that are currently facing professional sports." He claimed that revenue sharing would reduce player movement and franchise shifts and would lead to more carefully designed expansion. In the same article as Scully's comment, some owners disagreed with his viewpoint. Milwaukee Bucks president Jim Fitzgerald echoed the owners' refrain, saying, "There is a very real limit to the economic benefits of revenue sharing. Basketball, like any other product, particularly a product that competes for the discretionary dollar, must be promoted and sold. With excessive revenue sharing, the incentive to promote and field competitive teams is dulled."[53]

In the 1970s, when the American Basketball Association was seeking congressional approval to merge with the NBA, Kentucky Colonels owner Wendell Cherry testified before a committee chaired by Congressman Emanuel Celler, arch-foe of profit-seeking businesspeople. Celler questioned Cherry as to why the ABA (and NBA) did not have gate-sharing rules. Although Celler represented a New York City district, he thought the Knicks should subsidize teams with smaller arenas and population bases. Cherry admitted the ABA had a 15 percent gate-sharing rule for its first three seasons, but those owners rescinded the rule in the wake of pervasive losses. He stated:

> I think that the whole concept of gate sharing as some kind of magical solution to the economic disaster is foolish when you consider that this league, in five years of existence[,] has lost $20 million. Not a single club has made a dime in any given year. Gate sharing might be—and I think it should be in the province of the clubs—a viable approach to the question of helping weaker teams if you had a viable going business concern that made money. The idea of the nine ABA teams getting together and agreeing on 10 or 15 or 20 percent, when all of us are talking about disastrous losses every year, to me makes the question moot insofar as the ABA is concerned. We did have it and we did unanimously vote to change it.

Cherry probably revealed the source of the owners' animus toward gate sharing when he further testified, "When you talk about gate sharing you may be talking about dulling the incentive of a particular club which may not be doing its job. . . . what incentives do you produce in the club that may not be doing so well, to do better on its own initiative. A club can't make it in this business depending on another team forever."[54]

Owners' attitudes toward gate-sharing policies shifted with their circumstances. Eddie Gottlieb suddenly became a fan of revenue sharing when he

signed Wilt Chamberlain to a hefty contract. Some observers thought Gottlieb would have continued to earn a profit in Philadelphia, except for the
Chamberlain-sized salary Wilt was earning. Gottlieb complained, "Listen, I'm
paying this guy and you're getting rich off him."[55] Chamberlain was indeed
attracting large crowds to Boston and New York especially. Those owners
didn't want the Warriors to relocate to the West Coast, because they would
lose some lucrative dates with the Warriors.

Other owners' actions demonstrated malevolence toward weak teams.
When the NBA absorbed five NBL clubs for the 1949–50 season, Ned Irish
made sure that the Knicks did not host any of them, except for the Indianapolis team with its Kentucky and Olympic stars. He scheduled the other
"podunk" teams to neutral sites. His actions did not endear him to the other
owners. As Leonard Koppett pointed out, "There was no question of sharing gate receipts . . . but certainly the last group of National League teams
absorbed would have liked, and perhaps benefited from, a touch of the New
York exposure. In dollars and cents, Irish may have been absolutely right, but
his attitude didn't win him any allies among the owners who were struggling
to stay solvent."[56]

HOW AN NBA GATE-SHARING PLAN MIGHT HAVE WORKED

The BAA owners, some of whom were involved in the National Hockey
League (NHL), had three models to emulate. The NHL had no gate sharing. Major League Baseball had flat-rate-per-attendee rules; in the National
League, teams paid 22.5 cents on every full admission (later raised to 27.5
cents), while the American League stipulated 30 cents on each reserved
or box seat and 20 cents on bleacher and general admission seats. The latter plan effectively meant an average of 28 or 29 cents per full admission.
Baseball's revenue-sharing plans redistributed a much lower proportion of
gate receipts than the NFL's plan. Some sports historians believe the NFL's
"generous plan" fostered competitive balance. Football's gate-sharing plan
was less generous than the usual 60-40 percent split touted by these historians. First of all, the home team skimmed 15 percent off the top of gate
revenues for "stadium rental," an idea that may well have appealed to BAA/
NBA owners. The home team then paid the NFL 2 percent of the remaining 85 percent. The vaunted 40 percent share to the visiting team was based
on the remaining money. In effect, this meant the visiting team received 33
percent of the gate.[57]

Although many observers believe that gate sharing exists to redress differences in revenue potential between teams in New York and teams in smaller

cities, the owners' intent belies this.[58] Both baseball's and football's plans had regressive effects in the sense that weak-drawing teams often paid a higher percentage of their gate revenue to visiting teams than did strong-drawing teams. Baseball's plan was regressive because the flat rates per attendee did not address the fact that during the postwar period the New York Yankees got more revenue per attendee than did the St. Louis Browns, whether due to higher ticket prices or to a greater proportion of box seat and reserved tickets sold. Football's plan had a minimum payout of $20,000 per game. The football owners intended this minimum guarantee to be binding, since they had raised it several times. They enacted the $20,000 guarantee for the 1949 season and eventually raised it to $30,000 for 1968. The minimum guarantee meant that the struggling Chicago Cardinals paid a higher proportion of its home gate receipts to visiting teams than did the cross-town Chicago Bears.[59] Baseball and football owners appear to have been worried about fellow owners who might turn parasitic and live off their share of road revenue while keeping their payrolls low (and teams weak). American League owners castigated the St. Louis Browns for their frequent sales of players and terrible home attendance.

Major League Baseball owners made radical changes to their revenue-sharing plan during the 1990s. The most important change was to place the visitors' shares into a common pool that would be divided evenly. The earlier gate-sharing plans had the "perverse" effect of benefiting the New York Yankees and Brooklyn Dodgers. Both teams drew reasonably well at home, with the Yankees perennially leading the American League in attendance unless confronted by a Bill Veeck Jr.–run team in Cleveland or Chicago. The Yankees were such a strong draw on the road, though, that the team often ended up a net beneficiary under the gate-sharing plan. The Brooklyn Dodgers, while frequently leading the National League in attendance until the Boston Braves moved to Milwaukee, also benefited from the gate-sharing plan, as the team was a remarkably good draw on the road. Baseball's experiences suggested that a gate-sharing plan might not redistribute much money from the teams in the biggest cities to those in the smallest cities if strong teams attract bigger crowds on the road than do weak teams (with the underlying assumption that larger cities typically field stronger teams than do smaller cities). Winning NFL teams tended to draw somewhat larger audiences than losing teams, but the effect was not as dramatic as in baseball, possibly because of the greater proportion of season ticket holders in football.[60]

In the early days of the NBA, while the New York Knicks and Boston Celtics usually had winning teams, so did the teams in the smaller cities of

Minneapolis (Lakers) and Rochester (Royals). If basketball attendance was similar to that of baseball, then a gate-sharing rule might not have helped the bottom lines of the Waterloo (Iowa) Hawks, Sheboygan Red Skins, Anderson (Indiana) Packers, Tri-Cities (Rockford, Illinois, and Moline and Davenport, Iowa) Blackhawks, and Denver Nuggets. Irish had sixteen dates at Madison Square Garden for the 1949–50 season. Undoubtedly he could have shifted games with these small-city teams to the Armory with its seating for fifty-two hundred. The no-name teams might not have filled even the Armory. On the road, the Knicks, with their winning records, might have come close to filling the five teams' similarly sized arenas. Even allowing for differences in ticket prices, there is no guarantee that, given the circumstances, gate sharing would have saved the franchises in smaller cities. In the long run, having teams in these small cities was not viable, and, as ruthless and arrogant as Irish might have been, he probably was correct in a business sense.

Home gate receipts and gross receipts varied considerably between NBA teams. Even before the mid-1950s, BAA teams had considerable disparities in net gate receipts. Table 7 shows net home receipts for the 1946–47 and 1947–48 seasons. Given that most teams had payrolls in excess of $50,000 per season, some of the teams did not have much surplus after payrolls. The table shows how a plan for sharing gate revenue might have worked during the 1946–47 and 1947–48 seasons. The hypothetical plan assumes a one-third share of net home receipts put into a common pool. Teams receive equal shares of the pool. If BAA teams exhibited a similar characteristic as their Major League Baseball and National Football League peers, in that a team's ability to draw on the road was positively related to its win-loss record, then the common pool would have redistributed larger amounts to weaker teams than would a system whereby the revenue share went directly to the visiting team. Given that the BAA was hemorrhaging money, Wendell Cherry's remarks seem applicable. Throwing the teams from Cleveland, Detroit, Pittsburgh, and Toronto overboard instead of boosting their revenues by less than $20,000 each made more sense to the league's long-run viability.

Because Madison Square Garden hosted hockey and basketball, along with boxing, circuses, ice shows, and college basketball, open dates there were limited. Four of the Knicks' opponents did not play games at Madison Square Garden in 1946–47. Had there been a gate-sharing plan, teams stuck with games at New York's Armory would have received meager payouts.

The overall situation was not much improved in 1947–48, with the Providence Steamrollers and Boston Celtics struggling at the gate. Celtics owner

Walter Brown had sufficient capital reserves to weather his losses, but the Steamrollers eventually folded.

Gate sharing likely held little appeal for many of the owners who had sufficient capital to persevere in the face of continued losses. Those owners who were insufficiently capitalized probably would not have been saved by gate sharing.

Becoming the Best and Competitive Balance

As with baseball's National League in 1876, the BAA had to establish a reputation for playing the best brand of ball. This was especially crucial for drawing crowds in New York City, Boston, Chicago, and Philadelphia, where residents were used to the best in baseball, football, and hockey. Ned Irish and his compatriots envisioned a professional league based on already-publicized college stars. They recognized that the NBL initially had the best players. Over time, of course, the BAA owners could hope to outbid their rival NBL owners in acquiring the cream of the crop of future collegiate players. In preparing for the first season of head-to-head competition with the NBL, BAA owners signed a few NBL players and some top collegians, but the NBL held its own in signing collegiate talent. The BAA's salary cap may have limited the league in enticing NBL stars from switching leagues.[61]

Even the NBL could not definitively claim that their teams were the best. The Harlem Globetrotters were highly competitive even with the NBL's champion Minneapolis Lakers in the late 1940s. Some of the best Amateur Athletic Union (AAU) teams also claimed to be as strong as the top professional teams. Since several top college players passed up offers from both the BAA and NBL (Bob Kurland, Mikan's contemporary as a top big man, for instance), such claims could not be immediately dismissed. Other NBL players had initially played on AAU teams after college, including Don Barksdale, Jim Pollard, and George Yardley. Such AAU championship teams as the Phillips 66ers (Bartlesville, Oklahoma) and Peoria (Illinois) Cats might have proven competitive with many professional teams. The Denver Nuggets team was briefly an AAU club turned NBL/NBA team.[62] Even strong college teams believed they might give the pros a strenuous tussle if given the chance.

The BAA owners and coaches scrambled to find players before starting the league's inaugural 1946–47 season. Many of the teams were hastily thrown together. Since most of the owners knew nothing about basketball, their attempts to hire coaches and fill rosters were almost laughable.

Arnold "Red" Auerbach, a man with no collegiate or professional basket-ball coaching experience (he had coached a team of barnstorming profes-sional football players who were dabbling in basketball), brazenly assured Washington Capitols owner Miguel "Mike" Uline, "You need a coach. I can coach and I know enough guys to get a team put together quickly that will be good right away." Uline hired Auerbach for $5,000. Auerbach had met quite a few top basketball players during his World War II stint in the navy. In the parlance of the times, he dropped a few dimes making phone calls and recruited his players, including Bob Feerick, John Norlander, Fred-die Scolari, and Bones McKinney. In the latter case, Auerbach convinced McKinney that the Capitols would pay him the same amount as the NBL's Chicago American Gears. Since McKinney was from North Carolina, the prospect of playing for Washington and being closer to home proved allur-ing.[63] Auerbach proved adept at identifying talent, and the Capitols won 81.7 percent of their games, a percentage that would not be exceeded for twenty seasons. In an act of ingratitude and folly, however, Uline fired Auerbach after a few successful regular-season records and one championship series loss. The Capitols quickly disintegrated.

While a full-scale bidding war between the NBL and BAA did not break out, probably because of the BAA owners' decision to limit team salaries, the nascent league did sign twenty-three NBL players, including seven from Youngstown, four from Sheboygan, and four from Rochester. Youngstown had a losing re-cord in the NBL, but four of its five starters switched to the BAA. The BAA also signed a large number of untested players. Either the players weren't good enough, or they didn't enjoy life in the BAA, as 37.3 percent of the BAA play-ers never played another season in the NBL or BAA (see table 8). Part of this might have stemmed from the BAA's shrinking to eight teams the following season, but every team had at least three players who played just one season of BAA (or NBL) basketball. Less than two handfuls of the players had never appeared in a college game, which must have pleased Ned Irish. Of the thirteen players who carved out NBL/NBA careers of six or more seasons, five were former NBL players, including Kleggie Hermsen, John Mahnken, Mel Riebe, Ed Sadowski, and Dick Schulz. Mahnken and Sadowski were starting centers in the NBL. Schulz was a starting forward for the Sheboygan Red Skins. All three players, as well as Hermsen, were from winning teams in the NBL. Riebe was a starting forward for the Cleveland Allman Transfers, which ended up with four wins and twenty-nine losses. Teams hired and fired numerous players, as reflected by the relatively high number of players per team.

Another aspect of the BAA's initial set of players was the rampant provincialism. Owners and coaches appeared to have relied on players from local colleges. For some teams, such as those from New York, Philadelphia, and Chicago, such a strategy might have been sound. New York City was a hotbed of college basketball, while Chicago boasted DePaul University, University of Illinois, University of Notre Dame, and Loyola University. Detroit's players largely hailed from the states of Michigan and Indiana, with eleven of its fourteen players hailing from such schools as Valparaiso University, Indiana State University, University of Michigan, Michigan State University, and Wayne State University. The New York Knicks employed fourteen of their nineteen players from New Jersey and New York, including players from City College of New York (CCNY), New York University, Fordham University, Manhattan University, Princeton University, and Long Island University. The Providence Steamrollers featured five players from Rhode Island, while the Pittsburgh Ironmen had five from Duquesne University and a couple more from the University of Pittsburgh. The Boston Celtics, St. Louis Bombers, Toronto Huskies, and Washington Capitols went against the grain of provincialism. Red Auerbach had three Georgetown University players on his Washington club, but he also had four players who played for Santa Clara University, St. Mary's College, and University of San Francisco. The Capitols and the Bombers had very good records in the BAA's initial season, while the Celtics and the Huskies did not.

After the consolidation of teams in the NBA in 1950–51, players who survived the rigors of playing professional basketball had a reasonable chance of playing several years, as almost 40 percent of them would enjoy six or more seasons in the league. Only a few players lasted just one season, although this may have been deflated given the number of veterans remaining after seventeen teams shrank to eleven. The average age didn't increase by much. There were now just four players without college experience. Aside from the Indianapolis Olympians, with their University of Kentucky contingent, most of the teams were casting off their provincial nature, although the Minneapolis Lakers and Philadelphia Warriors still had four or five local collegiate stars on their rosters. Aside from Bob Cousy, the Boston Celtics, for instance, had players from the states of California, Ohio, Missouri, North Carolina, Oklahoma, and Minnesota on their roster. Rochester had three Seton Hall players and a CCNY player. By 1954–55, rosters stabilized further, and more than half the players would play for at least six seasons. The NBL influence was waning, as only twelve players remained from that league.

The BAA/NBA, then, needed to work on creating the image that it offered the best basketball to be seen. Red Auerbach, coach of the Washington Capitols and Boston Celtics, explained to Terry Pluto how difficult the league found establishing itself as top-flight basketball in the public's perception. "I had sportswriters tell me that Holy Cross was better than the Celtics. I said, 'Guys, you don't know what the hell you're talking about.' What saved us early was getting Bob Cousy. Then I set up some scrimmages with Holy Cross and invited the press to watch. We beat the hell out of Holy Cross, and that shut up that talk about a college team being better than the Celtics. But it still was hard to sell [pro] basketball to the fans."[64]

Some of the BAA's own players didn't help burnish the league's status in the basketball world's pecking order. St. Louis Bomber starter Bob Doll told reporters, "This might surprise you, but I think the Phillips 66 club, if it were in our league, might be the champion. They'd be tough for any of us to best, for they have what it takes in stars."[65] Ken Loeffler, Doll's coach, refuted his player's remark. "Our men are bigger, have had greater experience and have opposed better players. They are better poised and don't go frantic as college boys are apt to do. They have the usual advantage enjoyed by all professionals over amateurs. I would say that practically all pro league teams could take care of the collegiate teams." Loeffler also combated the public's perception that the "high-scoring" professional games implied a lack of defensive effort: "Fast scoring is the life of the game and of spectator interest. . . . Scoring today is built on fast action and improved technique and accuracy. . . . But you will never snore at a present-day [pro] basketball game."[66]

Whether any AAU team, such as the Phillips 66ers, could consistently compete with BAA or NBL teams remains a mystery. Since the AAU players worked at non-basketball jobs for much of the year, one is entitled to guess that their skills dulled over time.

Although the NFL's former annual game in Chicago with the College All-Stars usually ended in a rout of the collegians, professional basketball was not so fortunate. A Temple University coach cited the College All-Stars' success versus professional teams when the collegians won a sixth straight triumph over the pros by beating the Indianapolis Kautskys. Pro official Eddie Gottlieb quickly rationalized the defeats by replying, "That was a picked squad of college stars, some of whom had been out of college and played a year in professional ranks. And the Kautskys are only a fair professional team."[67] Regardless of the validity of Gottlieb's explanation, no publicist for the professionals would even want to have to field such a question. Eventually the Minneapolis Lakers so thoroughly demolished the collegiate all-star teams that the sponsoring *Chicago Herald American* had to relinquish the William Randolph Hearst trophy to the team.[68]

In the BAA's second season, the newly admitted Baltimore Bullets won the league championship. The team had earlier performed in the American Basketball League. With some NBL players and clever trades, coach Buddy Jeannette created a strong team. The fact that a team from another league could join the BAA and capture its championship did not bode well for the league's drive to capture public perception that it played the best basketball.

The Harlem Globetrotters loomed as potential claimants as the best professional team. The Globetrotters and the Minneapolis Lakers staged annual games between 1948 through 1952, with the Globetrotters winning the first two games and the Lakers the remaining five (two games were played in 1949). A final game between the two clubs occurred in January 1958, when the Lakers, sans Mikan, beat the Globetrotters 111–100. The first game, though, is of particular interest. According to author Stew Thornley, the game, played at Chicago Stadium, was the first half of a doubleheader on February 19, 1948.[69] The second game featured the New York Knickerbockers versus the Chicago Stags. The Lakers were not yet in the BAA, but the two leagues had agreed to share Chicago Stadium at times. The Lakers-Globetrotters game was an interesting contrast between the taller, and probably slower, Lakers and the ball-handling talents of the Globetrotters. The *New York Times* duly recorded the result of the BAA game but was silent regarding the Lakers-Globetrotters matchup.[70]

Some evidence arguing against the Globetrotters' superiority can be ascertained by NBA teams' experiences with former Globetrotter players. NBA teams began signing top African American players beginning with the New York Knicks' acquisition of Nat "Sweetwater" Clifton from the Harlem Globetrotters in 1950.[71] Even with Clifton, the Knicks eventually sank into basketball mediocrity, although the team did play in the championship finals for three consecutive years. The other early pioneers of integrating their teams did not become champions either. As the 1950s continued, aside from the signing of Wilt Chamberlain for a season before his college class graduated, the Globetrotters served more as leverage for talented African American players in salary negotiations than as top-flight basketball. The team began emphasizing entertainment more than true competitiveness (with the introduction of the Washington Generals exhibition team signifying the switch).

The World Professional Basketball Tournament, held between 1939 and 1948, offers a tantalizing glimpse into the relative merits of various teams. Right after World War II, the NBL's Fort Wayne and Indianapolis clubs easily defeated their rivals, the Oshkosh All-Stars and Toledo Jeeps. The Minneapolis Lakers had more difficulty in subduing the New York Rens, an African American club, in the final tournament. George Mikan scored forty points, while Nat Clifton, then playing for the Rens, tallied twenty-four points. The game attracted a crowd of almost 17,000.[72]

Ultimately, the BAA's biggest obstacle to basketball supremacy was the NBL's best teams, especially the Minneapolis Lakers and the Rochester Royals, who ended up in the same NBA division and could rarely, if ever, meet in the championship finals. During the first years of the BAA/NBL merger, top NBL teams dominated the league standings and championships. Many of the All-League players were former NBL stars. It took until the introduction of the twenty-four-second rule and George Mikan's (first) retirement for the old BAA teams to assert themselves, although, as mentioned, the New York Knickerbockers had a three-year string as runners-up in the championship series.[73]

By the mid-1950s, college coaches clearly understood that the pros were playing superior basketball. While urging his peers to adopt the pros' twenty-four-second shot clock, Howard Hobson of Yale said, "The pros have a better game, and we may as well admit it."[74] Sportswriter Jeremiah Tax was explicit: "On the rosters of the eight teams are 80-odd athletes who are the best of thousands who have played college ball during the past 10 years." He went on to describe the style of play as being superior, too, with "48 minutes of pulse-prodding action, continuous and flowing from climax to climax with the regularity of surf breaking on a beach and with the same scant seconds separating each crest." The following year he amended his commentary by pointing out that "even were Chicago allowed to start a team with the 10 top draft choices in any year, this collection of All-Americas [sic] would almost surely finish in last place for several seasons in a row."[75]

As late as 1960, though, some NBA officials coveted a few of the players outside of the NBA, including some in the National Industrial Basketball League (NIBL). Pistons general manager Nick Kerbawy observed, "Team to team, the NIBL can't stand up against the pros, but there are a few players in this league I'd like to have—and I'm going to try to get them." He identified former University of Kentucky player Johnny Cos as a potential NBA player. "He's one of a handful of NIBL players who could make it in the NBA. They have had the experience of playing the same type time game we play and figure to be of more immediate help than a kid just out of college for our purpose." Kerbawy noted the NIBL teams' chief allures of job security and training programs and remarked that two NIBL teams were readying offers for Oscar Robertson and Jerry West.[76]

Player Salaries

Owners of professional sports teams frequently bemoan player salaries. The histories of these organizations have common themes of player/management strife. The owners provided the necessary capital to stage the games and often held the whip hand with a one-sided interpretation of the reserve clause. The old-style professional basketball players were not capitalists and had to rent a place to play. As old-time player Dutch Dehnert recalled, "The biggest expense then was not the payroll, but the rental." The BAA owners possessed their own arenas. While Dehnert thought this eliminated the rental expense, an economist would point out that the owner still incurred an opportunity cost of using his arena for basketball instead of some other event.[77]

The salaries of professional players present interesting economic and managerial aspects. Player performance could be monitored by various statistics, which, even if imperfect, gave strong indications of productivity. Players also gained notoriety and could become fan favorites. While there was frequent strife between players and management, baseball and football players needed decades to form unions. Professional basketball players needed less time to form a union than their brethren in other sports, although their efforts were concurrent with those of athletes in other sports.

Basketball players differed from their baseball peers in that they were generally better educated. Because most basketball players during the 1950s and 1960s had college degrees, one could argue that their reservation salary, the minimum salary needed to induce them to play pro basketball, was higher than players in baseball could expect in employment outside of baseball. Several NBA-caliber players opted for jobs with large companies, such as Phillips Petroleum, that fielded semi-pro teams.[78] NBA president Maurice Podoloff told a congressional hearing that some of the industrial leagues were willing to pay between $9,000 and $10,000 for players in 1957, although he admitted these were rumored prices.[79] The combination of receiving a salary for playing basketball in addition to holding down a full-time job within an industry proved enticing to some players.

NBA players Ernie Vandeweghe and George Yardley, for instance, were trained in such lucrative professions as medicine and engineering. Vandeweghe, who completed his medical school studies while playing for the Knicks, had a contract that allowed him to skip road games with teams in western cities. Yardley opted to play with an AAU team for three seasons while working as an aeronautical engineer on guided missile projects. By the time the Fort Wayne Pistons exercised their draft rights to him, he was able to get $9,500 instead of the initial $6,000 offer. University of Kansas star Clyde Lovellette also opted for a detour via the AAU en route to the NBA.[80] Sportswriter Mark Leve commented, "The cases of Lovellette and [Chuck] Darling are typical of the numerous court stalwarts who believe that their brightest career lies in the field of business and that it's better to gain a foothold as soon as they leave college than to wait until their active playing days are finished, when their fame, too, will probably have diminished."[81] Lovellette, though, eventually played in the NBA.

Some basketball players, such as Lou Boudreau, Otto Graham, Gene Conley, Walt Dropo (drafted but not signed), and Chuck Connors, opted for other professional sports; Connors ended up as a Hollywood star in *The Rifleman* and numerous motion pictures. As late as 1958, NBA teams had difficulty signing their draft picks. Sportswriter Jeremiah Tax reported that the Syracuse Nats lost all four of their top draft choices to other employment.[82]

African American players had the chance of receiving lucrative offers from Abe Saperstein's Harlem Globetrotters. Wilt Chamberlain actually played one season with the Globetrotters in lieu of playing his senior year for the University of Kansas. Saperstein had earlier offered Bill Russell a reputed $50,000 salary, but Russell declined. Russell did say, "I'll say this—it was a good thing for me and it's a good thing for other Negro basketball players. When the Globetrotters bid for you, it helps you get a better deal with the pros."[83]

Many of the early BAA/NBA players did not intend to play for very many years. In the oral histories collected by Neil Isaacs, Charles Salzberg, and Terry Pluto, most players were content to spend a few years playing, acquire a nest egg, and then move on to jobs in industry or become self-employed. Indeed, league publicist Haskell Cohen trumpeted this facet: "The NBA is firmly established today. Almost every player is a college product. Each is serious and using his talents to his best advantage, so that, when his active days are over, he may be firmly established in some private enterprise or go into coaching to develop new players."[84]

Bob Davies was one of the higher-paid players. He recounted how he simultaneously coached basketball (and baseball) at his alma mater, Seton Hall, while playing for the Rochester Royals. With a bonus, he earned $15,000 for a season before signing a four-year contract for $50,000. Davies was a well-known collegiate and armed forces star, so he commanded bargaining leverage. Slater Martin, who became a perennial star, was relatively unknown out of college and settled for $3,500 with the Minneapolis Lakers. He related how the Lakers duped him by giving him a "$1,500 bonus" if the team won the championship. He later realized that he would have received the $1,500 when the Lakers won anyway.[85] Ed Macauley felt he had good leverage in bargaining with the St. Louis Bombers since he had been a collegiate star at St. Louis University. The Bombers were floundering in red ink, and the team hoped Macauley could resuscitate the franchise. They offered him $7,500 to sign and a $10,000 salary, which "Easy Ed" jumped at. He recalled getting an offer from the 66ers to play for just $300 a month.[86]

If these salaries sound modest, even for the immediate postwar period, it's because they were. Players and owners might exaggerate or minimize their salaries to the press for a variety of reasons. Given the limited salaries of the period, any such distortions would be a matter of a few thousand dollars for most players. Because pro basketball did not generate as large an audience as Major League Baseball, salaries of top basketball players were modest compared with the $90,000-$100,000 per season salaries earned by baseball's Joe DiMaggio and Ted Williams.

Aside from salaries, a few teams tried alternative forms of payment. The Chicago American Gears of the NBL tried a performance bonus scheme whereby George Mikan got five dollars for each field goal and two dollars for each free throw. The owner later applied the principle to his other players, but players would receive bonus payments only if the team won the game. The players responded by trying to pool the bonus payments for an even division, but one player balked. Because the owner said he would do so only if all the players agreed, the lone dissenter broke up the pool.[87]

The nascent BAA imposed a salary cap of $5,000 for any player and $40,000 total for all players on the roster. The league also tried to maintain a $5,000 salary cap for rookie players, but this quickly failed, as too many rookies had leverage in the form of other offers.[88] While Ned Irish may have earned the enmity of his fellow owners, his willingness to adhere to the salary cap cost him a chance to sign perennial all-star Dolph Schayes. When the league desperately needed well-known players, Irish refused to pay a $500 bonus in addition to the $5,000 salary, so Schayes signed with the NBL's Syracuse Nats.[89] Assuming all BAA owners adhered to the salary cap rules, their collective decision to impose such rules may have prevented an all-out bidding war for players.

In addition to their salaries, players could hope for a share of playoff money. At the league's inception, BAA president Maurice Podoloff disclosed that players participating in the playoffs would share $74,600. An additional $10,000 would go to players on the teams finishing in the top six in regular-season records. Two years later, Podoloff announced that

$70,000 was available for players on the top four teams. He made similar pronouncements as late as 1954.[90]

In any event, the NBA owners found themselves sandwiched with regard to player salaries. Players had relatively high reservation salaries because of their college degrees, which opened many outside opportunities. While the *Statistical Abstract of the United States* did not list earnings by educational attainment, the average weekly earnings for manufacturing workers was $59.33 in 1950 and $64.24 in July 1951. Players earning $6,000 or more in 1950 put their families well into the top 20 percent of family incomes.[91] Thus, while players earned more playing basketball than the average American did in his job and could augment their incomes by working during the off-season, owners could not cut salaries by very many thousands of dollars before the players would be earning similar amounts as manufacturing workers. Many of the best African American players had potential offers from the Harlem Globetrotters. The limited gate receipts set a fairly low ceiling for paying the stars. Basketball owners, then, had less leeway with regard to salaries than their baseball counterparts.

Even during the 1950s, team sports players generally earned lower salaries than other professional athletes. Sportswriter Myron Cope surveyed earnings in sports in 1964. He discovered that top bowlers earned far more than athletes in team sports. "The entrepreneurs—golfers, auto racers, thoroughbred jockeys, harness drivers, and bowlers—are Schedule C businessmen taxpayers who, for the most part, prosper according to the day-to-day frequency of their victories. . . . Curiously the big earners in sports demonstrate a paradoxical truth: The employee-athletes—the Mickey Mantles and Y.A. Tittles—are far more famous than their entrepreneur counterparts but far less prosperous."[92]

SOME INDIVIDUAL CASES

The NBL granted an expansion team to Chicago for the 1946–47 season. The American Gears quickly signed George Mikan, star center for DePaul University. Mikan signed a then-huge contract of $60,000 for five years, including an annual salary of $7,000 and a $25,000 bonus, payable over five seasons. Since the Consumer Price Index jumped by a factor of twelve between 1946 and 2010, Mikan's five-year package was worth roughly $720,000 in today's dollars, or less per season than modern Major League Baseball's minimum yearly salary of $400,000 in 2009.[93] Mikan chose the American Gears over the NBL rival Rochester Royals, because his college coach, Ray Meyer, was an advisor to the Chicago team. Mikan led the American Gears to a league title, one of the rare times when an expansion team captured the title.

The BAA apparently rescinded its $5,000 salary cap in subsequent seasons. By January 1948 the Philadelphia Warriors signed high-scoring Joe Fulks, an early practitioner of the jump shot. Ed Gottlieb, future owner of the team, signed Fulks for a bonus of $7,500 and awarded the player a reported $12,000 salary. Gottlieb heralded Fulks as a player who would "make you all sit up and take notice."[94]

George Mikan, though, remained the standard-setter for salaries. When the Chicago American Gears folded in 1947, the NBL's Minneapolis Lakers acquired the center. When the Lakers joined the BAA for the 1948–49 season, Mikan was receiving $15,000. By this time the BAA had a team salary limit of $55,000 and an individual salary of $9,000 (apparently Fulks's reported $12,000 salary was either a violation or an exaggeration). The NBL team owners were paying in excess of these limits, with the Lakers' total payroll being $75,000. Two players, Jim Pollard and Bob Davies, earned $13,000 and $12,000 respectively.[95]

Not all NBL players made five-figure salaries, of course, although some received supplemental payments. Fort Wayne Pistons player Jack Smiley recalled that he received a $5,000 salary to play basketball and a matching $5,000 salary to work for owner Fred Zollner's piston manufacturing company. He stated, "The amazing thing was that everybody on the team made the same."[96]

Hard Times and Upheavals

After four of its eleven teams folded, BAA owners increased the number of teams to a more convenient eight teams, when the owners approved the inclusion of a Baltimore Bullets team. The Bullets hailed from the American Basketball League, a league that the Philadelphia Warriors' eventual owner Eddie Gottlieb had abandoned. Koppett cites Gottlieb as a key addition to the fledgling BAA because of his previous experience as a professional basketball promoter.[97] The owners also voted to reduce the number of games from sixty to forty-eight, primarily to save on transportation expenses. The second season wasn't much better, and league president Maurice Podoloff had to rebut rumors that the league was folding after the season, although he admitted that "if such a tale had been told last year, there might have been something to it. But this season, we really have made progress."[98]

The league's Chicago outfit got a break when former NBL champion Chicago American Gears owner Maurice White had delusions of grandeur. According to his former player Dick Triptow, White wanted to—or rather demanded that he should—be president of the NBL. The other owners refused White's request. He decided the NBL wasn't big enough for his team and star George Mikan, so he launched a new league—the Professional Basketball League of America (PBLA)—with sixteen teams, including two southern teams. In an eerie parallel to baseball's three "major leagues" of 1884—National, American Association, and Union—three basketball leagues proved to be one too many. The *New York Times* reported that White quickly lost $600,000 and went bankrupt. The Gears players were fortunate to get fifty cents on the dollar for their back pay. The PBLA declared its players free agents, but the NBL was having none of that and assigned Mikan and Bobby McDermott to league teams, with the Minneapolis Lakers (formerly the Detroit Gems) getting the big prize in Mikan. Of such bizarre twists was an NBL/NBA dynasty formed.[99]

Improving the Product by Changing the Game on the Court

The standard interpretation of the NBA's history assigns primary credit for saving the league to the twenty-four-second rule, whereby the team possessing the ball must attempt a field goal within twenty-four seconds or forfeit possession. This rule certainly distinguished the professional game from college and high school versions for decades, but it wasn't until the league's ninth season that owners implemented it. There were several other rules, though, that were crucial.

Although the game's inventor, James Naismith, wanted to avoid rough play, all too often basketball became a more mobile form of wrestling, with players grabbing, shoving, pushing, gouging, and hip-checking opponents. While football and hockey suffer from excessive roughness and have rules regulating such, dealing with unnecessary roughness in basketball was problematic. Constant parades to the foul line in response to personal fouls infuriated fans and disrupted the fluid nature of the game. League officials found assessing the optimal penalty for personal fouls more difficult than anticipated. Coaches and players responded to personal foul rules in ways that economists would understand: more stringent foul rules led to changes in behavior.

Ted Williams, the great baseball hitter, liked to describe hitting against major league pitching as the most difficult thing in sports. In the early days of the BAA, hitting a field goal wasn't much easier than getting a base hit. While Major League Baseball hitters hovered around .260 to .270 (excluding pitchers' often futile swings at bat), professional basketball players were connecting on about 28 percent of their field goal attempts (see table 9). During the 1947–48 season, Bob Feerick led the league in shooting percentage at 34 percent, which in today's game is equivalent to a mediocre percentage for three-point shots. For the record, Williams batted .343 in 1947 and .369 in 1948. The BAA's shooting percentage jumped between 1947–48 and 1948–49 from 28.4 percent to 32.7 percent. Although the percentage did not rise continuously, the trend was generally upward through the 1950s. Not until the league's fourteenth season did the shooters collectively hit over 40 percent of their field goal attempts.[100] Even the great George Mikan had difficulty getting above 40 percent. Wilt Chamberlain, among his other astounding feats, occasionally topped 70 percent in his field goal shooting accuracy, well above his free-throw accuracy. Part of the difficulty in shooting could be attributed to the equipment. Players, too, were evolving their shooting styles, going from the two-hand set shot to the one-handed jump shot popularized by Jumpin' Joe Fulks. Leonard Koppett observed that the jump shot became more practical after the league rescinded the rule that a center jump must occur after every basket and after players got bigger (larger hands helped in shooting jump shots). The faster pace after the institution of the twenty-four-second shot clock may have exacerbated these trends.[101]

League owners would struggle for years to make their game more attractive. There were plenty of ways to alter the game in order to please fans.

THE BALL AND ARENAS

Some of the BAA/NBA's most pressing needs arose from the inadequate facilities and equipment. Since pro basketball was an afterthought to hockey, many of the arenas had not been designed for the former sport.

One reason shooting percentages were so low in the infant BAA and later in the NBA was because of imperfections in the basketball itself. The balls were not perfect spheres and lacked the wide seams of today's balls. Try sleight-of-hand stunts with an imperfect ball; the hardwood Houdinis would disappear or be embarrassed by the ball's erratic bounces. The imperfect rotation affected shooting percentages. In discussing the improvements in shooting, player and coach Joe Lapchick attributed the rising scoring in the mid-1950s to the twenty-four-second shot clock but also to better shooting and the ban on zone defenses. Players shot better as they adopted the jump shot. He cited the now iconic image of a solitary teenager shooting at baskets mounted on the ever-increasing number of garages in suburban and rural America. But he also credited the ball itself: "It's molded perfectly, and makes for better dribbling and shooting. There's no lace to bother you. And the fact that a team has half-a-dozen basketballs to warm up with instead of one, like we did in the old days helps it." Knicks official Nat Broudy recalled that the old balls were a little larger than the newer ones, and newer balls had wider seams that helped players grip the ball better. High-scoring George Yardley mused, "The basketballs were not molded until the late fifties and were often lopsided and not even rough, which made them more difficult to dribble and shoot with."[102] Certainly the outcry over the NBA's change of official basketballs in 2006 demonstrates the importance players attach to the most basic of equipment. Players disliked the new ball, which was discontinued mid-season.

Because most of the BAA arenas originally hosted hockey games, basketball was a poor relation. Bill Sharman, a master shooter, recalled:

> In Baltimore, we used to play in a roller skating rink. In Syracuse, we played in an old building at the fairgrounds that had a leaky roof, a warped floor, and very little heat. They had very few basketball arenas as they do today and most of them had poor lighting, all kinds of different, inadequate floors, bad temperatures, etc. Many were used for hockey and we would play right over the ice with no insulation except for the basketball floor itself. Suffice to say, with cold, stiff hands and fingers, it certainly didn't help the shooting touch and percentages.[103]

Conclusion

The BAA's birth was fraught with disappointment and difficulties. The owners' decision not to implement a gate-sharing plan may have helped keep surviving owners from becoming too discouraged. Since all owners claimed losses, having to subsidize owners with shallow capital reserves or whose territory was not remunerative might have forced the stronger owners to quit, too. The owners also succeeded in keeping bidding for players within reasonable bounds. Although the owners lost money, the lack of gate receipts and not overspending on players loomed as the chief culprit contributing to these losses. League owners took years to resolve the roughhouse nature of the game. Pro basketball was definitely a work in progress.

Another factor should be considered as well. Although I hesitate to indulge in "the great man" approach to history, especially as the nascent NBA lacked a truly great man, Maurice Podoloff looms as a critical figure in the league's survival and eventual prosperity. He had been involved in professional hockey, but he knew little about basketball.

Podoloff, league president during the era examined here, was easy to poke fun at. His diminutive, rotund figure certainly did not command respect. More than a few observers, though, credited him with being a crucial personality. His willingness to patiently absorb criticism and venomous barbs from owners and sportswriters, while mediating between the contrasting visions of the league, kept the owners unified (although he must have felt at times that he was herding cats). The sportswriters spoofed Podoloff with a song: "My name's Maurice Podoloff, Pumper-nick Podoloff . . . No genius will I ever be, My fame will come only, When I sell baloney, co-sponsored by Tom Gallery [NBC's sports director]."[104]

Certainly materials held in the Naismith Memorial Basketball Hall of Fame paint a portrait of a fussy man. His "NBA Bulletins" reveal much about his style of management. Podoloff was a micromanager before the term was coined. His duties included wrestling with schedules (along with Eddie Gottlieb), ordering basketballs, hiring referees, collecting gate-receipt information, and other issues. My favorite bulletins included number 49: "It would seem unnecessary to have to call to your attention the elementary rule that players and referees must not expectorate on the playing court." In number 66 he wrote: "I have had criticisms that some of the players, instead of running out on the floor, slouch on, and in this way destroy much of the effect that should be contributed by the team . . . [please instruct the players] to come out on the floor briskly and alertly and give the impression of being athletes rather than a bunch of old men starting in on an unpleasant job."[105] The schoolmarmish admonitions took a more serious note when Podoloff had to repeatedly hector owners and their officials to promptly return gate-receipt information. He even threatened the owners, saying, "It will not be permitted to teams to accumulate reports and in the event that a team has failed to make a remittance on time, the officials will be instructed not to proceed with the next game." He had to reiterate the point a couple of months later.[106]

Ned Irish's vision of the NBA as a classy, big-league operation was astute, and if he was not the best man to implement it, the league ultimately attained his vision. Though Irish and Podoloff may have feuded, as sportswriter Irv Goodman pointed out, "Generally, the owners feel there is no justification for anyone being after Podoloff's neck. If anything, they want him to assert himself more, to be firmer with rebels, to take a stand when he is attacked. They admire him for what he has done, and they will support him in a showdown."[107]

Podoloff was not the visionary that Pete Rozelle would be for the NFL during the 1960s, but he may well have been the glue that kept the ramshackle NBA together long enough for the innovation of the league's twenty-four-second shot clock, black stars, television, and contraction and relocation to coalesce the surviving teams into America's third major professional team sport. The league's infancy may well have sunk with a visionary at the helm. Sangfroid may have been Podoloff's lasting gift to the league.

There was a key missed opportunity, however, that Podoloff and the BAA owners might have exploited. When the Chicago American Gears' owner went bankrupt in the aftermath of his bold new league, George Mikan was theoretically a free agent, even though the NBL claimed it still controlled him. A concerted effort by the BAA owners to persuade George to remain in Chicago and to play for the league's Stags would have given the league instant credibility among the basketball cognoscenti. BAA owners might well have succeeded in persuading Mikan to join their league, as he preferred to play in Chicago and only reluctantly went to Minneapolis. In addition, Chicago might have been transformed into a solid franchise instead of one that needed bailouts to stagger through an additional season or two. The American Basketball Association recognized twenty years later how important signing Lew Alcindor would have been and pooled resources in an attempt to outbid the NBA's Milwaukee Bucks.

Getting Mikan would have weakened the NBL, or at least relegated it to a second-tier league over time. With Mikan as a gate attraction, Ned Irish's vision of the BAA as a big-city, class act might have become reality sooner than later. Of course, raiding the NBL of its biggest star would have broken the tenuous truce between the two leagues, possibly spurring a ruinous bidding war. However, energetic action on the part of Podoloff and the BAA owners could have significantly altered the course of professional basketball. Perhaps here is where a visionary leader would have paid dividends.

3

The Merger and Its
Aftermath (1948–51)

Because the NBL possessed George Mikan and other well-known stars, BAA owners faced difficulties in persuading the public that their teams played the best basketball. After two seasons the BAA owners had to decide whether to woo the more attractive NBL teams to join their league. The owners also faced the issue of racial integration.

The Merger

Although BAA owners concentrated on signing top collegiate talent, they were unable to overtake the NBL teams in talent. The NBL had already signed eleven college players by June 1947, so the two leagues agreed that the BAA teams would each get one choice before NBL teams began choosing players.[1] In this way the two leagues avoided a bidding war for players; their contemporary brethren in professional football were not so adroit. Owners in both basketball leagues were becoming aware that 1940s America was not big enough for two professional leagues. BAA owners decided to use the lure of playing in bigger markets and greater capital holdings to induce the best NBL teams to switch leagues. Unlike the contemporary sparring between football rivals NFL and AAFC (All-American Football Conference), by 1948 the BAA and NBL had no contested cities. A merger would not result in any team trespassing upon another team's territory. This absence made contriving a merger agreement much simpler and less acrimonious than in professional football. Throughout the spring of 1948, the *New York Times* published sporadic stories chronicling the sparring between the two leagues. Five of the

NBL teams refused in February to confirm that they planned to field teams for the 1948–49 season, and rumors abounded that Minneapolis, with George Mikan, was actively courting the BAA. Concurrently, Ned Irish had to dispel rumors that the Knickerbockers were calling it quits, saying, "We have no intention of giving up the BAA." He admitted that the team lost money again but attributed this to the sparse number of games held at Madison Square Garden: "We need the Garden for more contests, and while we can give the club more dates there next year the situation does not look too much better."[2]

Readers of the *New York Times* could be excused for being confused about the shakeup in the two leagues. You needed a scorecard to tell which teams were coming or going. Table 2 shows the roster of BAA and NBL franchises at the time. At first the leagues announced that only the Indianapolis Kautskys and the Fort Wayne Zollner Pistons would shift to the BBA, although Rochester and Minneapolis were possibilities.[3] The Royals and Lakers were not only teams playing in the larger NBL cities but were also among that league's strongest teams. A month later a report surfaced that three NBL teams were switching to the BAA, an action that threatened the NBL. A Kautskys spokesperson claimed the jumping teams wanted to play in a "tough league" with greater crowd potential and national publicity (which would be good for their other businesses). The reporter noted that the two leagues had previously existed amicably, even sharing billing at Chicago Stadium.[4] The teams from Indianapolis and Fort Wayne prepared to switch leagues. The Lakers decided to join the BAA, too, since it was becoming the only big fish in a shrinking pond. When the Lakers jumped, the Rochester Royals realized their own danger and pleaded to be admitted to the BAA. On May 10, 1948, the BAA announced the inclusion of the four teams, which it grouped in the league's Western Division with St. Louis and Chicago.[5] While in retrospect this was a pivotal day in NBA history, with the league getting such big-name stars as George Mikan, his teammate Jim Pollard, Bob Davies, and others, outside of die-hard professional basketball fans, America took scant notice.

The new additions hastened the diminution of Ned Irish's dominance of league affairs. The owners of BAA teams in smaller cities welcomed four new owners with similar interests. As Leonard Koppett relates, Irish wanted the league to do things with class. He was willing to lose money and was able to do so because the Garden had deep pockets, until it got things done with class, presumably mimicking Major League Baseball by having teams in only the largest cities. He lost even more influence through his "characteristic aloof, imperious, and humorless manner." This meant "He had no patience with the struggles of less affluent promoters, or the traditional scrambling for a few extra bucks or a slight competitive advantage that characterized the older pros."[6] Most of the other owners were not as willing to lose money. While baseball's Yankees and Dodgers dominated their leagues' affairs, the Knicks didn't have the influence to do so in basketball.

The NBL did not gracefully accede to the departure of its best franchises. League vice president Leo Ferris proclaimed war when the BAA offered a joint draft session with the NBL survivors. Even worse, Ferris threatened, "There will be no respect of player contracts and open war on signing players from now on." He claimed that players from the four defecting teams would now be assigned among remaining NBL teams, which would consider expanding to Des Moines, Denver, Dayton, and St. Paul. The NBL owners brandished the possibility of seeking an injunction to prevent these players from performing with their now-BAA teams, but the latter owners expressed indifference, and one said, "they [NBL] may not be in business long enough to worry about next season."[7] Nothing came of the threatened dispute over players, as the two leagues opted to respect each other's player contracts, thereby avoiding a potential financial disaster incurred from a bidding war for players.[8]

While the leagues sparred, sportswriters speculated on the effects upon player salaries. Sportswriter Bill Roeder predicted that Mikan, Pollard, and Davies would soon suffer cuts in pay, since "the BAA doesn't pay that kind of money and the monopoly arrangement would force the stars to take cuts or quit the games. With the Knickerbockers, for instance, they'd have to be satisfied with a $6,000 ceiling."[9]

After further negotiations failed, the two leagues played their 1948–49 seasons. The NBL was withering, but the BAA was not thriving either. On August 3, 1949, the two leagues merged and the BAA was renamed the NBA.[10] At first there were eighteen teams, and the league planned on having two divisions. Before the 1949–50 season opened, though, there were just seventeen teams, which were split into three divisions, as one of the original BAA member teams, the Providence Steamrollers, folded. The Indianapolis Jets (formerly Kautskys) folded but were replaced by the Indianapolis Olympians, a team partly owned by 1948 Olympians Alex Groza, Ralph Beard, and Wallace "Wah Wah" Jones.[11] At the insistence of Ned Irish and other surviving original BAA owners, the new refugees from the NBL were placed in the same division. This meant the Knicks, Celtics, and Warriors would not be irritated by playing the likes of the Sheboygan Red Skins, Waterloo Hawks, Anderson Packers, and Tri-Cities Blackhawks very often. As Leonard Koppett describes it, "The details of the merger were of staggering complexity, a conglomeration whose instability was obvious to the most casual fan as well as to those involved."[12] The division lineups were as follows:

> Eastern: Baltimore Bullets, Boston Celtics, New York Knicks, Philadelphia Warriors, Syracuse Nationals, and Washington Capitols
> Central: Chicago Stags, Fort Wayne Pistons, Minneapolis Lakers, Rochester Royals, and St. Louis Bombers
> Western: Anderson Packers, Denver Nuggets, Indianapolis Olympians, Sheboygan Red Skins, Tri-Cities Blackhawks, and Waterloo Hawks[13]

With all of the bewildering developments, perhaps it was fortunate that the new NBA was obscure. For an established major league to experience such upheaval would have seriously undermined its credibility.

Although all seventeen teams completed the 1949–50 season, a miracle of sorts, it was clear that many of the new entrants had no future in the league. The league bid adieu to Anderson, Denver, Sheboygan, and Waterloo. Unfortunately, original BAA members Chicago and St. Louis went out of business, too, with Washington, Baltimore, and Indianapolis to follow. When the league stabilized in 1954–55, only three of the original eleven BAA franchises were left. The other five survivors had NBL antecedents.

The mix of teams surviving the upheaval created tension as owners sparred over the length of the regular season. The original BAA teams had large arenas and weren't keen on extending the regular season, due to other bookings and added travel expenses. Owners of teams in smaller cities wanted more games, and they had more votes. The season gradually increased to eighty games by 1961–62.[14]

After the tumultuous 1949–50 season, the league shrank to eight teams by the 1954–55 season. Some of the survivors of the 1949–50 season barely hung on. The Chicago Stags pleaded for help, despite a winning season in 1949–50, and got it in the form of new players from the St. Louis and Anderson teams that folded. The infusion of new players was not enough, however, to enable the Stags to stagger on, and the Chicago-based team folded before the 1950–51 season.[15]

Sportswriter Terry Pluto believes the league's split identity was exemplified by the 1954–55 championship series between Fort Wayne and Syracuse.

> Yes, they were basketball's best, but that still didn't stop a lot of people—especially those powerful snobs in New York City—from asking, "How can the NBA be a big-league sport when Fort Wayne and Syracuse are in the Finals?" Of course, the answer was that they beat out the Knicks, but the truth hurt.

Adding to the NBA's little league national image was that Fort Wayne could not get into its own building for the Finals; it had been taken over by a pro bowling tournament. The New York wise guys had fun with that. So Fort Wayne set up shop in Indianapolis.[16]

Whether or not Pluto's theory of northeastern snobbery is true, some of the league's owners must have been pleased when the Philadelphia Warriors won the 1955–56 championship over the Fort Wayne Pistons. After this series, big-city teams would dominate the championship series, with St. Louis (1957–58 and 1960–61) and Minneapolis (1958–59) being the smallest cities with teams participating until 1971 when the Milwaukee Bucks played the Baltimore Bullets. The Boston Celtics, Philadelphia 76ers, Los Angeles Lakers, San Francisco Warriors, and even the New York Knicks would dominate championship play during the 1960s.

If imitation is the sincerest form of recognizing profitability, then the NBA was going in the right direction. New leagues kept popping up and, aside from the American Basketball Association of the late 1960s to early 1970s, disappearing quickly. After the relocations of the Rochester Royals and Fort Wayne Pistons, businessmen in those cities still aspired to professional basketball and met with optimists from eight other cities, including the Tri-Cities of Davenport, Rock Island, and Moline, to form a new league.[17] This league never threatened the NBA. The American Basketball League, founded by Abe Saperstein, lasted just one full season (1961–62). The American Basketball Association began play in 1967–68. The league used the three-point shot and a tri-colored basketball (much beloved by many basketball fans) but was established with a marked lack of capital. Despite exciting stars such as Connie Hawkins and Julius "Dr. J" Erving, who were perhaps more exciting than the stars in the NBA, only four ABA teams would be absorbed into the NBA a decade later.

The chaotic 1949–50 season saw many, even most, of the clubs struggle at the gate. Sportswriter Stan Baumgartner cited the Philadelphia Warriors as a team that was struggling, while the teams from Rochester, Syracuse, Boston, New York, Fort Wayne, Minneapolis, and the Tri-Cities were faring well. He predicted that the league needed to shrink to twelve teams.[18] Even by the 1951–52 season, fan interest remained disappointingly low.[19] Baumgartner attributed the attendance woes to the games themselves, saying, "Astronomical scores have apparently dampened fan interest." Continuing in this vein, he wrote:

> To get this spectator appeal the pros concentrated on scoring more baskets and high totals. Totals rose from the 60s to the 70s, 80s, and now above the 100s. The moguls created a Frankenstein, which now threatens to destroy

them. Today pro basketball is a battle of points, not teams. There is no thrill in a pro game, until the final five minutes and then only if the contest is close. It is merely a spectacle of sharpshooters. . . . Pro basketball players have become so proficient they have taken the "kick" out of the game. It has become an exhibition rather than a contest.

He added, "High prices, high taxes, less money for luxuries—and pro basketball is a luxury—are factors. Gamblers, loud-mouthed, abusive, crude, who chase decent people away in such towns as Philadelphia, Baltimore, and New York, are another factor."[20]

Scanty Revenues to Share

After the shakeup of NBL and BAA teams, NBA teams continued to have difficulty drawing large crowds (see table 10). Historian Robert Peterson believes league games averaged around 3,300 during the 1950–51 season, a number not too different from the 1946–47 figure. The Syracuse Nationals and Minneapolis Lakers outpaced the New York Knicks and Philadelphia Warriors. The New York Knicks figures differ from those reported in the *New York Times*. Historian Donald Fisher presents data from the June 19, 1951, "NBA Bulletin" that shows average attendance per game during the 1950–51 season to be 3,600.[21]

The NBA records at the Naismith Basketball Memorial Hall of Fame contained game-by-game net (after admission taxes) gate receipts for most of the 1949–51 seasons (see table 11). The table shows that in 1949–50, the Knicks and Lakers likely would have been the biggest losers from a gate-sharing plan. Some of the teams in large cities, though, would have been net beneficiaries. Surprisingly, such small-town teams as the Syracuse Nationals and Tri-Cities Blackhawks would have been net losers under most types of revenue-sharing plans. During the 1950–51 season, the Knicks, Lakers, and Nationals would have continued to be net losers under revenue sharing. The ill-fated Washington Capitols might have received a proportionally large boost from a common-pool revenue-sharing plan, such as today's Major League Baseball boasts, but the team's tepid attendance on the road would have limited its gain under a plan similar to the contemporary baseball and football plans. Whether the Capitols would have received enough of a subsidy from revenue sharing to survive is an interesting question.

For teams in smaller cities, though, enthusiasm for a potential gate-sharing plan would have been tempered by two facts. Table 32 contains a fixed-effects regression equation for the 1950–51 season with gate receipts as the dependent variable and several independent variables. The visiting team's win-loss record positively affected the gate receipts, similar to what occurred in Major League Baseball and the National Football League. The difference between a visiting team sporting a .600 win-loss record versus one with a .400 record was roughly $1,325 in net gate receipts per game. Owners of weak teams in small cities might not have received much succor from a 1950s-style baseball or football revenue-sharing plan. In addition, table 12 shows that the Knicks amplified the larger crowd size at games played in Madison Square Garden by scheduling the top teams, such as the Minneapolis Lakers, Rochester Royals, Syracuse Nationals, and Boston Celtics, at Madison Square Garden. The Indianapolis Olympians, Fort Wayne Pistons, and Milwaukee Hawks rarely appeared in Madison Square Garden. In fact, the Knicks often consented to transfer their home games against those three teams to other venues as part of doubleheaders.

If the intent of a proposed gate-sharing plan was to get the New York Knicks, with that team's greater potential to generate gate receipts, to share with the teams in the smaller cities, these findings suggest that a common pool approach, such as used in Major League Baseball today, would have been more effective than a plan similar to baseball's plans of the 1950s. Since the Knicks relegated the poorer teams in the league to games in the 69th Regiment Armory, any plan that was similar to the contemporary baseball or football plans would not have greatly helped those teams.

The Perils of Ownership

Aspiring owners of professional basketball teams in the immediate postwar period did not have to be wealthy (but it helped), nor did they have to know anything about running a sports team (but, again, it helped). Ownership in the BAA-cum-NBA became a revolving door. Many potential owners were lured by the siren call of profits or glory, but few attained either.

For a mere $25,000, an investor could gain membership in the NBL. Les and Jack Harrison decided to upgrade their barnstorming team and become a member of the NBL as the Rochester Royals. They paid $25,000 for an expansion franchise in late 1945. In today's dollars this would be approximately $300,000.[22] In joining the NBL the Harrisons had to sign players to a standard players contract.[23]

Of course, an aspiring owner needed to own a stadium or obtain a contract with a suitable stadium. The nascent BAA had even cheaper franchise fees than the NBL, but the BAA owners had arenas. Each of the eleven owners of the original BAA teams paid $1,000 to join. In some cases the arena owners executed a policy of benign neglect, as in the case of the Chicago Stags, where the Norris family who controlled much of the National Hockey League allowed Judge John A. Sbarbaro to run the Stags' operations.[24] The judge and the hockey interests quickly learned that basketball required more effort than they were willing to invest. Despite having winning records in each of its four seasons, the Stags failed at the gate.

Leonard Koppett believes the BAA owners' idea was a sound one:

> A professional team, as a tenant in a privately owned or municipally built arena, must not only pay rent but compete for favorable dates. After all, scheduling a game for a Monday afternoon, even if it's a terrific match-up, won't do much good. You need a weekend date, or an appropriate weekday night (which varies with each town) to really pull in customers. So it is an ideal situation if the same company that owns the arena can own the team. This is precisely the idea upon which the BAA was founded in 1946. In this circumstance, the arena can control bookings so that its own team gets favorable dates, and the whole operation can be centralized. And basketball games, played frequently, familiarize the public with the building and help other events. But where that kind of ownership is not possible, the promoter must get a good deal from whoever owns the building to stay in business. Usually this is possible because a basketball team can contract for many dates, and the landlord usually makes extra money from the concessions sales of programs, hot dogs, and beer when large crowds come to his building.[25]

However, Koppett's analysis is fundamentally flawed. If a businessman owns both an arena and a team, he still faces the opportunity cost (defined as the best alternative use of a resource) of having his team use the arena. If other, more lucrative events could be booked at his arena, he faces the same decision as would separate owners. If there were no viable bookings for, say, Madison Square Garden, Knicks games, even if they lost money, might be financially beneficial. As long as the Knicks' revenue more than compensated for the expense of holding the game at Madison Square Garden, the game was useful even if it did not cover its share of overhead.[26] What is different between explicitly renting an arena and owning both an arena and a team is that the owner of both businesses internalizes the decisions; he is, in effect, renting to himself. The Knicks demonstrated this situation, as the Garden owners frequently reserved weekend dates for ice shows, hockey games, college basketball doubleheaders, and other events instead of Knicks games.[27]

Having a large arena was no guarantee of a team's financial success. Other owners of arenas in larger cities might send their team to play home games in other arenas; for instance, Boston played games at the Boston Garden and in Providence, Rhode Island.

The Baltimore Bullets exemplified the risks inherent in owning a franchise. The team was the BAA champion in its first season. By April 1951 the *New York Times* reported the franchise had been sold for the third time for an undisclosed amount. The real question was "Who wants to buy the Bullets?" Three years later the team's finances continued to bleed red, and Podoloff set a deadline for the franchise. Some Baltimore businessmen attempted to jump-start the team with an infusion of $125,000. A group of sixteen stated their willingness to each buy $2,500 worth of stock if thirty-four others would join them.[28] A week later the league granted permission for the franchise to suspend operations while allowing the team to perform the following season if the owners could get solid financing. Once again the surviving NBA owners held the league's equivalent of a wake by dispersing whatever desirable players the franchise had.[29] At least the Baltimore owners' fellow NBA owners wanted the team to succeed financially, while these same peers showed no mercy to teams like the Anderson Packers and Sheboygan Red Skins of the league.

For a more dramatic move, Washington owner Mike Uline tried to fold two teams at once. He had hoped for better tidings during the BAA's second season, but continued financial losses, despite a winning basketball team, induced a more drastic decision. He decided to fold both his BAA Washington Capitols and his hockey team, the Washington Lions. Uline cited a novel reason for some of his losses. "Uline's decision was based upon alleged financial losses of more than $200,000 in the last six years and 'unfair government competition.' His reference to Government competition was based upon use of the National Guard Armory for some sports events. Uline said seven basketball teams which formerly had staged home games at his arena were using the armory. He said that meant a loss to him of $1,000 a game. Uline will convert the arena into a cold storage plant."[30] Apparently Uline reconsidered, and his basketball franchise staggered through a few more seasons before folding midway through the 1950–51 season. The team's lack of fan support can be seen in the fact that its last four home games generated just $3,832 total in net gate receipts, of which $700 would have been paid out as the league's minimum share.[31]

Not all of the owners were capitalists. The second Indianapolis team, the Olympians, and the Denver Nuggets were player-owned franchises. The Nuggets were incorporated, and the team's stock was distributed to the players on the heretofore AAU team. "The value of this stock will depend on the team's success. As the team's manager put it, 'The harder we work at the game, the more we get out of it.' No player was guaranteed a salary, but it was agreed that profits, if any, would be distributed whenever feasible."[32] Unfortunately, this player-owned team failed both financially and on the court.

The Indianapolis Jets fared better. Five former University of Kentucky stars played on the United States Olympic team during the 1948 games. Upon their return, they found the existing Indianapolis NBA team in disarray.[33] The league encouraged the five Olympic players to replace the Jets by granting them $30,000 in seed money. The players borrowed $30,000 from the city of Indianapolis and rented the Butler University Fieldhouse for $800 per game. They renamed the Jets as the Olympians. The players became the corporation officers. Ralph Beard, one of the team's stars, recalled: "That was considered the greatest floor in the league at that time. And the fans really embraced us. Whenever we'd play Minneapolis, or Anderson, or Fort Wayne, we'd pack that Butler Fieldhouse—15,000 fans. Boy, we were really in the tall cotton then. We were rolling. By the end of our first year in the league, we had paid off our $30,000 debt to the city; we'd paid ourselves the generous salary of $5,000 each for five months; we'd given ourselves a $5,000 bonus each, and had $28,000 in the bank to boot."[34] As sportswriter Angelo Angelopolous pointed out, "They're doing all right at the spacious Butler University Fieldhouse gates, averaging close to 5,000 paid spectators. That's a considerably healthier box office than many of the rivals who have been in the pro basketball business for years."[35] The story ended unhappily when some of the Kentucky players' past actions while collegians caught up with them and they admitted to point shaving by not playing their best. The league forced the guilty players to divest, and the franchise staggered through two more seasons before folding.[36] However, the figures in table 11 conflict with Beard's recollections and paint a less favorable picture.

When several former NBL teams folded after the 1949–50 season, not all of their owners went quietly. For sheer temerity, the owners of the unwanted Anderson Packers team went down kicking, presenting a list of conditions for staying in the league, but the league refused to meet these conditions. As league president Maurice Podoloff blandly stated, "So the league purchased the Anderson franchise and disposed of it."[37] Exit Anderson.

Three other former NBL franchises failed to post a $15,000 cash performance bond and left the NBA. These disgruntled owners, along with the owners of the Anderson team, vowed to resurrect the NBL. Unfortunately for these rejected teams, the surviving NBA teams obtained some of their leading scorers; Anderson's leading scorer, Frankie Brian, ended up with the Tri-Cities Blackhawks.[38] Concurrent with the resurrected NBL, the American Basketball League, centered in the states of New York and New Jersey, staggered on.[39] The NBA was soon standing alone in the professional basketball world.

The NBA revealed its preferences by bidding adieu to these teams in smaller cities while struggling to maintain teams in larger cities such as St. Louis and Chicago. One could almost hear Podoloff chortling when he announced, "We are now boiled down to a good working organization." The league purchased the St. Louis Bombers' players and announced its intent to retain a franchise in the city for another three years. Eventually the Milwaukee Hawks would relocate to St. Louis. The league made special dispensation to the Chicago Stags, who were having difficulty in posting the $15,000 performance bond. An anonymous *New York Times* sportswriter wrote that the league had contributed $40,000 to the Stags the previous season.[40]

Despite its dismal financial record, the Chicago franchise remained attractive. Harlem Globetrotters impresario Abe Saperstein initially announced he would operate a rejuvenated Stags franchise (renamed the Bruins, continuing the ursine motif among Chicago sports teams), but he eventually gave up, blaming the "total failure of the NBA to deliver the franchise and the players in accordance with the promises made by its representatives when I offered to purchase." Podoloff retorted that Saperstein would not operate a club in Chicago. The president issued the usual statement that the remaining Chicago players would be distributed among the remaining clubs.[41]

The Chicago Stags did not pass quietly into the night. The Chicago basketball club filed a circuit court suit against the NBA seeking restoration of the franchise and $150,000 in damages. The plaintiffs alleged that the league tried to finagle transfer of the franchise from them to Abe Saperstein. Although Saperstein offered to buy the franchise, the league refused to meet his conditions, so the league suspended the team for the 1950–51 season.[42] Chicago was now effectively without a professional basketball team.

The reasons for the high rate of attrition in the NBA were apparent. Pioneering professional basketball owners often lacked sufficient capital reserves (or the stomach for chronic losses) and promotional savvy. The NBA's upheavals were not for the fainthearted. Baseball and football, however, had endured similar growing pains as owners sought locations that were willing and able to support teams. Those owners who survived could either congratulate themselves or wonder at their masochism.

Despite this tumultuous beginning, better days were coming. By 1961 the NBA placed a price tag of $200,000 on the aspiring Chicago and Pittsburgh franchises.[43]

Salaries

After the BAA and NBL merged, competition for players diminished. Owners hoped for a scaling back of salaries. Emory Jones, general manager of the soon-to-be-defunct St. Louis Bombers, thought the average player earned more than $5,000. With team rosters of eleven players, a coach, and a trainer, the payroll might amount to $70,000 or so. "Every club's top player, its No. 1 box office man, deserve[s] proportionate pay, and its next two or three best somewhat less, but the average player should get no more than about $3,000 or $3,500 and I know some others who agree with me. Ability to pay has to be a big factor in any business."[44]

Instead of falling, however, the salaries of top NBA players began rising. Max Zaslofsky, a high scorer for the Chicago Stags, demanded $14,000 per season for five seasons. Sportswriter Harry Sheer dubbed him the league's first holdout. The team eventually signed him for $10,000 a season, with a bonus bumping the total to $12,000. Sheer estimated that Zaslofsky would make about $40 for every field goal he scored.[45]

In a May 18, 1950, bulletin, Maurice Podoloff disclosed payrolls for twelve teams during the 1949–50 season. His report listed salaries for 182 players. The salaries ranged from $2,700 to $17,500 (probably George Mikan), with an average salary of $5,618. Only eight players made $10,000 or more. The figures, though, raise some questions. First, there were seventeen teams playing during the season. Second, one team reported salaries for thirty players, with fourteen of them receiving $4,000 each, while other teams reported only eight or nine salaries. Historian Robert Peterson reported these figures in his book *Cages to Jump Shots*, but he did not discuss the quirks in the data.[46]

Some players were creative in negotiating salaries. Tom King of the Detroit Falcons, a team that only avid NBA fans know about, recalled how he became the highest-paid player in the league. He had a degree in business management, so he asked owners Jim Norris and Arthur Wirtz if he could also be the team's publicity director, business manager, and traveling secretary. In addition to his $8,500 salary and signing bonus for playing, he earned another $8,000 for these jobs. As King laconically noted, despite his being the highest-paid player, "I certainly was not the best player."[47]

While George Mikan remained the league's highest-paid player, at a reported $20,000 during the early 1950s, Bob Cousy slowly caught up; by the 1955–56 season his salary was reputedly $17,000. Cousy remembered telling owners that unless he played for the Boston Celtics, he wasn't playing professional ball. He had opened a gas station and a string of driving schools in Worcester. He figured he needed at least $10,000 from basketball before he would quit his other businesses. Ben Kerner, owner of the Tri-Cities Blackhawks, drafted him and offered $7,000, which Cousy turned down. "I was honest and told him that I didn't even know where Tri-Cities was. . . . I said, 'Mr. Kerner, I'm going to pump gas and teach ladies to drive.'" Kerner traded rights to Cousy to the Chicago Stags, but that team folded before signing him. The Celtics won rights to Cousy in a lottery.[48]

Players also faced an element of risk during the early years of the NBA. A number of franchises folded, some during mid-season. The uncertainty surrounding salaries prompted players to press for guarantees. When the Baltimore Bullets folded after the 1953–54 season, the owner owed two weeks' pay to some of the players. League president Podoloff stepped in and announced that these players would be paid by their new teams or by any resurrected Baltimore franchise.[49]

The league also tried different limits on rosters, although generally the limit was ten players. In the opening 1946–47 season the league allowed each team to have twelve players, but later reduced this to ten (nine of which must be in uniform for a game). The more generous roster limit of 1946–47 was useful, as coaches and owners were uncertain of their new players' abilities and rosters changed quickly. The owners bumped the limit of players to eleven, but after the upheaval of the 1949–50 season they reverted to the ten-player limit.[50]

Coaches received higher salaries than did most of their players. Al Cervi earned $12,000 during 1949–50 as coach of the Syracuse Nationals. The Nats led their division and had, by NBA standards, good-sized crowds of five thousand.[51] Some team owners tried to reduce their payrolls by designating a player as coach. Player-coaches appeared sporadically throughout the NBA, culminating in the Boston Celtics' selection of Bill Russell as player-coach for three seasons in the late 1960s.

Competitive Balance

The NBA is renowned for dominant teams such as the Boston Celtics, Minneapolis/Los Angeles Lakers, and Chicago Bulls. The New York Knickerbockers, charter members of the league, have won only two championships. In this the

NBA differs from baseball's American League with its repeated dominance across decades by the New York Yankees. There was no "New York State of Mind" in the NBA, although the Boston Celtics came close.

Basketball's Boston Celtics and Minneapolis/Los Angeles Lakers have certainly dominated the NBA, winning thirty-three titles between them through 2010, or roughly half of all titles. There does not appear to be the same sentiment to break up the Celtics and Lakers as there was in baseball to break up the New York Yankees. Even before the NBA, the barnstorming professional teams such as the Original Celtics and New York Renaissance compiled lengthy winning streaks, albeit against opponents of wildly varying quality. Celtics player Joe Lapchick remembered the disparity: "Long before anybody thought of breaking up the Yankees, the Celtics were broken up. We were in the American League in those days, and the club owners decided that we were too strong. I think it was a confession of weakness on their part, but they voted to break us up. With [Dutch] Dehnert and Pete Barry, I was sent to the Cleveland Rosenblooms."[52]

The Minneapolis Lakers, with George Mikan, dominated the early NBA, winning in five of the first six seasons George played in the league (his teams won a couple of championships in the NBL, too). Eddie Gottlieb of the Philadelphia Warriors complained, "Our league is fast getting to be like the American League in baseball with the Minneapolis Lakers dominating the circuit in New York Yankees fashion—and unfortunately the domination is affecting the top of the league as well as the bottom. The Lakers are running behind in attendance and we at the bottom are faring equally disastrously. Only two factors are keeping us in business—doubleheaders and the Harlem Globetrotters. The Trotters are really keeping the circuit going."[53]

The NBA's early years as the BAA and the subsequent merger of the BAA and NBL accounted for much of the imbalance among teams in the late 1940s and early 1950s. The winnowing of weak teams redressed the differences in win-loss percentages. Table 13 shows that the league's ratio of actual to idealized standard deviations narrowed during the mid-1950s. In 1956–57 the actual standard deviation was less than the idealized standard deviation. However, after that season the Celtics and Hawks began to dominate, and the actual standard deviation resumed being more than twice the idealized standard deviation.

There is one drawback with using standard deviations. Much of fans' discontent about the Yankees was not about their win-loss percentage per se, but about the monotony, especially during the 1950s, of the club winning the American League pennant fourteen times in the sixteen seasons between 1949 and 1964. During the 1950s the Yankees' win-loss records were not outstanding for pennant winners, and the team rarely ran away with the pennant. A league with a lower ratio of actual to idealized standard deviation might still be perceived as imbalanced if the same team finished first relative to another league with a higher ratio but churning among teams. In a sense, this is similar to arguments about income distribution in the United States. Yes, those in the top 10 percent make much more than those in the bottom 10 percent, but many if not most of this year's top 10 percent will not be in the top 10 percent a few years hence.

The New York Yankees of the 1950s had their Cleveland Indians, perennial "bridesmaids" as the sportswriters liked to say. The Minneapolis Lakers had a fierce rivalry with the Rochester Royals in the same division. During Mikan's six full seasons with the Lakers in the NBA, the team averaged just one regular-season win more per season than the Royals. The Royals won or shared the division title three times. The Lakers won 67.6 percent of their regular-season games between 1948 and 1954, but the team shone during the playoffs by winning 72.1 percent of its games. The team lost only one playoff series, in the spring of 1951, when the Royals prevailed three games to one.

The Minneapolis Lakers' continued success appeared to bore the team's fans. Although information is not available for 1948–51, the team's gross and home receipts fell between 1951–52 and 1953–54. Their profit and loss figures were relatively stable across the three years, although 1953–54 was the worst year of the three. The league's total home receipts fell between 1952–53 and 1953–54, but, again, it is difficult to know what the trend was.

Four factors loom in explaining the wide swings in some teams' win-loss records: (1) the winnowing of six teams between 1949–50 and 1950–51; (2) the introduction of the twenty-four-second shot clock for the 1954–55 season, which coincided with George Mikan's first retirement; (3) the wave of talented (mostly black) stars in the late 1950s; and (4) home-court advantage. The latter three factors are discussed in chapters 4, 5, and 6.

The bizarre scheduling and divisional lineups of 1949–50 help explain the disparities among teams for that season. Teams had lopsided proportions of games at home, on the road, and at neutral sites. The 1949–50 schedule was bizarre on another dimension. The clubs played sixty-two, sixty-four, or sixty-eight games, with the Sheboygan Red Skins, Waterloo Hawks, and Denver Nuggets, perhaps mercifully, having just sixty-two each, while all of the Central and Eastern Division teams (aside from the Syracuse Nationals with sixty-four) played sixty-eight games. Essentially, the established NBA clubs tried to avoid playing the newcomers.

Between the 1949–50 and 1950–51 seasons, surviving NBA teams experienced large changes in their rosters due to the dispersal of players from franchises that folded. These roster changes engendered large swings in some teams' performances (see table 14). The Boston Celtics were the primary beneficiary of the dispersal drafts of players held when some franchises folded after the 1949–50 season. The Celtics acquired Bob Cousy and Ed Macauley. They later added Bill Sharman after the Washington Capitols collapsed the following season. The Celtics improved their win-loss percentage from .324 to .565.

The Syracuse Nationals' fall from grace was surprising. Although the Nationals benefited from a favorable schedule in 1949–50 (playing against the other recent NBL refugees, since Ned Irish didn't want them playing in New York), this wasn't the full story of the team's remarkable .797 win-loss percentage in 1949–50. The team's win-loss record was 35-9 against Western Conference teams (the Nats were in the Eastern Division) and 16-4 versus the Eastern and Central Conference teams, virtually identical win-loss percentages. One might surmise that playing a slate of games against the likes of Anderson, Sheboygan, Waterloo, and Denver left the Nats refreshed and ready to take on more formidable rivals in the two established conferences. The Syracuse Nationals team returned its top six scorers in 1950–51, and all played most of the team's sixty-six games. The team's plummet is difficult to explain.

The New York Knickerbockers finished second in the division but thirteen games away from first place. The Knicks played only twelve games (winning eight) with the inept Western Division clubs and claimed that the Syracuse Nats had an unfair scheduling advantage (although, of course, Ned Irish presumably had agreed to the schedule before the season began). Given Irish's vision of the now NBA being a "big league" circuit with teams only in larger cities, the reader can only imagine his fear of hosting, say, the Waterloo Hawks team at Madison Square Garden with a possible ensuing headline, "Knicks Meet Their Waterloo at Garden." One does not have to be a New Yorker to recognize the problems inherent in such matchups with Anderson, Sheboygan, and other teams that might have presented similar marquee disasters. Waterloo and Sheboygan each appeared at the Garden once, and both times the teams were part of the first game of a doubleheader playing a team other than the Knicks. The Knicks avoided scheduling the Anderson Packers in New York by playing them as part of a doubleheader in Philadelphia.[54]

The Western Conference's two best teams in 1949–50 sported winning records mostly because they feasted on the three bottom feeders in their division.

Indianapolis' 39-25 record reflected its 26-9 record against the Western Conference and 13-16 against everyone else. Anderson's record was 25-12 against Western Conference foes and 12-15 versus the remainder of the league. Sheboygan, Waterloo, and Denver, the three worst teams in the division, contributed to the division's overall 157-221 win-loss record. None of the six Western Division teams had winning records in interdivisional play, and the group collectively had a 50-114 win-loss record against their Eastern and Central Division rivals. Any team that got to play the Western Conference teams an inordinate amount of times figured to compile a gaudy record. The Fort Wayne Pistons, as with most of the incumbent BAA teams, feasted on the newcomers from the NBL, thereby accounting for some of the improvement in their 1949–50 records.

Although the BAA/NBA's reserve clause was not as formal as that of Major League Baseball, owners nevertheless dictated player movement. Aside from the traditional mechanisms of trades and sales, pro basketball's volatile history meant that player dispersal drafts loomed as a major source of player movement. With frequent folding of teams, desirable players on those teams were exposed to a reverse-order draft. Of course, many, if not most, teams that folded were not endowed with a surfeit of talent to disperse.

In the immediate postwar era, players were frequently signed as free agents. Coaches would call players and ask them to join their teams. Eventually the NBL and BAA developed drafts of amateur players. To forestall players jumping contracts, the NBL ruled that players who jumped would be barred from league play for life. The BAA had earlier announced such a policy. An economist might view the twin announcements as a violation of antitrust laws, but the league owners were probably pleased with the results, as a ruinous bidding war did not erupt.[55]

The NBL and BAA merger occasionally created confusion as to which team possessed a right to a player. The Fort Wayne Pistons, desperately seeking a center, first signed Don Otten of Bowling Green (Ohio) State University. "All they got for their money was the privilege of watching him loaf." The team then paid the former NBL and briefly NBA Waterloo Hawks team $20,000 for Charlie Share while awarding him a $10,000 contract. The Boston Celtics, who had drafted Share in the 1950 draft, cried foul. To appease the Celtics, the Pistons bought Bob Brannum from the Sheboygan Red Skins for $15,000 and Bill Sharman from the Washington Capitols for $3,000. They sent Brannum and Sharman to the Celtics.[56]

Because of the reshuffling of rosters, even top players moved around. Table 15 shows the experiences of the NBA's best players from 1946 to 1962. In this case, because there is no comprehensive rating for NBA players of this era as there is for baseball players, players who appeared on the end-of-season NBA First and Second teams are considered "Top Players."[57] Between 1946 and 1962, fifty-six players received these honors at least once. Some would continue to win such honors (West, Baylor, Robertson, Russell, and Chamberlain). Of the fifty-six, twenty-two (39.3 percent) spent their entire career with only one franchise. This proportion was higher than that for the most productive Major League Baseball players through 1998 (19.0 percent). The basketball proportion would have been higher except that Bob Cousy played a few games after his retirement when he coached the Kansas City Kings. George Mikan played on two teams because his first team folded. Baseball and basketball teams' likelihoods of retaining star players are not strictly comparable. Baseball's likelihood ratios include some players who performed during free agency, when they were not under contract with a specific team, while basketball's upheavals during the NBA's first decade triggered a lot of player movement, despite being a strict reserve-clause regime.

Examining the twenty-two NBA players who rated First- or Second-team honors three or more times between 1946 and 1962, the proportion that remained with a single franchise rose to 59.1 percent. Of baseball's most productive 261 players, about a quarter remained with one team for their entire career. Granted these are small samples, but NBA owners appeared loath to transfer the very best players. The nine players who moved include the aforementioned Cousy and Mikan, as well as Wilt Chamberlain, Richie Guerin, Johnny Logan, Ed Macauley, Slater Martin, Bill Sharman, and Max Zaslofsky. Logan spent all but his final season with the Blackhawks/Hawks, while Sharman's initial team, the Washington Capitols, folded after his first year. He then spent the remainder of his career with the Boston Celtics.

In a sense, this relative stability of the very best players defies the Coase/Rottenberg theorem. While the New York Knicks attempted to acquire top-flight players from teams in the smaller cities, they had mixed success and settled into a decade-long funk. The Knicks have not exemplified buying a team's way to championships, but the Los Angeles Lakers have obtained Wilt Chamberlain, Kareem Abdul-Jabbar, and Shaquille O'Neal from teams in smaller cities (Philadelphia, Milwaukee, and Orlando respectively).

DISPERSAL DRAFTS

Modern fans of the NBA are used to the reverse-order draft of collegiate and international players, which ostensibly helps teams with poor win-loss records rebound. The early BAA had a similar draft. Given the number of teams that folded, the BAA/NBA also held a number of dispersal drafts in its first decade. In some of these drafts, owners of surviving teams acquired good players.

The dispersal drafts began on July 10, 1947, after the Detroit Falcons franchise folded.[58] In the last dispersal draft, the remaining eight teams scavenged the Baltimore Bullets' roster. The Milwaukee Hawks had first rights and selected Frank Selvy, a high-scoring player. Selvy provided a temporary attendance boost for the Hawks.[59] Between these dispersal drafts, though, were some of greater impact. How the Celtics obtained Bob Cousy is an amusing story that exemplifies the slightly crazed aspect of the league's early history with its frequent dispersal drafts. Red Auerbach wanted a center, so he passed on exercising his territorial right to Cousy to get Charlie Share. The Tri-Cities Blackhawks drafted Cousy, but Bob made it clear he didn't want to play in that area. The Blackhawks then traded Cousy to the Chicago Stags for Frankie Brian, but the Stags immediately folded. In the meantime, the St. Louis Bombers also folded, although Ned Irish attempted to buy the team in order to acquire center Ed Macauley. The other owners would not allow this acquisition and dispersed the Bombers' good players via a "draft." Boston got Macauley, negating the need for Share, while Red Rocha went to Baltimore and Johnny Logan went to Tri-Cities. Chicago's big assets were established stars Max Zaslofsky and Andy Phillips. Cousy was also available. As sportswriter Leonard Koppett put it, "New York, Philadelphia, and Boston were equally insistent that the welfare of the league, not to mention of the whole Western World and perhaps the universe as we know it, depended entirely on being given the rights to Max."[60] Podoloff decided the three owners could draw names out of a hat. For once Irish got lucky. He drew first and got Zaslofsky, a native New York and Jewish star. Eddie Gottlieb got the second draw and got Phillips. Brown, Auerbach, and the Celtics got Cousy. The three players cost their owners $15,000, $10,000, and $8,500 respectively. Auerbach and Cousy certainly ended up best off, as Cousy proved to be a productive and exciting player for more than a decade. Auerbach now had some of the players needed for his fast-break style of basketball.

The dispersal drafts were an embarrassing facet of the league's early days, but they affected competitive balance. The Boston Celtics and Red Auerbach became a winning combination with the acquisitions of Macauley and Cousy from the draft. In subsequent years, the NBA's drafts would comprise only collegiate and, eventually, high school talent.

Avoiding a Gambling Scandal

Because basketball had the fewest players on the court or on the field at any one time of the major team sports, it was attractive to gamblers, especially those who liked their odds favorable. While baseball players had long been suspected of hippodroming, the old-fashioned term for throwing games, the White Sox players' fix of the 1919 World Series led to drastic action. The baseball owners sought the perception, if not the reality, that the games were honest. To restore public confidence, they concentrated power in the hands of Judge Kenesaw Mountain Landis. Landis quickly banned the eight White Sox players involved in the plot, including one whose only offense was not reporting the fix. Although some disquieting rumors persisted, the public believed the games were on the level, and the 1920s became a prosperous decade for baseball.

Gamblers were among the NBA's best and most troublesome fans. While most fans attended the games purely for the sport, gamblers wanted more involvement in the game. Sportswriter Arthur Daley believed that gamblers were initially leery of professional basketball: "the bookies viewed it with jaundiced eye. The players were so skilled and so consummately clever that the betting gentry was afraid of them. So there was no wagering on the pro dribblers for the longest while. But then it became obvious that this was a completely honest game and the bookies were accepting bets on the pros when they were refusing them on the collegians."[61] Old-time BAA/NBA players painted a different picture, recalling the antics of gamblers throughout the league from the beginning.

Leonard Koppett believed the essence of basketball is deception: deceiving the defender. "Unhappily, this basic feature of basketball brings with it some undesirable consequences, and there is no point in avoiding them. Actions that deceive an opponent can also deceive a referee, adding to a burden of decision already greater than officials in other games face. And it is not a coincidence that the worst fixed-game scandals to hit any team sport have hit basketball. The highly developed ability to mask intent can be, like any ability, misapplied, to dishonest ends."[62] Since there are only five players on the court, a gambler needs to induce only one or two players to shave points, and the fast pace of the game makes it very difficult to ascertain malfeasance (especially in the era before games were videotaped).

> How, then, are fixes detected? By external evidence only. Never by examination of how a game was played. . . . And when is suspicion justified? Never

on the basis of an unexpected result. Never. Every imagined fix can easily be a legitimate upset. . . . Again, the basis for suspicion must be external. That external evidence lies within the betting world. To fix a game, the fixed must hope to gain. He can only gain by collecting his bet. To collect it, he must first make it. And the bet must be a sizable one to warrant the bribe and the risk.

None of the 1951 college scandals used on-floor game evidence, but rather relied on confessions and testimony of a conspiracy to fix a game. Koppett also pointed out that professional players were less likely to jeopardize their salaries than a collegiate player, who theoretically received no explicit cash payment.[63] Charles Rosen describes how the honest bookies investigated suspicious goings-on: "Crooked games are anathema to an honest, workaday bookie. They prevent him from evening out his bets and make him vulnerable to a big loss should the 'wrong' team win. A bookmaker would much rather work on commission and never lose money. The New York bookies were in a bind and were forced to make a move. . . . Several of them pooled $5,000 and hired a private detective to try and run down all the specifics of the fixed ball games."[64]

Sports historian Neil Isaacs believed that the college basketball scandal of 1949–50 "created a vacuum in public support which the NBA was prepared to fill." He lauded Maurice Podoloff's willingness to ban any player implicated in point shaving or betting on games as assuring the public that the games were honest. Other historians are not quite so laudatory, citing some cases where players whose only guilt lay in not telling the authorities their teammates were fixing games were banned from the league.[65]

Ned Irish became rich and well known by promoting college basketball doubleheaders at Madison Square Garden beginning in the 1930s. For many years these collegiate doubleheaders were the pinnacle of the basketball world. The BAA faced stiff competition for spectator dollars in New York City from the collegians.

Gamblers were not reticent about their presence at college basketball games throughout the country, and they were especially notorious at Madison Square Garden. Only the most naïve could believe there was not potential for an unseemly scandal. Fixing a basketball game was not too difficult. Because the bets were based on point differentials, gamblers could convince players that they weren't actually throwing games, just manipulating the score. Clever and skillful players could shave a point or two here and there without too much suspicion, especially when there were few game films to check their behavior.

As early as 1944, college coaches were sounding the alarm that a scandal was imminent. Famous Kansas coach Forrest "Phog" Allen warned that Madison Square Garden was rife with trouble, citing an attempt to fix an NCAA championship game between University of Utah and Dartmouth College. Ned Irish, the Garden's acting president retorted, "If Allen has any proof of dishonesty in basketball games at the Garden, he'd better come through with it." Allen apparently sent Irish the name of a player who had sold out and been expelled from college. Irish's response was to increase police presence at the game, with orders to prevent all known gamblers from entering the Garden.[66]

The college basketball scandal supplied headlines for months in 1950–51. Irish finally had to confront the situation at Madison Square Garden. He temporarily considered dropping the sport. Reporter Warren Moscow reported, "It was understood that, while the Garden was loath to lose the revenue from a sport that ranks with hockey, the circus, the rodeo and other attractions, there were some who felt that the apparent impossibility of policing the sport was bringing the Garden a bad name. There was another opinion that banning the sport would be a concession of defeat, and that rigorous attempts at ending the evils should be made first."[67] While Irish and the Garden scaled back college basketball doubleheaders, the games continued throughout the 1950s.

At first BAA and NBL owners were just as willing as the college coaches and administrators to ignore potential gambling problems. While pro basketball may have attracted fewer gamblers than its more popular college counterpart, gamblers made up a small but loyal segment of the fan bases of many teams. Even so, player reminiscences frequently centered on characters in the stands yelling and screaming when someone scored a "meaningless" basket near the end of a game. Although such baskets might not affect the final outcome, they could affect the point spread, the predicted difference in scores between two teams. Player and later coach Alex Hannum recalled, "In my first game at Madison Square Garden, we were up by eight points over the Knicks and the fans yelled like hell. Then the score was tied, and the place was quiet. We later learned the point spread was eight. We also sensed that our salaries were being paid indirectly by the gamblers because a lot of the fans buying tickets were there to bet on the game."[68]

In the league's third season, a gambling incident popped up. High-scoring Joe Fulks of the Philadelphia Warriors claimed that a man by the name of Morris "Moxie" Fleishman offered him "easy money to throw games." Since Fulks was the league's second-highest scorer that season, despite making only 31.1 percent of his shots, he had plenty of opportunities to miss just one more shot. Who would be able to discern the difference? Since professional players differed from college players in being given explicit payment for their services, gamblers had to finesse their pitch. Fleishman allegedly said, "Other people are making easy money by off-setting games. Why don't you make some easy money while you are able. You can't go on playing professional basketball all your life."[69]

Although wagering on sporting events was illegal in many jurisdictions, figuring out what protections were owed gamblers was a thorny issue. Under then-existing Pennsylvania law, there was no law specifically outlawing attempts to bribe basketball players (the legislators had not included such athletes in the law). Instead, Fleishman was arraigned on a misdemeanor law stating that anyone who "offers or gives to an agent, employee, or servant of another . . . any valuable thing without the knowledge and consent of the employer . . . as an inducement, bribe or reward for doing or omitting to do any act [to the prejudice of the employer] is guilty of a misdemeanor."[70] Fleishman's attorney successfully argued that the law did not apply to professional basketball players. The presiding judge acquitted Fleishman, because the state's attorney failed to prove money was offered to throw games.[71] In the aftermath the Pennsylvania legislature and governor revised the law concerning bribery in sports events.

In another strange event, NBA referee Arnie Heft received a telegram advising him that his assignment in Syracuse was canceled. The telegram had Walter Kennedy's name on it, but Kennedy, in charge of assigning referees, denied sending it. League officials were never able to ascertain who sent the telegram or for what purpose.[72] League officials were, of course, properly suspicious of the incident.

Untangling the effects the college basketball scandal had upon the NBA is difficult. The league's winnowing process of 1949–53 argues against the story that patrons switched allegiance between college and professional hoops. Since the surviving owners did not supply profit/loss or attendance data for 1948–51, comparisons with the 1951–57 figures they did provide are impossible.

There were, however, some connections between the recurring college basketball scandals and the NBA. While historian Neil Isaacs claims, "No NBA game was ever shown to have been fixed, and the appearance of integrity was preserved," the league had several close calls.[73] Unbeknownst to the league, some point-shaving players were performing in it. Olympians and former University of Kentucky stars Ralph Beard and Alex Groza not only played for the Indianapolis Olympians, but they also shared ownership of the team.

Although their college coach, Adolph Rupp, declared that gamblers could not touch his boys, allegations evolved into admissions that three of his players accepted $1,500 to fix a National Invitation Tournament championship game at Madison Square Garden on March 14, 1949. To their credit, Podoloff and the owners reacted quickly and decisively by suspending Beard and Groza. Since all of the Olympians players combined owned 70 percent of the stock in the team, the league had to purchase Beard's and Groza's shares. In addition, the league allowed the team to select some replacement players from other NBA teams. While there were no allegations that Beard and Groza ever threw NBA games, the league had to be worried about the repercussions. The Indianapolis team staggered through two more seasons, and the remaining players actually posted a better record in 1951–52 than in Beard's and Groza's last season of 1950–51.[74]

One ramification of the college betting scandals was that the New York Knicks suffered diminished benefits from the territorial draft rule. Five prominent New York City colleges eventually suspended their basketball programs, effectively wiping out the territory. The Knicks were waiting for Long Island University's Sherman White, a 6′7″ center whom sportswriter Leonard Koppett believed would have helped the Knicks win some championships and change the league's development. Unfortunately, White was implicated in the gambling scandal and forfeited any NBA career he might have had.[75] The college basketball desert that was now New York City meant the Knicks did not exercise a territorial draft pick for more than a decade until selecting Bill Bradley in 1965.

Kentucky center Bill Spivey was another casualty of the gambling scandal. Spivey proclaimed his innocence but was indicted for perjury even though his trial had ended in a hung jury. As with the Chicago White Sox players, his ambiguous legal status made him too risky for the NBA to touch, and he was barred from the league.[76] The league would also later ban Connie Hawkins, whom many thought was not guilty of wrongdoing.

There was a potential risk from banning too many prominent players: an outlaw league might use such marquee players to achieve quick recognition from the public. Indeed, Spivey and Hawkins played in the short-lived American Basketball League, and Hawkins later dazzled fans in the ABA.

From the league's standpoint, the stringent measures, while potentially unfair to individual players, seemed necessary. Not long after barring Beard and Groza, the league was confronted by a nasty situation: accusations of a dishonest referee. NBA fans likely can recall the 2007 mess surrounding convicted referee Tim Donaghy (who pleaded guilty to two felony charges in connection with illegal betting on NBA games). Similarly, in the early 1950s district attorney Frank Hogan, the same DA who investigated Beard and Groza, accused Sol Levy of taking $3,000 in bribes in connection with three games he had refereed. Levy allegedly was supposed to keep Boston from winning by more than the point spread versus, ironically, the Indianapolis Olympians. In the third game he supposedly called an inordinate number of fouls against the New York Knickerbockers (forty-six versus twenty-nine) to help the gamblers.[77] While such disparities in fouls might raise the hackles of coaches, proving that the disparity marked dishonest refereeing was difficult. As the case unfolded, Levy was alleged to have been on Salvatore T. Sollazzo's payroll, although Hogan admitted that the referee failed "to come through" for Sollazzo. In addition to the three games identified earlier, Hogan claimed Levy was supposed to fix a Lakers-Capitols game. The referee was supposed to foul out some Lakers players, presumably George Mikan, but was unable to do so. The Lakers won by six points.

As the case unfolded, prosecutors had difficulty finding a law under which to indict Levy. He was tried on a seven-count criminal information instead of an indictment, "because 'a careful study' of the Penal Code's bribery statue showed it did not cover bribery involving officials at games." District Attorney Hogan recommended to the state legislature that they amend the statute "to cover this defect." "Levy was charged with violation of Section 439 of the Penal Law, which involves the corrupt acceptance of a gift, or promise of a gift, for acting in a particular manner towards one's employer."[78]

During the trial, Sollazzo testified that he conspired with Levy to rig points on six NBA games.[79] A special three-judge court eventually found Levy guilty on six of the seven counts against him, but even here there was controversy. One justice did not believe that Levy came under Section 439, because she considered him an independent contractor of the NBA. Apparently she stated that "deliberately fouling out basketball players was not a punishable offense." Levy was sentenced to serve up to three years in the city penitentiary. A month later Levy's sidekick, Salvatore Sollazzo, pled guilty in federal court of evading income taxes totaling $264,455 for 1944 and 1945. The incident appeared to be an isolated event, and the league's prompt handling of it prevented serious public relations problems. A year later Levy's conviction was unanimously reversed by the appellate division of the New York Supreme Court. The justices did not deny that Levy acted corruptly but ruled that Section 439 did not apply to a referee in professional games or sports.[80]

Shortly after Levy received his sentence, another ugly scandal arose. Major League Baseball had its Hal Chase, a slippery infielder with a golden glove and an apparently less than golden sense of ethics. While it was difficult to convict Chase, many of his teammates remained convinced that he was throwing games. Jack Molinas, another suave athlete, would fight the NBA for years. With his legal training, Molinas was a more formidable foe than many of the collegians implicated in gambling scandals. He had been Columbia University's basketball captain. The New York Knicks could have selected Walter Dukes of Seton Hall, Ray Felix of Long Island University, or Molinas as a territorial pick after the 1953 season. The Knicks opted for Dukes, who signed with the Globetrotters when that team offered him a $17,000 bonus that the Knicks refused to match.[81] Dukes would play for the Knicks in subsequent seasons. The Fort Wayne Pistons selected Molinas.

Midway through the 1953–54 season, Molinas admitted placing bets on games, including some Pistons games. While Maurice Podoloff characterized the situation as "a minor aberration that will not affect the league . . . not a big operation, involving diabolical genius," he was sufficiently concerned that he suspended the player on January 10, 1954. Molinas thus forfeited his reported $9,600 salary. At no point did anyone accuse Molinas of rigging or throwing games. Sportswriter Arthur Daley was less charitable, however. He described Molinas's antics as a "brazen search for trouble" and a calculated action, saying, "If the point spread was favorable enough, he'd place a bet. If it wasn't, he'd decline to wager." The writer alleged that bookies refused to accept bets on Fort Wayne Pistons games in late December and early January: "Something must have aroused their suspicions."[82]

A Bronx grand jury and chief assistant district attorney George Tilzer admitted, "Despite painstaking and exhaustive investigation, we were unable to unearth any evidence of crime committed. No evidence was unearthed involving any player being influenced by professional gambling."[83] Molinas periodically pressed for an appeal, but the courts denied him such. He later filed a $5 million suit against the league, because he had been denied reinstatement. Podoloff blandly stated, "The same thing that happened before will happen again. We will be upheld. It will just cost us some additional fees." Molinas said the league was depriving him of an opportunity to make a living, although he also had to admit that the Bar Association had not deemed betting on games serious enough to prevent him from practicing law.[84] Whatever sympathy people may have had for Molinas disappeared in the 1960s when he became a pivotal figure in yet another college gambling scandal. This time he was accused of fixing games.

Years later, Fort Wayne Pistons star George Yardley told Charles Salzberg: "That year [1955] we lost by one point to Syracuse in the finals. We were up by 17 at one point in the first half, then led all the way through the second half. We had the ball with thirty seconds to go, then fifteen seconds to go, and then we throw it right to Syracuse's George King, who goes in a for a lay-up. I don't know about that. . . . Some of the players on our team were friendly with Molinas." Yardley went on to describe another scandal that was not publicized but in which two Pistons players, among others, were forced to retire. "I don't know whether it had anything to do with that scandal [presumably referring to the playoff loss]. . . . We all think that in our own minds we're great and we have a couple of stiffs out there that were hurting us."[85]

In December 1955 Maurice Podoloff had to investigate bribe offers to NBA coaches. In one incident an unknown person phoned from Minneapolis and asked for Syracuse coach Al Cervi. After four attempts to reach Cervi, the caller said, "Tell Cervi to lose this game, or not to win it by more than six points. Tell him there will be $1,000 in it for him and a couple of hundred for yourself [referring to the office attendant answering the phone]."[86] Two other coaches received similar phone calls during the same time period. Podoloff remarked, "Even though I feel this is the work of a crackpot, I am doing everything possible to trace down the caller. Right now I am stabbing in the dark."[87]

In retrospect, scholar Fletcher Gregory's summation of the NBA's actions is astute. The league may well have been unfair to some individuals, but the overriding need to assure the public that the games were honest may have justified such draconian policies. Bill Spivey and Connie Hawkins were cast as unwilling "Shoeless Joes" (the Chicago "Black Sox" star who was banned for life from baseball for conspiring to fix the World Series), but such characters as Jack Molinas, Ralph Beard, and Alex Groza merited strong punishment if the league were to maintain its reputation.[88]

With gambling even more ubiquitous today than in the 1950s, basketball and other sports remain vigilant for gambling situations. Newspapers and the Internet make access to point spreads and odds easier than ever. How the league would fare under another gambling scandal remains to be seen, but based on the popularity of college basketball, for instance, sports fans would likely forgive if not forget any future transgressions.

Integration

Jackie Robinson has been acknowledged as the first African American player of the twentieth century in Major League Baseball, joining the Brooklyn Dodgers in 1947. The NBA's integration story has not been as publicized, however, possibly because it lacked the drama played out in Brooklyn and her fellow National League cities (and by Larry Doby of the Cleveland Indians in the American League later that summer). The NBL had begun integrating teams, with players such as Dolly King, before the merger with the BAA. In addition, after the initial four NBL teams jumped to the BAA, the remaining NBL teams invited the all-black New York Rens to join the league, becoming the Dayton Rens. This team was neither an artistic or financial success, folding after a mediocre 14-26 record.[89] The Rens had earlier played the Minneapolis Lakers in the championship game of the World Professional Basketball Tournament.

There were several differences between basketball's and baseball's integration experiences. Many of the NBA players performed for colleges and universities in northern cities and were used to playing with and against African American players. Of the 131 white players performing in 1950–51, just 29 played for schools in the South, many from Kentucky. While racial prejudice undoubtedly lurked in northern universities, players at those universities nevertheless were likely to have played against black players. Former NBA player Walt Budko recalled: "There was no racial tension in pro basketball. The difference from baseball was both the ethnic and the geographical makeup. New York wasn't the be-all and end-all of basketball, but that's where much of its fame emanated from. And in that area the blacks started coming in right before the war. So most of us played on teams with blacks and thought nothing of it. A lot of the fellas were in the service with blacks and played with them there. I never heard anyone cussing anyone out with racial stuff." Perhaps buttressing Budko's positive spin on racial integration was Wat Misaka's experiences. Misaka, a Japanese American who was interned during the war, played for the University of Utah. During the NCAA tournament, his defensive efforts thwarted the University of Kentucky's Ralph Beard. The crowd loved the small player (5'7"), so the Knicks signed him. There were no untoward incidents during Misaka's brief NBA career, although the *New York Times* account of the college game read, "Little Wat Misaka . . . was a 'cute' fellow intercepting passes and making the night miserable for Kentucky." The Knicks cut Misaka early in the 1947–48 season, along with their previous season's leading scorer, Sonny Hertzberg.[90]

While baseball's Negro Leagues played in many big cities and were fairly well known, even by whites, none of these teams had the cachet that the Harlem Globetrotters possessed. Abe Saperstein's Globetrotters drew large crowds throughout America and the world, although they weren't always welcome in the American South.[91] The team's control of top African American players would complicate the integration of professional basketball, both because NBA owners, needing the lucrative appearances by the Globetrotters, were wary of offending Saperstein by competing for top black players and because the team provided black players leverage in salary negotiations versus NBA owners. Since Saperstein employed only a handful of players, though, his domination of this supply would not survive the 1950s.

Professional African American basketball teams appeared almost as quickly as their white counterparts. Certainly there would have been no excuse for white coaches and players to deny the abilities of top black players. As late as 1948 the Harlem Globetrotters defeated the Minneapolis Lakers in serious competition, and Saperstein's team would provide top-flight competition for a few more years. Why the BAA/NBA waited until 1950–51 to integrate remains unclear, although, as mentioned, owners may have hesitated in deference to Abe Saperstein's corner of the market for black players. The owners' decisions to integrate their teams, however, were clearly pivotal ones, although the benefits were not immediate.

Three black players—Chuck Cooper, Earl Lloyd, and Nat "Sweetwater" Clifton—simultaneously integrated basketball. Cooper was the first black drafted; Lloyd was the first to play in a regular season game.[92] Ned Irish signed Clifton from the Globetrotters, paying between $10,000 and $12,500 for his contract. The *New York Times* said Clifton was reportedly receiving $10,000 a year from the Globetrotters.[93] Lloyd appeared in an NBA game the day before Cooper, but of the three pioneers, Cooper has received the most attention. Playing for the Boston Celtics, Cooper received a "tremendous ovation" from the Rochester fans, according to the Rochester Royals program.[94] Neil Isaacs, Terry Pluto, and Charles Salzberg's collections of pioneering NBA players' oral histories paint a generally benign picture of integration, although many white players recalled some of the indignities suffered by their black teammates. One must view their recollections carefully, since white players may not have witnessed or understood the pressures under which their black teammates endured. Sportswriter Ron Thomas ably chronicles the journey of the NBA's black pioneers in his book *They Cleared the Lane*. Although these players recounted a relatively peaceful introduction to the NBA, they still bore scars from the segregation they experienced in many cities. These players also expressed a belief that they had to sublimate their games—less flash and more attention to basketball's dirty work of rebounding, setting draft picks, and playing defense. Some believed black players were purposely denied opportunities to score a lot of points.

While there is no way to prove or disprove that white owners, coaches, and players did not want black players to be the top scorers, it is interesting to note that Don Barksdale became the first black NBA player to lead his team in scoring. He led the Baltimore Bullets in scoring in 1952–53 (the third season of integration). He also became the first black player to appear in an NBA All-Star Game. He had earlier been the first black player to be on a U.S. Olympic team in 1948. A year later he was playing for the Boston Celtics. He noted that it was "comical" that even though there were literally (two) handfuls of black players in the league, "it seemed like they always ended up guarding each other in a game."[95] He cited Bob Cousy as one of the whites who became friends with many black players.

After Barksdale led his team in scoring, the next two black players to do so were Ray Felix and Maurice Stokes. Both led their teams in scoring during their rookie seasons. Stokes quickly established himself as a gifted player, earning Second-Team All-NBA honors in each of his three years as an active player.

While the Boston Celtics, New York Knicks, Tri-Cities Blackhawks, and Washington Capitols integrated their teams in 1950–51 (Tri-Cities only for a few games with Hank DeZonie), it took several seasons for the remaining teams to do so. After shifting his franchise from the Tri-Cities to Milwaukee, owner Ben Kerner signed another black player, Bob Wilson, for the 1951–52 season and Dave Minor for the 1952–53 season. The Baltimore Bullets became the fifth team to integrate by signing Don Barksdale and Dave Minor during 1951–52. The Syracuse Nationals integrated by acquiring Earl Lloyd in 1952–53. The Philadelphia Warriors integrated in 1954–55 with Jackie Moore. The Fort Wayne Pistons, Minneapolis Lakers, and Rochester Royals signed their first black NBA players during 1955–56, thereby completing the initial integration. By comparison, Major League Baseball owners did not fully integrate until the Boston Red Sox became the last team to field a black player, Pumpsie Green, in 1959. The NFL waited until 1962, when the Washington Redskins signed a few African American players.

The Rochester Royals had earlier integrated their NBL team during the 1947–48 season with Dolly King. Royals owner Les Harrison, who often sought white ethnic players such as those from Italian or Jewish backgrounds, warned King of the abuse he would face: "If you're gonna play, you're gonna have to accept the abuse; if you'll take a chance, so will we." Along with a few other black players in the NBL, King received the bulk of the abuse from opposing fans.[96] Unfortunately, an interracial fight broke out between players Pop Gates and Chick Meehan, with fans swarming the floor; the incident led to a one-year absence of black players, as NBL owners feared more violence. Both players denied the fight was racial, and, given the number of fights between white players, an interracial fight did not have to be spurred by racial factors. The owners, though, were hesitant to risk another such situation.[97] Harrison signed Maurice Stokes, Ed Fleming, and Dick Ricketts for 1955–56 and added Sihugo Green for the following season, giving the Royals a league-leading four black players.

The 1953–54 Minneapolis Lakers would be the last all-white champions. The 1954–55 Syracuse Nationals and 1955–56 Philadelphia Warriors championship teams both had black players.

Table 16 shows that four of the nine teams that integrated suffered declines in gate receipts, but each of these teams also declined in terms of win-loss percentages. Of the five teams experiencing increases in gate receipts immediately after integrating, three also had increases in win-loss percentages. The evidence regarding integration's effects upon gate receipts was ambiguous.

Once the next wave of black players—Stokes, Russell, Chamberlain, Baylor, and Robertson—arrived, they dominated statistical categories. After Bob Pettit won the scoring title in 1958–59, Wilt Chamberlain won the next seven titles. Aside from single scoring titles won by Rick Barry, Jerry West, and Pete Maravich, all subsequent scoring titles have been won by African American players. Stokes, Russell, and Chamberlain wrested the rebounding title from Bob Pettit beginning in 1956–57. Only during the late 1970s did white players such as Bill Walton and Swen Nater interrupt black players' leadership in this category. A similar situation, although not as pronounced, occurred with assists. African American players dominate the lifetime categories.

Conclusion

The BAA owners' decision to absorb the most attractive NBL teams obviously looms large in the league's development, although the move and subsequent merger could not save several BAA franchises. By ghettoizing the later NBL refugees, BAA owners may have ensured the demise of those teams. The 1949–50 season was probably one best forgotten, as the chaos did no one credit. Fortunately, there weren't too many people paying attention to the league's upheavals. The league's integration did not initially create much excitement either.

One benefit from the NBA owners' acquiescence to the unwieldy seventeen-team league was the absence of an antitrust lawsuit as occurred twenty years later with the ABA. By demonstrating that the Waterloos of the world could not sustain a top-level basketball franchise, the surviving NBA teams avoided a lengthy, expensive lawsuit and potential congressional scrutiny. Years later, when the NBA allied with the National Football League and National Hockey League in petitioning Congress for partial or full antitrust exemptions, the league was not embroiled in lawsuits that bedeviled the older leagues.

The streamlined NBA still struggled to entice fans. The game on the court was not obviously different from or superior to the collegiate brand. In many ways the professional players' experience and savvy led to brutal, foul-plagued games that alienated fans. While the owners confronted indirect situations of gambling, they avoided an outright scandal such as plagued and would continue to plague college-level basketball.

4

Shakedown (1951–54)

With the NBL gone, along with some of the original BAA franchises, the surviving owners hoped consolidation would provide stability if not prosperity. However, the elimination of six weak teams did not immediately create prosperity for the remaining NBA teams. Three more teams folded before the league settled into an eight-team circuit. The owners, seeking to reduce costs and bolster attendance, decided to rely on doubleheaders. They also worried about the growing roughness of league games and worked on trying to improve the product.

Attendance Blues

NBA president Maurice Podoloff attributed the attendance doldrums of 1951–52 to football, television, and public distrust of basketball emanating from the point-shaving scandal in college basketball. He also admitted that the general economic conditions during the Korean War and inadequate promotional efforts contributed to the downturn. His plaint echoed those of Major League Baseball owners facing steep declines in attendance after 1949. Hockey owners, too, faced shrinking crowds.[1]

Although modern critics of the NBA decry its marketing of individual stars instead of teams, the tactic is as old as the league itself. Ever since the league enticed George Mikan and the Lakers from the NBL, it has emphasized marquee players. The famous Madison Square Garden marquee, "Tonite: George Mikan vs. The New York Knicks," is as vital today as it was in the early 1950s.[2] Perhaps Knicks fans were sore at George for humiliating their centers, as he had set scoring records against them. Mikan and the Lakers, however, had not been a particularly popular draw at Madison Square Garden between 1949 and 1951, as the team never attracted more than 10,000 fans for any of its games there. Even in Minneapolis, with its mid-sized arenas, the team rarely generated crowds in excess of 10,000. But during Mikan's three remaining full-time seasons, he and the Lakers drew Garden crowds in excess of 16,000 three times and proved one of the better draws.[3]

Sportswriter Leonard Koppett believed that Bob Cousy, the 6'1" guard was a key player in popularizing the game. While most fans could not relate to the NBA centers, Cousy, while still taller than the average American male, was not a "pituitary freak."[4] "What the big men did, however successful, was the result of natural endowment; what Cousy did, looking so small among them, constituted the triumph of the common man. . . . Cousy did so much to establish, in the American imagination, the status of pro basketball. Black players were still few, so it was Cousy who displayed a truth that was already a cultural norm among the blacks and would be, eventually throughout the game: that in basketball, style is as important to the fan as sheer result." The addition of Cousy and Ed Macauley transformed the Celtics into a winning team, albeit one that fell short of advancing to the NBA finals until Red Auerbach added Bill Russell. Boston fans responded by boosting attendance at the Boston Garden by more than 60 percent between 1949–50 and 1950–51.[5]

Owners began to realize that a player did not have to be like Mikan to draw crowds. Ben Kerner, owner of the struggling Milwaukee Hawks, found that when he inherited rookie Frank Selvy from the defunct Baltimore Bullets he received an attendance boon, if only temporarily. Selvy scored thirty-five points in his first home game with the Hawks. In the next game 5,026 paid attendees watched Selvy score thirty-one points. Kerner gushed, "That's just under 9,000 paid for two games. The best week I've ever had here. I've gone eight, nine games before without drawing many more than that altogether."[6] He certainly needed an attendance boost. He had transferred his Tri-Cities Blackhawks to Milwaukee for the 1951–52 season. While the Blackhawks played thirty-five home games in 1950–51, Kerner scheduled only twenty home games for 1951–52. When the Boston Braves baseball team transferred to Milwaukee for the 1953 season, fans flocked to see them, leaving the moribund Hawks even less appreciated. Then again, the Hawks were a poor team on the court.

ATTEMPTS TO BOOST THE GATE

The sad truth for BAA owners was that their product simply did not generate large enough crowds to be profitable. Owners, especially of teams in smaller cities, quickly grasped this reality and responded by employing various promotions.

Early in the league's existence, owners relied on the Harlem Globetrotters to ensure a relatively full arena. As Leonard Koppett wrote, "The Globies were available, a couple of times a year, to stir basketball interest in any town they visited, to make a good payday for the arena (even after the Globies got their cut), and to help bring in crowds to see a BAA game by playing their own game as a preliminary."[7] Historian Michael Schumacher points out that initially the Globetrotter-Laker game was played first, then the BAA game. However, when fans started leaving after the Globetrotter game, BAA owners made the Globetrotter game the second game of the evening. The Globetrotters were quite popular, although some observers wondered how their attendance would hold up if the team had a home arena where it played thirty or forty games each season.[8]

The Washington Capitols attracted their largest crowd of the 1949–50 season—6,105—when the Globetrotters appeared in a doubleheader, but the Trotters could not save Washington. The Trotters usually created crowds in excess of 18,000 at Madison Square Garden, although regular NBA doubleheaders sometimes drew 16,000 or more.[9] Chicago Stadium did well when the Globetrotters appeared. A game between the Globetrotters and the Minneapolis Lakers filled the stadium with 20,000 fans, while doubleheaders with NBA teams in 1950 and 1951 attracted only 11,000 fans per game.[10] The Globetrotters, then, were a formidable gate attraction, but the mix of showmanship and humor, not the team's absolute level of talent, may have accounted for the crowds. NBA teams needed years to shed their Globetrotter dependency.

In an attempt to boost attendance, NBA owners revised a page from Major League Baseball's book. Baseball doubleheaders, now a vanishing aspect of the game, were once a hallowed institution. On the three major summer holidays—Memorial Day, Fourth of July, and Labor Day—Major League Baseball teams held doubleheaders. Aside from the lackluster St. Louis Browns, these doubleheaders were by far baseball owners' best paydays; in most cases the holiday doubleheaders generated much larger crowds than two single games would have. The NBA initially featured doubleheaders where a high school game, a Harlem Globetrotters game, or even a rival NBL game would be staged before the main event.

The struggling Chicago Stags broached the possibility of staging four-team BAA doubleheaders, but the owners tabled the suggestion for the remainder of the 1946–47 season because of difficulties in adjusting the schedule. Double-headers, of course, meant that some teams would forfeit a home game. If the doubleheader were staged in a city with a large arena, the gate receipts might surpass those of two individual games at smaller arenas. The difficulty of getting four teams to one location, along with the added transportation expense, discouraged many owners from trying the plan in the late 1940s.[11] Murry Nelson describes how the NBL/BAA agreed to stage twenty-two doubleheaders at Chicago Stadium once the NBL's Chicago American Gears folded. Unfortunately, he did not discuss how the gate receipts were split among the teams. The Chicago Stags eventually got their wish, as the other teams each agreed to give up one of their home games in return for playing in a doubleheader at Chicago Stadium.[12]

Some owners did not bother much with promotional innovations. The NBA did not produce an equivalent of baseball's Bill Veeck Jr. or Larry MacPhail. The Rochester Royals' owners, Les and Jack Harrison, were content to nearly fill their small Edgerton Park by fielding winning teams. They worked out a deal with some local retailers to sell tickets. As historian Donald Fisher writes: "With little need for entrepreneurial marketing innovations, the Royals' mode of promotion stagnated. The team was filled with stars, won a high percentage of its games, and most importantly, unfailingly filled Edgerton Park. . . . Royals management saw no need to plan for the future in terms of an innovative marketing program utilizing modern public relations techniques." Fisher's in-depth case history of the Royals contains an analysis of the team's programs. He noted that the number of pages and number of advertisements declined steadily. The companies buying advertisements also changed over time. Instead of advertisements catering to businessmen and members of the professional class, the later advertisements were for home appliances, alcohol and tobacco, and other products. Fisher noted that automobile dealers, at least, were fairly loyal advertisers.[13] The team relied upon a coterie of season ticket holders. Some observers believed that the reliance eventually boomeranged, as the team did not expand its base of fans. Fisher also cited the 1950s phenomenon of suburbanization; with Americans earning higher incomes, they purchased automobiles and homes in the suburbs. He concludes, "For many Royals fans of the late 1940s, the drive to Edgerton Park on the city's west side may have simply become an inconvenience."[14]

In contrast to the Harrisons' staid approach, Ben Kerner knew that while fielding a winning team was paramount, an owner also had to promote the team. Whereas Veeck occasionally used his sideshows to divert attention from the horrors on the field (such as his St. Louis Browns), Kerner used promotional gimmicks as a bonus for his fans. He noted, "All the extras in the world aren't worth a plugged nickel if you don't have a winner." Kerner figured that the Hawks lost 15 percent of their patrons each season as a result of moving out of the area and switching to other entertainment venues. Kerner told Lowell Reidenbaugh that he needed to find 1,500 new Hawks fans annually to fill Kiel Auditorium, saying: "Our average take for 33 openings was only slightly below that of New York's. But you have to remember that the Knicks have a greater capacity in Madison Square Garden . . . and their ticket scale has a $6 tops while ours is only $3. Among the $40,000 worth of attractions that helped the Hawks draw a club record of 270,000 fans the past season, an increase of 23 per cent of the 1958–59 gate [were big musical bands]." Kerner's attendance boost was matched by an increase in his expenses. He once figured $160,000 in revenue was sufficient to break even, but with higher salaries (his Hawks were not perennial contenders until the late 1950s) and other expenses, he now figured $500,000 was needed to break even.[15]

The Minneapolis Lakers sent Podoloff a lengthy letter explaining their promotional efforts. The team proposed a children's television show with George Mikan, distributed Lakers comic books, gave passes to high school teams, did radio promotions, and organized Greyhound bus tour packages.[16] A few owners also employed baseball's tactic of "cultivating" children as attendees. Fred Zollner admitted children for fifty cents a ticket in an effort to "grow" his fans.[17]

Certainly league president Maurice Podoloff was aware of the need to generate favorable publicity about the league. In one of his bulletins to the owners, he cited press clippings collected by his assistant (and later NBA president) Walter Kennedy. They were hopeful of upcoming articles in such popular periodicals as *Time, Life, Look, Colliers*, and the *Saturday Evening Post*, although in some cases their optimism proved premature and the articles did not appear.[18]

The league drew relatively large crowds for its East-West All-Star games. The first game generated a crowd of just over 10,000 at Boston Garden. While baseball and football owners might have disdained such a turnout, basketball officials were ecstatic. Boston Celtics owner Walter Brown was a driving force for the game. Podoloff gushed that the gross gate receipts were $13,250, while the net receipts were almost $11,000. He pointed out that a recent Boston-Minneapolis game on a Sunday had gross gate receipts of just $8,700. Two years later the game grossed $21,500 and netted just under $18,000.[19] While the league enjoyed the big gate receipts, Brown had to host the second game in order to convince them of its long-term viability. The league also attracted crowds in excess of 5,000 for charity purposes, such as the game to raise funds to pay Rochester Royals player Maurice Stokes's burgeoning medical expenses in the wake of his tragic injury in 1958.[20] By the end of the 1952–53 season, though, owners still had not succeeded in generating adequate revenue.

Travel

The owners' obsession with travel costs was indicative of the league's financial plight. In a sense transportation costs were relative. Basketball teams faced lower transportation costs per mile than baseball or football, since basketball teams' entourages were considerably smaller (a dozen players at most, a coach, and perhaps a couple of other people versus twenty-five baseball players, a manager, some coaches, and other people; football had even larger entourages). The basketball owners may have had reason to worry, although some of their woes were self-inflicted. Baseball's American and National Leagues scheduled three- and four-game series, so traveling players could look forward to a few days in a city. Basketball players, however, faced a more peripatetic existence, as teams played just single games in each city during road trips. The basketball league's penchant for doubleheaders also exacerbated travel. A baseball team playing seventy-seven road games might have only twenty-one to twenty-eight actual destinations during the season (visiting each opposing team three or four times), while basketball teams had more than forty stops during the regular season. By the 1960s the schedule typically consisted of seventy-two to eighty regular games. Teams played more than half of these games on the road, whether as regular visiting teams, participants in a doubleheader, or in a "home game" at another site (such as the Philadelphia Warriors' famous game with the New York Knicks at Hershey, Pennsylvania, when Wilt Chamberlain scored his one hundred points).[21] Fort Wayne Pistons coach Charley Eckman begged schedule makers not to "ask us to travel from the eastern division to the western, or vice versa, within 24 hours."[22]

Since professional sports teams often paid by the mile for train travel; aggregate miles traveled gave some idea of relative travel expenses. For the shorter 1947–48 season, with only forty-eight games, teams averaged around $8,000 each in travel costs. The St. Louis Bombers incurred $16,000 in railroad fares during the longer 1949–50 season. Because of the Bombers' geographical isolation, that team probably incurred greater transportation costs than any other NBA club, save Denver.[23] A year later sportswriter Bill Mokray calculated that baseball's Philadelphia Phillies and Pittsburgh Pirates traveled roughly 24,000 miles during the season. He discovered that every NBA team logged at least 2,000 more miles during their seasons than the two baseball teams, with the Minneapolis Lakers traveling more than 42,000 miles. Mokray's article detailed the experiences of the Boston Celtics, who saw transportation expenses roughly double between 1946 and 1958. Of course, some of this was due to the general increase in prices between those years as well as to more regular season games. The Celtics' and Warriors' officials estimated that they incurred travel expenses of one dollar per mile traveled. Two years later Mokray presented a chart showing that Minneapolis had traveled 60,000 miles during the 1959–60 season, while New York traveled just 30,000 miles. The combined league travel rose from 265,862 miles in 1957–58 to 299,368 miles in 1959–60, an average of 37,500 miles per team.[24]

The league sometimes attempted to mitigate differences in travel costs by practicing a limited form of expense sharing. Owners submitted their travel expenses, which would then be equalized across teams. Those paying above the league average received compensation from those paying below the average. For the 1947–48 season, the Baltimore Bullets, Boston Celtics, and St. Louis Bombers received compensation from the other four teams. The league had an independent arrangement with the Chicago team with regard to travel expenses.[25]

In addition to the transportation expenses, teams incurred expenses for hotels and meals. The NBA owners agreed to issue seven dollars per day meal money for players beginning with the 1957–58 season, which was an increase from the four dollars per day paid in 1946–47 and five dollars per day starting in the 1947–48 season. Baseball players received twelve dollars a day during the 1960s until it was raised to fifteen dollars a day in 1968.[26]

Although owners frequently complained about travel expenses, one is entitled to skepticism. Only two of the eight teams reporting financial data to Congress covering the 1951–57 seasons listed transportation expenses. The New York Knicks' "Travel Expenses" rose from $21,000 to $30,000 between the 1952–53 and 1956–57 seasons, while the Philadelphia Warriors' went from $20,000 to $25,000 during the same time period.[27] These figures may contradict Mokray's estimates presented above. It is unfortunate that the other teams, especially those in Minneapolis and St. Louis, did not report similar data. Given their relative isolation, it is likely that the western teams incurred greater transportation expenses, but these travel expenses pale beside the player payrolls. The reader is also reminded that owners had voluntarily incurred greater transportation expenses by setting up the numerous doubleheaders during the 1950s. Apparently the gains from playing such events outweighed the increase in transportation costs.

Today's NBA players have no conception of what a rough lifestyle their predecessors endured. Because passenger jet travel was not available for the league's first decade, teams traveled by trains, buses, and propeller planes. The classic travel story of the league's early days concerns teams traveling to Fort Wayne. After a game in, say, Rochester, a team would catch the westbound *20th Century Limited* toward Chicago.[28] The players would not even enjoy a full night's sleep but would have to get off at a nonscheduled stop in rural Indiana at 5 A.M. As Knicks official Marty Glickman recalled the situation:

> The only thing there was an uncovered wooden platform. Traveling with the Knicks, I knew that our instructions were to walk on a two-lane blacktop road toward a blinking yellow light a half-mile away. That turned out to be the only light at a crossroads where there were ten or twelve buildings, nothing taller than two stories. Then we were to look for the plate glass window with the sign of the Green Parrot Café. Carl Braun was our designated shooter of the pebbles up to the second-floor window, because he had the softest touch. After two or three pebbles hit the window, a frowsy-haired woman would look out and say, 'Oh, the Knicks.' She'd get on the phone, and in a little while four or five cars would gather and drive us the forty miles into Fort Wayne. We'd go right to bed and get up for the game that day or night. That was the only way to get to Fort Wayne from Rochester.[29]

With the introduction of passenger jet planes and the developing interstate freeway system, passenger rail service began to wither. As early as 1958, NBA president Maurice Podoloff was citing the difficulties arising from the reduced number of scheduled trains.[30]

A few owners tried to ameliorate their team's travel woes. Although Ben Kerner, owner of the wandering Hawks, was especially frugal, he did lease a DC-8 passenger airplane for his team's use during the 1958–59 season. Other teams chartered planes for occasional travel, but air travel was not a panacea. The Minneapolis Lakers almost replicated the tragic fate of Buddy Holly, J. P. "The Big Bopper" Richardson, and Richie Valens when their chartered plane was forced to land in an Iowa cornfield.[31] During the mid-1950s, most of the flights were on non-jet aircraft that often sat fewer than fifty passengers. Even non-emergency situations could result in frustrating delays. Sportswriter James Murray provided a detailed look at jet travel in the NBA by riding along with the Los Angeles Lakers on a nine-day road trip, a trip that included inconvenient flight times, bad weather, frequent stops, and dreary hotels.[32]

Despite these inconveniences with traveling, owners continued to stage doubleheaders. There was a limited form of gate sharing with respect to doubleheaders, although owners would have christened it "expense sharing." The owners recognized the trade-offs involved in staging these doubleheaders: a potential of much larger crowds versus increased travel expenses. The Celtics, Knicks, and Warriors apparently worked out a reciprocating deal where they swapped home dates for doubleheaders on an equal basis. In referring to rescheduling some games between the Baltimore Bullets and Boston Celtics, Podoloff wrote: "I don't know how the teams would prefer to handle the matter of payment for the games. Boston, New York and Philadelphia, which have exchanged a number of games, can, of course, treat these reciprocal obligations as wash transactions without making any adjustments. However, if these cities and all the others involved so desire, this office can act as a clearing house for all payments."[33] In general, though, the league devised an informal policy. "When the doubleheader program was originally proposed, it was agreed that a game between two teams of the same division played in that division would require a payment of $1,000 from the franchise holder where the game was being played. It was assumed that a game between two members of one division played in a city of the other division would necessitate additional travel and therefore, the cost was increased to $1,500 per game for such games." In other words, the home team agreeing to play its game as part of a doubleheader reaped $1,000 or $1,500. The putative road team received nothing. Podoloff allowed owners the possibility of staging doubleheaders for playoff games, but it is unclear whether any owners took advantage of the offer. What also remains unclear is how NBL and BAA teams split gate receipts from games played at Chicago Stadium.[34]

Scheduling

Scheduling of games is an often neglected aspect of competitive balance. Most professional sports leagues attempt to balance the number of home and road games. The National Football League is unique in overtly manipulating its schedule to help weaker teams. Major League Baseball, with its interleague play, now features unbalanced schedules, where teams play different rivals for varying numbers of games. The New York Mets, for instance, always play six games with the New York Yankees. For the Mets, this is a disadvantage in terms of win-loss, but, of course, it's an advantage in terms of gate appeal. The owners' decision to schedule doubleheaders affects competitive balance.

Being the NBA schedule maker was a thankless task. Since Philadelphia Warriors executive Eddie Gottlieb often set up the schedule, his detractors claimed he gave his team a break. Gottlieb's task was made more difficult as the league began staging doubleheaders with four NBA teams instead of doubleheaders with two NBA teams and a high school, college, or Globetrotters game. Ned Irish, imbued with the success of his pioneering collegiate doubleheaders at Madison Square Garden, sought the same with the NBA. The Knickerbockers had long staged doubleheaders at Madison Square Garden, even including, in its early years, a game between NBL teams. To invite teams from a rival league to share a bill with one's own team revealed how much Irish wanted to fill the Garden. Unless every team staged an equal number of doubleheaders, such activities necessarily led to imbalances between home, road, and neutral games between teams.

Owners of teams with smaller arenas were not keen on doubleheaders, since they could often nearly fill their stadiums with single games. The league staged sixteen doubleheaders during 1948–49. The number slowly rose, and doubleheaders didn't disappear until the 1974–75 season. Indeed, Koppett pointed out the tension between owners of teams in larger cities and those in smaller cities. He cited the needs of the Knicks, Warriors, and Celtics to fill a large stadium as favoring the doubleheaders. These teams, too, might have faced lower transportation costs in arranging such affairs. The western teams, most with smaller arenas, would not benefit much from hosting a doubleheader and faced greater transportation costs in doing so. The owners agreed to lengthen the season to sixty-eight games while allowing more doubleheaders.[35] When the league shrank to nine teams, teams played a seventy-two-game schedule, but the schedule was imbalanced. Teams played rivals in the same geographical division ten times and rivals in the other geographical division eight times. Western Division teams played a couple of extra games to fill out the seventy-two-game schedule.[36] Ned Irish complained about that schedule years later. He especially lamented the bucolic pace of two games per week for November and December and then the frenetic pace during the remainder of the season. He wanted to revert to the sixty-game schedule with twenty-two home games and twenty-two road games, with the remaining sixteen being doubleheaders. He claimed the Knicks lost $5,000 every time they left the Garden to play in the 69th Regiment Armory. Because of the other events scheduled for the Garden, the club scheduled the team to play in the Armory "to maintain continuity of promotion and fan interest." He chided the owners of teams in smaller cities for their selfishness in wanting a longer season.[37] The owners of teams in smaller cities continued to press for more regular-season games, and the league eventually ended with eighty-game seasons by 1961–62.

Gottlieb's scheduling headaches included recognizing that some teams drew better on one day of the week than another. Some teams favored Saturday home games while others favored Sunday home games. Because of blue laws, Gottlieb's Warriors and the Syracuse Nationals were legally prevented from playing home games on Sundays, adding to the scheduling complications. Trying to satisfy such disparate demands while keeping traveling manageable was difficult.[38] Whatever his efforts, Gottlieb received more brickbats than applause. Boston columnist Dave Egan—notorious for tormenting baseball player Ted Williams in Williams's ongoing feud with reporters—was one of the detractors, claiming that Gottlieb manipulated the schedule for his Warriors' benefit. Gottlieb responded that league president Podoloff assisted with and ultimately approved the schedule. "Each club gives the league its dates for its home court. Usually, these are controlled by which dates the team can get. There are either ice hockey games, ice shows, or some other events going on in the building that limit the availability of home dates for a lot of our teams. The schedule is then put into its final form from those dates, and must be approved by each club." Gottlieb noted that Boston owner Walter Brown approved the schedule.[39]

Podoloff seconded Gottlieb's description of the scheduling process:

> We must arrange 288 games within 142 days under conditions that give us less than 142 available dates. . . . Besides, we must arrange the schedule so that we book 46 doubleheaders to the satisfaction of all the clubs. . . . We tried hard not to schedule a team for more than three games on three consecutive days . . . [and] also tried to rotate the appearance of the teams at regular intervals over the entire season. We also had a fifth problem. We tried not to schedule a team appearing on a Saturday afternoon telecast after playing the night before. If a team has a game scheduled the previous night, we have to make sure that the club—without difficulty—arrives for the Saturday afternoon game by train in ample time for a 2 o'clock starting time . . . certain teams draw best on particular days. . . . It would be an utter waste for the Boston Celtics, with their tremendous appeal to face the Knicks at the Armory with its limited seating capacity.

Compounding these factors was the aforementioned shrinking number of passenger trains between NBA cities.[40]

St. Louis Hawks owner Ben Kerner suggested trying two-game series instead of the prevalent one-game stands. He believed the change would reduce player fatigue and transportation costs. He emphasized the potential savings in the latter as the chief virtue: "Our operating expenses for a season are approximately $400,000. That includes player salaries, promotion, auditorium rental and travel, which means transportation, hotels, meals, cab fares, etc. Now we can't expect to cut down on salaries, rental or promotion. . . . As it is, we have to start promoting all over again [with the one-game stands]. We lose the cumulative value of home stands such as baseball enjoys." The league never implemented Kerner's proposal. While baseball teams typically played three- or four-game series with one rival, baseball differed from basketball in that starting pitchers changed with each game, creating a distinctly different game each time. Kerner admitted that his plan wouldn't save much more than $6,000 or $7,000 per team in transportation costs, but he was so hard-pressed that he wasn't "about to look down my nose at six or seven grand [from saving even just five or six road trips per season]."[41]

Kerner's idea appealed to some of his fellow owners. Eddie Gottlieb saw merit in the idea but noted that some teams couldn't schedule two-game home series. Otherwise he thought the other owners would approve the plans. The players also applauded the plan. Ed Macauley, St. Louis Bombers player and coach, said: "Playing games on successive nights isn't a problem. We've been playing on consecutive nights for years, often as many as four or five nights in a row. But what does sap a player's stamina is the travel between games."[42] Whether fans would attend a second game with as much zeal was a question to which no one seemed to have a definite answer. When the Minneapolis Lakers moved to Los Angeles, the league staged two-game series in Los Angeles to save on travel costs, although the eventual relocation of the Philadelphia Warriors to San Francisco mitigated the travel issue.

Competitive Balance

The Minneapolis Lakers continued to win championships, but the Rochester Royals were at least a worthy foe. The three original BAA teams that survived had yet to displace the two former NBL teams as champions. Home-court advantage and referees were two factors affecting competitive balance. In addition, the New York Knicks continued to fail to win a championship.

The National Basketball Association had a pronounced home-team bias, especially after the league absorbed former NBL teams. Between 1949 and 1957, the home team won at least 64.3 percent of the games each season, sometimes winning almost 75 percent (see table 17). During the postwar era, home-field advantage was not as pronounced in Major League Baseball or in the National Football League. During the 1953–1955 seasons, NFL home teams had win-loss records of 38-31 (.551), 43-27 (.614), and 46-23 (.666). Between 1952 and 1956, home teams won 54.1 percent of Major League Baseball games.[43] In college basketball's Big-Ten Conference, home teams won 75 percent of the games during the late 1940s. By the late 1960s and early 1970s, home teams won less than 60 percent of the NBA games. Leonard Koppett attributes this to "some degree of up-grading of the league: large arenas in larger cities producing less intimidation and hysteria, better travel arrangements, and so forth."[44]

Observers thought that the intimacy of basketball arenas contributed to the home teams' lopsided advantage. Fans could literally trip referees and players. Coaches could yell in a referee's ears as he ran down the court. Terry Pluto's and Neil Isaac's collections of player reminiscences testify to the intimidating nature of crowds around the league. The home-court advantage may have partially become a self-fulfilling prophecy; some players, recognizing the near-futility of trying to win on the road, took it easy. Former Lakers player Kevin O'Shea recalled the differences in attitude between George Mikan and Jim Pollard.

> Mikan, you got to give him credit, he put out all the time. Jim Pollard, who was a good friend of mine, wouldn't put out on the road. He would save himself for the home games, which would frost the hell out of George. He'd get mad as hell at that. That was George's style, he wanted to win every place. By the same token, some of the players didn't play that hard on the road. It wasn't worth it—you weren't going to win on the road. You could win some, but you'd have to beat the hell out of that team to do it."[45]

If a team didn't get its share of home games, it operated at a distinct disadvantage. The NBA's practice of scheduling doubleheaders with four teams at an arena might have been lucrative, but the practice created disparities in schedules.[46] Taking the 1954–55 season as an example, the Milwaukee Hawks played just seventeen home games while playing twenty-five games on the road and thirty games at neutral sites. The Syracuse Nationals got to play thirty-two games at home against twenty-six on the road. Their remaining fourteen games occurred at neutral sites. While the Nationals won the championship and the Hawks accrued the league's worst record on merit, the unbalanced schedule probably exacerbated any latent difference and affected the standard deviations shown in table 13. The Nats typically had more home games than any other team in the league. In subsequent seasons the league reduced the disparity in home games. By 1956–57 every team had thirty-one games at home, thirty-one games on the road, plus ten games at neutral sites.

Table 18 shows the disparities in home and road records. The Syracuse Nationals had the best home win-loss record in the league. Throughout the oral histories collected by Salzberg, Isaacs, and Pluto, Syracuse was designated as one of the roughest places to play, and the team's home record confirms this. Dolph Schayes attributed the Nats' home-court advantage to the difficulty opposing teams had in getting to Syracuse (although this argument would seemingly apply to Syracuse players, too) and the partisan crowds' reveling in being the Davids versus the New York, Boston, and Philadelphia Goliaths.[47] The Fort Wayne Pistons and the Rochester Royals also had fairly large numbers of home games. The teams in the big cities tended to have the fewest home games. One exception was the meandering Hawks team. The team had a respectable win-loss record in its home games while it was based in the Tri-Cities of Illinois and Iowa. Once the team moved to Milwaukee for the 1951–52 season, however, it played the fewest home games of any team and had a sub-.500 record at home (37-46). Of course, the team's road record was even worse. No team participated in more doubleheaders than did the Hawks. The Hawks, already a mediocre team, were not helped by the lopsided unfavorable schedule, but owner Ben Kerner probably figured the paydays from the doubleheaders benefited him more than additional home games in Milwaukee.

REFEREES

Although no one explicitly said that referees were partly responsible for the home-court advantage in the 1950s, the idea was implied.[48] The rowdy crowds could intimidate the staunchest referee. The league's use of freelance referees and occasional failure to back them contributed to the referees' sense of frustration.

If players and coaches experienced rough conditions, imagine the plight of the referees. While players could hope to have friendly crowds at home games, referees were reviled everywhere. Players who disliked traveling at least got some time at home, but referees were perpetually on the road during the season.

At first the league hired referees on a freelance basis. Many of them were experienced college or high school referees. The players engaged in much rough play, and trying to call the game was often difficult for the two referees. They wondered whether the league would support them in penalizing flagrant player violations and in contretemps with owners and coaches, many of whom were abusive.[49]

The National Basketball League was no stranger to player/referee fights. That league fined and suspended Syracuse Nationals player Jerry Rizzo for the remainder of the season after he punched referee Ralph Fowler. Rizzo's coach, Al Cervi, was fined fifty dollars for running onto the court and "pushing officials around."[50]

League coaches could intimidate referees by demanding that the league president not assign any "offending" referees to work their teams' games. Naturally this tactic demoralized referees, and referee Ronnie Gibbs resigned, saying, "When the league doesn't back up its officials any more than that, I felt it was time for me to get out."[51]

The BAA appointed Pat Kennedy to be chief referee. Kennedy stated that he hoped the league would eventually have a full-time staff of referees, similar to Major League Baseball's umpiring staff. Progress toward a full-time permanent staff was slow. Three years later, aside from Kennedy, just one referee was working exclusively NBA games: Sid Borgia. Under the $50-per-game compensation policy, Borgia could make in excess of $5,000 for the season.[52]

Respected referee John Nucatola told reporters in 1954 that league officials were still unwilling to back the referees. Syracuse Nationals owner Danny Biasone demanded that Podoloff keep "those New York [City] referees" out of a Syracuse–New York Knicks series. Podoloff responded by saying, "Your statement constitutes a grave and unwarranted reflection on the integrity of some of the best officials of the association. If you are correctly quoted, you have to either prove your statement or retract with adequate apologies to the men involved." Biasone issued a halfhearted apology, saying he hadn't besmirched any referee by name, before concluding, "Why should New York referees always handle our games?"[53]

Concurrent with player efforts to organize, referees also struggled to negotiate better working conditions. In 1958 the referees requested a formal contract to replace the per-game payment basis (adjusted for years of experience). The per-game policy left the referees with no protection against injury or illness. The hockey owners gave their referees contracts stipulating a minimum of $6,000 a season, regardless of how many games they worked, although they also had an opportunity to work additional games to increase their salaries to between $8,500 and $12,000, in addition to their pension. A year later the league still hadn't agreed to contracts and continued to pay between $40 to $75 per game. Referees agitated for a minimum of $6,000 per season, a figure that corresponded with what the lowliest player earned. While the league increased the per-game amounts, by 1960 it still refused to issue contracts.[54]

WHY NO NEW YORK DOMINANCE

While the Knicks made the championship finals three years in a row between 1951 and 1953—mostly because the Eastern Division lacked the Lakers and Royals—the franchise pretty much disappeared from the playoffs until the late 1960s. The team took in more gate revenue than any other team in the league, so it had the purchasing power to buy good players from owners with struggling finances. Why did Ned Irish fail? Leonard Koppett argues that Irish antagonized many of his fellow owners. In some cases the owners practiced charity toward fellow owners in dire straits (granting Gottlieb the territorial rights to Wilt Chamberlain), but they were unwilling to help Irish.

When the St. Louis Bombers were about to crash, Irish attempted to buy the franchise for $25,000 to $50,000. Similar to the baseball owner who attempted to buy the Detroit Wolverines back in the 1880s just to get star hitter Dan Brouthers, Irish wanted to get the Bombers' center, Ed Macauley. The other owners prevented the sale, perhaps to spite Irish for his past arrogance. Sportswriter Dick Young caustically wrote, "The league voted Ned down, something to which Irish has long become accustomed."[55] The archrival Boston Celtics got Macauley, helping transform the Celtics into perennial playoff contenders.

Knicks center Nat Clifton believed Irish's failure to reserve open dates during the playoff period hurt the team. "Every time we'd get ready to play in the playoffs they would switch us from the Garden to the Armory. It was because of the circus or the rodeo came to town. I think they had some kind of contract with the Garden. I think we'd have won the championship a lot of times, maybe three, if they'd kept us in the Garden, because that was our floor and there we were fast and we were good."[56] Clifton's memory was accurate; the Knicks played their home games during their three championship series between 1951 and 1953 at the 69th Regiment Armory, not at Madison Square Garden. According to game-by-game accounts in the *New York Times*, the Knicks had win-loss records of 40-11 at Madison Square Garden and 24-1 at the Armory during the 1950–53 regular seasons; however, the team played most of its home games against the tough Rochester and Minneapolis teams at the Garden. In Irish's defense, most of the Knicks' February and March regular-season home games were played at the Armory, so the players should have been acclimated. Irish undoubtedly lost gate receipts from scheduling the playoff games in the Armory compared with Madison Square Garden, but then again, holding the games at the Armory and, say, a rodeo at the Garden may have created *two* sell-outs—in other words, the team had its playoff games and rodeo, too. In later years, when the Knicks consistently failed to make the play-offs (winning that opportunity only once between 1955 and 1967), it made sense to book Madison Square Garden for events that would occur with certainty rather than risk the uncertain fate of the Knicks.

Bill Russell reigns supreme as basketball's championship player. He led the Celtics to eleven titles in thirteen seasons. Only baseball's Yogi Berra has a similar record in professional sports (fourteen American League titles and ten World Series championships in eighteen years), although Joe DiMaggio came close (ten American League titles and nine World Series championships in thirteen years). The Knicks' inability to win the championship emanated from its mediocre centers. The team's guards and forwards were usually of sufficient caliber, but lacking a Mikan, Russell, or Chamberlain, the team became an early version of the Los Angeles Lakers (circa Elgin Baylor and Jerry West).

According to Fuzzy Levane, a one-time Knicks coach, and Lenny Lewin, a reporter for the *New York Daily Mirror*, Rochester Royals owner Les Harrison offered to trade his pick in the 1956 draft to the Knicks. The Royals had the very first pick in the draft (Russell was not in anyone's territory, having played in San Francisco). Then Knicks coach Vince Boryla tentatively negotiated a deal with Harrison: the Knicks would trade Walter Dukes and $15,000 in exchange for the Rochester Royals drafting Russell and then trading him to the Knicks. Irish repudiated the deal, saying, "Dukes, OK, but $15,000? Tell them to shove it."[57]

Irish's search for a top-flight center included Nat Clifton and Ray Felix. Irish had earlier displayed a penchant for drafting the wrong guy. Koppett recounted a situation where, after the Chicago franchise folded, Irish went for the top-scoring player instead of the better, all-around (and crowd-pleasing) Bob Cousy.[58] Irish selected Max Zaslofsky, a former high scorer, who gave the team two or three decent seasons.

Irish might have been an astute promoter, but he clearly misunderstood the nature of constructing a championship club. Unlike his New York Yankees counterparts, who relied on baseball experts such as Ed Barrow and George

Weiss, Irish lacked a basketball guru who would guide him on the path of basketball enlightenment.

Owners occasionally addressed the issue of competitive imbalance. Some of their proposals were eccentric. The owners considered implementing a "bonus draft," similar to the NFL's rotation of the top pick, but ultimately rejected the proposal.[59] NBA owners were so concerned about the Lakers' dominance during the early 1950s that they tried to devise solutions. "One was to prevent the first five teams from drafting men for two years. Another was to give the lower brackets two draft choices, the upper bracket one. Still another was to toss the ninth-and tenth-man on each club (as designated by the owner) into a grab bag and allow the lower clubs to put in claims." Years later, when his team was dominating the league, Boston Celtics owner Walter Brown echoed these proposals to aid weaker teams by suggesting the league give the four worst teams two collegiate draft picks each before the top four clubs got any draft picks. "I think my plan would enable struggling clubs to better themselves sooner," he said.[60] Ned Irish suggested an ingenious if futile idea: requiring each team to play two or three new players each season in order to foster competitive balance.[61]

The owners generally accepted the Lakers' and Celtics' dominance. They may have felt that teaming Mikan or Russell with any set of nine NBA players still would have resulted in those two players winning.

Innovation

In the early 1950s, the game of basketball was devolving into something less than appealing. Roughness, stalling, and other antics robbed the game of its fluidity and athletic grace. The game had yet to capture the fancy of many basketball fans, much less the general public.

CURBING BIG MEN'S ADVANTAGES

As basketball coaches sardonically explain, "You can't coach height." While "small" players such as Bob Cousy, Isiah Thomas, John Stockton, Allen Iverson, and Steve Nash have been stars, the game's chief characteristic is the prevalence of tall—very tall—players. Compared to some of the tallest centers in basketball, baseball's Randy Johnson was short, and even at 6'9" Ed "Too Tall" Jones of National Football League fame was too small to handle most

NBA centers. Seven-foot or taller centers such as Wilt Chamberlain, Kareem Abdul-Jabbar, Shaquille O'Neal, and other giants have dominated the game.

Mikan typically ranked in the top two or three in scoring and was a strong rebounder. To slow him down, league coaches and officials decided to widen the free-throw lanes from six to twelve feet. Nat Holman, longtime player and coach, led the charge to change this aspect of the game. The rules for international competition, such as the Olympics, already used a wider free-throw lane, so the NBA was not the pioneer. Other basketball officials, such as coach Phog Allen, wanted to raise the baskets from ten feet to twelve feet. Holman, surprisingly, eschewed the higher baskets. The NBA experimented with the wider lane early in the 1950–51 season. "It is thought the greater distance will eliminate the 'cheap' basket . . . and also gives those 6-3 'runts' a better chance grabbing rebounds."[62]

The owners voted to widen the free-throw lane for the 1951–52 season. Observers attributed the change to a "stop Mikan" sentiment. Mikan responded, "It's the best thing that's happened to basketball since the elimination of the center jump."[63] Though Mikan professed to be pleased with the wider free-throw lane, his statistics fell between 1950–51 and 1951–52. In the latter season he scored 4.6 fewer points per game and hit only 38.5 percent of his shots compared with 42.8 percent the season before. He also grabbed fewer rebounds. Whether his statistical deterioration was a result of the rule change is unclear. His 1950–51 season may have simply been his peak. Fellow centers Ed Macauley and George Ratkovicz saw some declines in their statistics, too, although Nat Clifton, Larry Foust, and Don Otten had improvements. In any event, Mikan's Lakers regained the league championship with the rule change.

Some people advocated neutralizing the taller players' advantage by raising the baskets, a somewhat illogical suggestion. There was one official NBA game played with twelve-foot baskets; the Minneapolis Lakers and Milwaukee Hawks battled to a 65–63 score on March 7, 1954. The Lakers reportedly had difficulty hitting the basket, and layups were an adventure. Center Clyde Lovellette laconically noted, "He [the tall player] was still closer to the basket than the six-foot guy."[64] This game also featured an experiment whereby free throws in the first and third quarters were shot at the end of those quarters.

The NBA was not unique in grappling with the issue of dominant big men. Some international basketball officials called for an informal agreement to limit players to a maximum height of 6'5″. The international basketball community naturally failed to enact such an agreement. Longtime pro player Al

Cervi suggested a quota on "big men." Each team could have two men 6'6" or taller on the court. "There'd be a lot more action, because the little man is faster, you'll have a faster game, and there'd be more play-making."[65] One can only imagine Cervi's chagrin when giant Wilt Chamberlain would rewrite the record books. Thus, while fans may have professed to dislike big men's dominance, the league did little to stop them.

CONTROLLING ROUGH PLAY

Sports fans are familiar with the image of hockey players sporting memorable dental configurations. Basketball players, too, suffered from rough play. The observation "I went to a hockey game and a fight broke out" applied equally to professional basketball. Although the game's creator, James Naismith, had envisioned an indoor game that would not have unnecessary roughness, pioneering players quickly discovered the advantages of rough play. Longtime NBA star George Yardley recalled: "I must have had about 80 stitches in my face, all from things that happened on the court. Guys would hit you with a clenched fist, just cutting your skull open. Over the years, I played with at least 40 different guys and I can't name one who had all of his own teeth."[66] Jerry West was famous for having his nose broken multiple times. Veterans routinely tested rookie players, even rookie teammates. In his autobiography, *The Inside Game: Race, Power, and Politics in the NBA*, Wayne Embry, certainly no one's idea of a meek player, described how veteran players used rough tactics to test the mettle of young players.[67]

Ned Irish, executive vice president of the New York Knickerbockers, bemoaned the rough play that he witnessed. He made the incredible threat that the Knicks would "not be represented in the . . . NBA and there will be no professional games in Madison Square Garden next season" unless officials reduced such tactics. His fellow owner, Danny Biasone, of the Syracuse Nats, accused Irish of indulging in "pure malarkey" and suggested that Knicks basketball would be improved if "the Garden managers and Knickerbocker people would try to win their games on the hardwood and not at the luncheon table." Irish remained a vocal critic of roughness in the NBA. A few years later he disputed whether referees were willing to call intentional fouls.[68] Sportswriter Everett Morris recalled the bad old days of professional basketball before World War II:

> The roughhouse, the cute little illegalities which prevented an opponent from making a good play and the heaping of abuse on officials, to cover up their own physical and technical deficiencies, were the stock in trade of players.

... The big city public simply wasn't buying such goods and so the dreary apology for basketball stayed in its dance halls and tank towns. Then along came what is now the NBA with its big league fanfare, big arenas in big cities and promise of big-time basketball played along the college lines by young men fresh from the college ranks. This was what the basketball fraternity had been waiting [for] ... the NBA game has retrograded to the point where it bears an alarming similarity to that which eked out an existence in the bushes not so long ago. The games are much too rough. The premium is on fouling instead of the spine-tingling play.[69]

Sportswriter Arthur Daley bemoaned the intentional foul trading between teams as they tried to regain possession of the ball, and argued that with proper incentives most players could play a cleaner game. "Deliberate foul-trading was strangling the goose that had hatched golden eggs.... It's a worth-while exchange strategically but a horrible thing from the standpoint of public relations and crowd appeal. There's no fun for a genuine fan to watch a parade of goons to the line for a foul-shooting contest instead of basketball he [the fan] paid to see." Daley reported that just prior to the 1954 NBA All-Star Game, Maurice Podoloff warned players and coaches that such tactics were forbidden. Daley drily reported, "They followed instructions because they are so clever they don't have to violate the rules. Why doesn't that happen in every game?"[70]

Limiting the numbers of fouls a player could incur might have curbed the rough play. However, when the NBA adopted four twelve-minute quarters instead of college's two twenty-minute halves, the league officials quickly *increased* the number of personal fouls an individual player could incur before being eliminated from the game from five to six fouls.[71] Maintaining a five-foul limit per player might have mitigated some of the fouling. Then again, fouling star players out of the game always risked antagonizing fans, who wanted to see their favorite stars play for as long as possible.

Complaints about rough play culminated in Wilt Chamberlain's retirement near the end of the 1959–60 season. He had recently lost two teeth from errant elbows, and he felt the league officials were not stopping the unnecessary roughness. Wilt's coach, Neil Johnston, supported him, at least in public: "They're getting away with murder against Wilt. It would help if he would belt a few, but he's only fought back a couple of times when he got mad."[72]

Bob Cousy quickly chided Chamberlain, especially the latter's insinuation that part of the roughness was due to racial prejudice. Cousy, who had a reputation for befriending black players, dismissed this aspect. Citing the fact that even with the rough play Chamberlain was averaging thirty-six points per game, Cousy stated: "Frankly, whether Chamberlain is playing or not is a point of complete indifference with me. I feel that everybody in the league, with the exception of Eddie Gottlieb, thinks the same as I do. . . . Wilt is the biggest complainer ever to hit the NBA. Standing 6 feet 1 inch, it is difficult for me to feel sorry for a man 7 feet tall." Cousy later added a swipe at Wilt's dunk shots and blocking tactics, saying, "If Wilt Chamberlain quits the league, we can all go back to playing basketball again."[73] Cousy might have expressed the other players' emotions, but Eddie Gottlieb's panic certainly was more accurate. Chamberlain had proven to be a magnet for crowds, which benefited all of the players. He had attempted 991 free throws, 200 more than any other player, proving that he was indeed getting fouled. One doesn't need much imagination to think that rival centers were trying to get their foul's worth by fouling hard.

Chamberlain elaborated about his retirement a few days later: "I couldn't play in the NBA without losing my self-respect. If I were to go back next year and get into three or four fights it would reflect on me and then indirectly upon my race. If I were subjected to the same conditions that existed in the league this year I might degrade myself by my conduct."[74] He denied that there was a racial component to his withdrawal from the league and pointed out, "I never complained about anything but the officiating and I don't think it was an unjust complaint." Apparently friends and family persuaded him to return to the NBA (one wonders about his self-respect): "I received letters from people all over the United States asking me to reconsider. Some were Warrior fans, some were NBA fans. Some were just television fans in places like California and Miami. All of them asked me to continue playing basketball."[75]

BIZARRE AND REVOLUTIONARY PROPOSALS

NBA owners cannot be accused of a staid conservatism with respect to the game itself. League officials proved willing to try a variety of innovations, some of which may strike modern readers as ludicrous.

As mentioned above, in the same experimental but official game in which players shot at twelve-foot-high baskets, the referees called fouls as usual. However, players attempted free throws at the end of the first and third quarters (the second and fourth quarters were played normally). Players shot fifteen free throws at the end of the third quarter, a result that undoubtedly contributed to the experiment's immediate demise. Eddie Gottlieb, owner of the Warriors, had advocated for this idea of shooting free throws at the end of quarters for a few years.[76]

Referees sat around during an official game between the Milwaukee Hawks and the Baltimore Bullets in 1952. The referees sat in tennis umpires' chairs. Although a *New York Times* reporter said the two officials "treated the experiment seriously and both appeared pleased with the result," the league did not repeat the experiment.[77]

Pro officials also did not implement a Tulane University coach's suggestion that halves be determined by points instead of time. The coach had suggested ending the first half when one team reached forty points and ending the game when one team reached eighty points.[78]

One earlier change, originating in college basketball, does survive to the present: having defensive players assume the inside positions on both sides of the lane on free-throw attempts. The earlier rule stipulated that the defensive team have one inside position and the offensive team have the other (I was not able to ascertain how the teams determined which inside position they were to assume).[79]

All of these situations failed to create as much excitement as hoped. Thus, owners would continue to seek improvements to the game.

Conclusion

The NBA owners struggled to increase demand for their product. The elimination of weak franchises was a definite case of "addition by contraction." The remaining teams, if not prospering, at least no longer had to subsidize or endure unviable teams. Concurrent with the growing stability in franchises, however, games were becoming less attractive, whether because of the Minneapolis Lakers' dominance or because of the continuing mayhem on the court.

The league's competitive balance was not marred by a dominating New York team, although the Knicks made three consecutive appearances in the championship finals. While Minneapolis was not the league's smallest city, the Lakers certainly did not capture the nation's imagination. To a great extent, basketball success revolved around a dominating center. The owners' attempts to create parity foundered upon the scarcity of great big men, George Mikan merely being the pioneer. Mikan was a great player, but he did not possess the sheer physical skills of Wilt Chamberlain and Bill Russell, or the flash and excitement that later-day players such as Oscar Robertson, Michael Jordan, and LeBron James did. Bob Cousy would eventually introduce this fan-pleasing style to the game, although other players, such as Bob Davies, certainly had the skills to do so earlier. Owners willingly traded competitive fairness for revenue when they scheduled doubleheaders. The doubleheaders (or their absence) created skewed home/road schedules and gave the Syracuse Nationals a big advantage over the St. Louis Hawks.

The owners' somewhat timid remedies regarding playing rules had failed to jump-start demand. Fans attending games ran the risk of watching a dull, ugly sort of contest, wrestling without the ring, as it were. Stability would not evolve into prosperity without further innovation.

5

Stability (1954–57)

With the NBA down to eight teams, owners still faced inadequate revenues. They continued to grapple with the unattractive aspect of the league's end games, where fouling and rough play were still the tactics of choice. How to reduce the primitive aspects of the game remained a difficult problem, but it was one with an elegant solution. The owners also needed to assess whether television would prove to be a friend or a foe.

The Tough Times Continue

Even in the league's ninth season, some teams were barely surviving. Ben Kerner, owner of the Hawks, hired Marty Blake as its general manager after the team moved from the Tri-Cities to Milwaukee. Blake later reminisced that the team was $94,000 in debt when he signed on for the 1954–55 season.[1] Kerner wanted to sell the team for $75,000 but received an offer of only $50,000 from an investor who wanted to move the team to Indiana. Kerner eventually moved the team again, this time to St. Louis (he would later move it to Atlanta, where the team's wanderings ended). The St. Louis business community apparently assured Kerner that there would be at least 1,000 season ticket holders; Blake claimed there were only 55. "So we scrambled for money. We played a million exhibition games. We promoted before promotion was fashionable. I mean, we had acts such as Count Basie, Guy Lombardo, the Four Freshmen, Tommy Dorsey—all big names and they all played after our games. We gave away prizes."[2] Kerner later boasted that he would sell 3,500 season tickets for the 1960–61 season. He exercised his imagination in offering women patrons a jar of coffee costing $1.08 for each one-dollar ticket purchased. "If you [a woman] hated basketball you could still make an 8-cent profit. And this is a woman's sport. To see those guys running around in their shorts, that's really something. I should have thrown in bus fare."[3]

The Hawks gained a measure of prosperity when they played in the 1956–57 NBA Championship Series. Kerner estimated he had lost $100,000 since buying the Buffalo NBL franchise in 1945, including $36,000 during his last season in Milwaukee (where his team took second fiddle to the newly arrived baseball Braves). Because the Hawks were his sole source of income, Kerner could not absorb large losses for as long as Walter Brown of the Celtics had.[4]

Even as late as 1955, a sportswriter could claim, "Profits in the NBA have been almost nonexistent, even for the big-city teams." The reporter believed the Fort Wayne Pistons might show a profit because of the loyal fans from the city and its neighboring towns who filled the team's 9,500-seat Coliseum. The team also played games in Elkhart and Kokomo, Indiana, and in Miami, Florida.[5]

In the wake of the stabilization of teams and the twenty-four-second shot clock, NBA owners began to experience a measure of prosperity. Sportswriter Jeremiah Tax reported that the Boston Celtics' "gross receipts" rose eightfold between 1946–47 and 1956–57. He also mentioned that the defunct Chicago Stags and St. Louis Bombers teams could not even elicit bids of $30,000 for either franchise in 1950, while surviving teams were turning down offers of $200,000 by 1957.[6] In addition to the twenty-four-second shot clock, Tax thought the "TV Game of the Week" on Saturday afternoons was boosting attendance.

In an earlier article, Tax discussed baseball player Marty Marion's efforts to obtain an NBA franchise. Tax listed operating expenses of $215,000, which he thought could be defrayed by charging an average price of $1.50 for 3,500 seats at thirty home games. In addition, a prospective team owner would get some revenues from selling rights to radio broadcasts and shared television money from the league's sale of telecasting rights.[7]

In 1957 *Sporting News* reporter Bill Mokray also heralded rosier prospects. He believed the Boston Celtics were still in the red for their first ten years of operation, but that the team was valued at $350,000. The team averaged about 7,500 attendees per home game.[8]

Syracuse, too, experienced a transformation from red to black ink after a strong showing in the 1958–59 playoffs.[9] Les Harrison was another owner of a team in a small city. He also had a lack of capital. His Rochester Royals were his sole commercial interest.[10] He, too, struggled to remain solvent. When the Royals' star players faded after 1954–55, the franchise became untenable in Rochester.

THE PROFIT AND LOSS DATA SUPPLIED TO CONGRESS

While much of the anecdotal evidence applies to the earliest years of the BAA/ NBA, the evidence supplied to Congress for its 1957 antitrust hearings paints a rather dismal picture. Table 19 shows the profit/loss figures supplied to Congress during the mid-1950s. Since the Consumer Price Index was relatively stable during this time period, the figures are in nominal dollar amounts.

At first glance it appears the New York Knickerbockers stood alone as they consistently reported profits. The other two "large-city" teams, the Boston Celtics and the Philadelphia Warriors, also came close to breaking even over the six seasons reported, although the Warriors probably incurred a loss between 1951 and 1957 if the team had reported its 1951–52 figures. The Minneapolis Lakers and the Fort Wayne Pistons were the big losers, even though the Lakers were league champions three years in a row (1951–53). The three teams that folded during or after the 1951–55 seasons did not supply information. Because these teams folded, there is a strong presumption that they were losing money up to the time they folded. Inclusion of these teams' losses would have made the league figures even worse.

The profit figures, though, require care in interpretation. The New York Knicks included a note with their figures: "No rent or any part of Madison Square Garden general overhead or administrative salaries [is] included in the above expenses. Had this overhead or rent been charged for each game, operations for 1952, 1953, and 1954 would have resulted in a loss and 1955 and 1956 would have about broken even." A similar note held for the 1956–57 information the team supplied separately; this note said the team would have incurred a loss had the rent and overhead expenses been included.[11]

Not all team owners also owned the arena in which their teams played. In these cases, the owners paid a rental fee. Most of the teams reported home gate receipts after netting out federal amusement tax and arena rental. Unfortunately there is no way to ascertain the rental fees for some of the teams. The Boston Celtics, Rochester Royals, and St. Louis Bombers divulged their rental fees, which ranged from $5,000 to $102,000 but were clustered around $50,000 per season. The rental fees appear to have been a mixture of fixed base and per attendee. Even if an owner owned an arena, he still incurred an implicit "rent" in terms of the foregone rent he could have charged, say, for an ice show or rodeo. Madison Square Garden could have charged the Knicks an explicit rent.

The losses may be understated for two other reasons. First, while most of the owners also owned other businesses besides their basketball teams, the time these owners spent working on their teams was time spent away from these other businesses. An owner could have legitimately paid himself a salary for services rendered to the basketball team. The teams from Boston, Fort Wayne, and Rochester specifically showed administrative salary costs of zero for most seasons, although the Celtics listed $25,000 of such expense for 1956–57. The teams from New York, Philadelphia, and Syracuse did not list "administrative salary" in their recap of expenses. The Hawks showed $5,000 of administrative salaries for three seasons, none for two seasons, and $17,000 for 1956–57. As with the Celtics, the Hawks' owners may have decided to reward themselves for a lucrative year (both teams reached the NBA finals in 1956–57). The Minneapolis Lakers' administrative salary expense fluctuated wildly. For 1952–53 the team listed $48,000 in such expenses, but less than $10,000 for any of the subsequent years. Second, any capital an owner invested in his team might have been invested elsewhere and earned a rate of return. Many of the owners had paid only nominal amounts for their franchises, so this implicit expense may have been small. The foregone earnings from investing their capital in safe bonds could have been considered an expense from an economics point of view.

SOURCES OF GROSS RECEIPTS

Table 20 shows the teams' gross receipts, using data from *Organized Professional Team Sports* (1957), except where noted. While a team's population base mattered, with the Knicks garnering the most gross receipts in every year surveyed except 1951–52, the relationship was not perfect. Until 1955–56 the Philadelphia Warriors' gross receipts lagged behind those of every team except the Milwaukee Hawks. When the Hawks moved to St. Louis, the team's gross receipts jumped. The Minneapolis Lakers experienced a free fall in gross receipts after George Mikan retired.

For most, if not all, teams the home gate receipts were the largest source of income. Since there was no gate sharing in the NBA, this secondary source for Major League Baseball and NFL teams was not available. Of course, for the league as a whole, visitors' shares were just a redistribution of and not an accretion to home gate receipts. Teams reported home gate receipts differently. Five of the eight teams reported the gross receipts (net of the admission tax). They did not adjust the gross receipts for arena rental, league fees, and other overhead. The Fort Wayne, Philadelphia, and Syracuse teams reported home gate receipts after subtracting the arena rental and association shares.

Therefore, the figures in table 21, which shows net rather than gross figures for home gate receipts are not strictly comparable. New York's advantage in home game receipts is offset somewhat by not being adjusted for arena rental or association shares.

NBA owners were grateful for even the meager amounts television and radio stations were willing to pay to telecast and broadcast games (see table 22). Ben Kerner claimed, "You got to have your extras, your sponsor, your game program, or you can't open. You can never take in enough at the box office to pay your overhead."[12] The New York Knicks received the largest amount of media revenue in most seasons, although the St. Louis Bombers began receiving a comparable amount. The Pistons, Nationals, and Royals typically gained little from this source. Even in terms of today's dollars, NBA owners in the mid-1950s would have been getting well under a million dollars a season from media sources.

Although players complained about exhibition games, such games were typically a minor source of income (see table 23). League owners collectively received almost as much from exhibition games as they did from media revenue, although exhibition game receipts fell off markedly after the 1954–55 season. The Minneapolis Lakers and the St. Louis Bombers were the main beneficiaries of exhibition game revenue. While regular-season home receipts might have increased over the period surveyed, the decline in exhibition game receipts partially offset the increase.

Unlike their fellow owners in Major League Baseball, very few basketball team owners received revenue from concessions. Since a number of the original BAA franchises were owned by arena owners, they may have accounted for the concessions revenue under the parent company. Out of the eight teams in the NBA, the Pistons were the only team that reported concession sales and averaged only $10,000 per season from such sales.[13]

For owners of successful teams, there was the uncertain hope of profits from participating in the play-offs. The early NBA play-offs sometimes confounded observers with haphazard arrangements. Apparently some owners were dubious that play-offs generated a net financial benefit. League president Podoloff tried to allay fears: "Some of the members of the Association have been disturbed as to whether or not the playoffs will take care of themselves. Preliminary figures . . . indicate the following: Net receipts after taxes = $145,883. From this will have to be paid the players' pool of $70,000.00 and a maximum of 42.5% or $62,000.00 for rent, leaving $13,883.00 to cover expenses of the playoffs. I think the expenses will exceed this sum but at any rate there is no imminent danger of an assessment being levied."[14]

Competitive Balance and the Territorial Draft

Competitive balance improved as the BAA/NBA stabilized. Table 24 shows the win-loss records over the extended period of 1946–62 along with the number of championships won. Six of the eight surviving teams had won at least one championship. The Knicks and Pistons had at least reached the championship finals. Table 25 shows that most NBA teams experienced very rapid changes in fortunes. Concentrating on the eight franchises that survived the upheavals of the early 1950s, six experienced improvements in win-loss percentage (W-L Pct.) of .200 or more across two or three seasons, but several experienced rapid declines. The Philadelphia Warriors' win-loss percentage bounced around more than that of most other teams.

The BAA team owners quickly approved a reverse-order draft of amateur players, similar to that of the National Football League. The NFL draft had one twist: over the course of twelve seasons, each team would get the number-one pick via a rotation. The team with the worst record would get the second pick. The BAA developed its own twist: the territorial draft. The basketball team owners figured that allowing teams to have a special right to select college stars from nearby colleges would boost the audience. According to longtime NBA observer and Knicks official Nat Broudy, "All the teams tried to maneuver so they could get ballplayers from their area."[15] The New York Knickerbockers initially stood to gain from the rule because of the number of top-flight college teams in the New York metropolitan area. Chicago had DePaul and Loyola Universities and Boston had College of the Holy Cross. Other teams might not have many good college teams in the area. The league eventually modified the territorial limits, so the Boston Celtics received the entire New England area to choose from, while the Detroit Pistons were allowed to choose from colleges in the state of Michigan.[16] The college betting scandals of the early 1950s effectively wiped out New York's benefits from the territorial draft, as many New York colleges dropped big-time basketball from their varsity sports programs.

Although the owners didn't express it outright, since they spent remarkably little money on scouting collegiate players, the territorial draft was doubly attractive because it economized on such expenses. The primitive nature of acquiring college talent is remarkable. Of course, it took baseball decades to develop a scouting system. According to draft information compiled in *The Official NBA Basketball Encyclopedia*, no team exercised a territorial pick until 1956 when Boston chose Tommy Heinsohn from College of the Holy

Cross.[17] The Celtics had previously eschewed using a territorial pick in order to acquire Bob Cousy.

While the basketball encyclopedia listed territorial picks as beginning only in 1956, other sources cited territorial picks being used as early as the 1949 draft, when the Minneapolis Lakers selected Vern Mikkelsen from St. Paul's Hamline University. The Lakers and Warriors exercised the most territorial draft picks before the 1956 draft. The two teams obtained seven players via such picks. The Lakers got Mikkelsen, Myer "Whitey" Skoog, and Dick Garmaker, while the Warriors got Paul Arizin, Bill Mlkvy, Ernie Beck, and Tom Gola.[18] In addition, the St. Louis Bombers got Ed Macauley and the Knicks got Walter Dukes with territorial picks. While Mikkelsen, Macauley, and Arizin quickly became all-star players, and the others became solid pros, none tipped the scales as much as later territorial picks Wilt Chamberlain and Oscar Robertson. In later years the Cincinnati Royals selected four territorial picks, including Robertson, Jerry Lucas, Tom Thacker, and George Wilson. The Warriors got Guy Rodgers and Chamberlain, while Detroit took Dave DeBusschere and Bill Buntin. When the Lakers transferred to Los Angeles, they had access to UCLA stars Walt Hazzard and Gail Goodrich. Fortunately for the league, the territorial draft system ended before Lew Alcindor, aka Kareem Abdul-Jabbar, graduated. Bill Bradley was one of the last territorial picks, going to the New York Knicks.[19] The territorial draft even influenced owners' decisions about where to relocate. Part of the rationale for the Rochester Royals' shift to Cincinnati was the promise of obtaining the territorial rights to Oscar Robertson.[20]

On occasion, teams would not exercise their territorial picks and instead retained their regular first-round pick. The Knicks did this by refusing to select Fordham University's Ed Conlin in the 1955 draft; they drafted Kenny Sears instead.[21]

As the years passed, some owners began to complain about the territorial draft. Hawks owner Ben Kerner, now ensconced in St. Louis, argued:

> When the league was founded back in 1946, there was a good reason to have such a rule on the books. Pro ball was new and it stood to reason that if a club could reserve college talent within a 50-mile radius of the city, it would be an excellent shot in the arm for attendance. But we've outgrown those uncertain times. We're established now and we're only hurting ourselves with the rule. Besides, how often do teams make territorial picks because they fear unfavorable fan reaction? There are a number of instances in which club owners tried to cotton to fans by grabbing a local standout, and then regretted it when the fellow didn't measure up.[22]

Kerner's complaint was, of course, self-interested, as aside from producing Ed Macauley, the universities within the city of St. Louis were not a bastion of collegiate talent.

Red Auerbach, too, urged discontinuation of the territorial draft in 1957, saying, "It's true that an occasional top-flight player will be turned out by colleges in those clubs' territory, but there's no steady flow as there is in Philadelphia and New York, where they produce ready-made professional players like an assembly line."[23] Ned Irish disagreed: "If you have a college player in a certain city where he has done well and is a favorite, and has filled buildings with fans, it certainly makes sense to keep him in that city." Irish went on to say that even if a local college hero bombs in the pros, "he will at least create a temporary boost in attendance."[24] Boston and New York, though, were no longer the meccas of college basketball. Midwestern and southern schools were producing top-flight talent, and, of course, UCLA would dominate the college game between 1964 and 1975.

Innovation

The NBA's search for an improved product continued as the 1950s reached mid-decade. The owners were not passive in the face of the game's deterioration on the court.

ATTEMPTS TO SPUR ACTION

Viewers of football will notice a similarity between most games. In the fourth quarter the trailing team usually resorts to a higher proportion of pass plays instead of running plays. The team with the lead tends to become more conservative, literally running out the clock with running plays. Basketball is similar, as time constraints force clubs to alter their tactics. Basketball teams possessing the lead try to milk the clock by stalling. Teams that are trailing resort to incessant fouling, being willing to trade free-throw attempts for possession of the ball. These tactics make sense and are certainly legitimate. Football has built-in breaks in the action, but basketball, with its continuous play, suffers from the delay imposed by lining up and attempting free throws. Although free-throw attempts can be dramatic (as in the 1986 Gene Hackman movie *Hoosiers*, where benchwarmer Ollie hits the two free throws to win a crucial game), they rarely appear in ESPN's "Top Ten" highlights. While fans try to get involved by waving their big foam-rubber "No. 1" hands or, in the old days, pulling wires that made the backboards sway, most fans probably rank watching a player shoot a free throw with watching a baseball pitcher intentionally walk a batter or a football quarterback spike the football to stop the clock.

Pro coaches eventually took the infinite loop that passed as basketball's fourth quarters to extremes. While NBA teams possessed greater parity than many college teams, coaches of inferior teams usually wanted to reduce the number of possessions in any game rather than let the "law of large numbers" shrink their hopes of victory. The game that supposedly forced the NBA to implement its twenty-four-second rule occurred on November 23, 1950. The Fort Wayne Pistons decided to stall against the hometown Minneapolis Lakers, who were the defending champions. The Pistons' stall tactics worked, as they snapped the Lakers' streak of twenty-nine consecutive wins at home and won their first game of the young 1950–51 season. The final score, 19–18, though, was an embarrassment to the league. Readers should note, however, that the NBA's twenty-four-second shot clock did not debut until the 1954–55 season. Red Holzman, New York Knicks coach, recalled a game with six overtimes played in 1951. He thought that was the game that helped instigate the shot clock. According to him, whoever got the ball at the start of an overtime period held it for the last shot. "It was usually us, and I held the ball while the fans booed the shit out of us. Finally we lost 75–73."[25]

The evil twin of stalling was roughhouse fouling in hopes of getting possession as the game waned. Between stalling, fouling, and marching to free-throw lines, NBA action languished. The owners, aghast at their coaches' antics, initially tried a "gentleman's agreement" against stalling and fouling. Even a contributing writer to a team program excoriated the owners' inability to curb their coaches' tactics, writing: "[The owners] called it the Honor System and they were proud of the maneuver that was to drown the complaints of the paying customers who didn't like their basketball dragged out. It seems to me that this solution lasted about two weeks before the hammering and howling started all over again." The writer's scorn was justified. An earlier article in the New York Times described the league's action taken in January 1954: "The NBA board of governors decided last night that putting its coaches on an 'honor system' was the best way to reduce excessive fouling. . . . Unable to agree on any of the numerous suggestions advanced to curb deliberate trading of fouls in the closing minutes of games, the board put upon the coaches the burden of controlling the foul situation." The reporter ended with the laconic observation, "It will be interesting to see if this works."[26]

The honor system failed to prevent ugly repeats of the November 23 Lakers-Pistons game. Owners passed new rules, hoping to maintain the fluidity of the game in the fourth quarter. Sportswriter Dick Young jeered, "Things have reached the stage in the NBA where, whenever a time out is called during a game, one of the newspaper men in the press row yells facetiously: 'Let's have a quick meeting of the rules committee and change something before they start playing again.'" Young expressed some sympathy for the owners, but he could not understand why owners did not either reduce the number of fouls a player could commit before being disqualified or employ a shot clock. He concluded, "Such a change would require the employment of a special timer, with a stop-watch, at all games. This costs money, and any rule which costs money has a tough time passing."[27]

Owners tried such tactics as changing the dimension of the backcourt, a team's defensive area, and awarding two free throws for fouls incurred in the backcourt for the 1953–54 season. At first Eddie Gottlieb, president-manager of the Philadelphia Warriors, lauded the rule, saying, "It has not only sped up the actual play on the court, but has shortened the over-all time required to finish a contest." Gottlieb's opinion was seconded by Philadelphia sportswriter Stan Baumgartner.[28] Although the rule dropped the NBA's number of personal fouls by 12 percent and free-throw attempts by 8 percent, the number of field goal attempts and scores also fell.

Sportswriter Leonard Koppett recounted a playoff game that was more proximate to the drastic change inherent in the shot clock. The Boston Celtics played the New York Knicks on March 20, 1954, on national television. "The game encompassed all the repulsive features of the grab-and-hold philosophy. It lasted three hours, and the final seconds of a one-point game were finally abandoned by the network. The arguments with the referees were interminable and degrading. What had been happening, as a matter of course, in dozens of games for the last couple of years, was shown to a nationwide audience in unadulterated impurity."[29] The owners decided that a drastic change was needed to prevent another such embarrassment as the ugly playoff game in March 1954.

THE TWENTY-FOUR-SECOND SHOT CLOCK

The league passed the rule adopting a twenty-four-second shot clock a month later. Syracuse Nationals owner Danny Biasone devised the rule by dividing the complete game time of forty-eight minutes by an average number of field goals attempted during a game. Apparently Biasone had tried earlier to convince his fellow owners that a shot clock would alleviate many of the woes occurring late in the game.[30] Biasone was not alone in advocating for a shot clock; referee Eddie Boyle and Boston Celtic Ed Macauley both urged implementing some sort of time limit on possessing the ball. Macauley told a luncheon audience: "Make us shoot the ball within a certain time and you'll see a better game. Imagine the feeling of fans at the game or at home listening on the radio, when they know the other club has to shoot the ball and their team can get possession late in a game with a resultant chance to tie or win."[31] As with baseball's choice of ninety feet between bases, the NBA's twenty-four-second rule seems a perfect choice in balancing offense and defense. Olympic and college games eventually chose variations on the rule, with college basketball waiting decades before implementing a shot clock. The league also changed the number of team fouls per quarter before assessing penalty free throws. Initially the rule stipulated that a team would be allowed two free throws for every foul committed on the team over six in any quarter (with suitable adjustment for overtime periods). Owners, coaches, players, and fans quickly embraced the new rules.

Within a year the twenty-four-second shot clock received praise such as, "It is this rule that can be singularly pointed to today as re-establishing the spectator interest that has now been rejuvenated in America's most popular wintertime activity."[32] Sportswriter Harold Rosenthal commented in 1958: "The freeze and its various stalling overtones were putting the game 'on ice' in more ways than one. The proceedings had degenerated into an ugly exhibition of late hacking and fouling. . . . [Implementation of the shot clock means that] today no lead is safe in the last two minutes. Few indeed are the customers who will leave before the final buzzer, no matter how cock-eyed the margin seems to be at the moment."[33]

Abe Saperstein, owner of the Harlem Globetrotters, swam against the shot-clock tide. He quixotically urged a restoration of the jump ball after every basket.

> A fellow goes to a sport to blow his top. He can't do it in a factory. But at an athletic contest he can, and nobody will arrest him. With goals so cheap, he doesn't have time to cheer. To stir up interest among the spectators, I'd give them an opportunity to yell like hell. The way it is now, a shot is made, the ball is taken out of bounds and thrown down to the other end of the court for another basket. Fans are developing swivel necks. There's no time to cheer, no time to savor a goal. Even the scorekeepers can't keep up with the baskets."[34]

Even as clever an entrepreneur and promoter as Saperstein undoubtedly was, he, like everyone else, is entitled to a few bum ideas. Cleveland Pipers coach John McLendon also disliked the thirty-second shot clock in the National Industrial Basketball League. "Rules of this type have no place in sports.

Coaches spend endless hours teaching boys something, in this case gaining possession, and just because of a time buzzer, they are forced to surrender the ball by shooting it toward the hoop."[35]

What effects did the twenty-four-second shot clock have? Leonard Koppett highlighted the immediate jump in scoring.[36] Teams averaged 93.1 points per game in 1954–55 as opposed to 79.5 in 1953–54 (see table 9). Part of this was because of improved shooting accuracy from the field and at the line. While most observers recall that players and coaches adapted immediately to the rule changes, the statistics paint a different picture. While play in the BAA was undoubtedly inferior in 1946–48, especially before the arrival of NBL stars like Mikan and Davies, the games featured more field goal attempts and fewer free-throw attempts than even in 1954–55 and 1955–56, the first two seasons with the shot clock. The shot clock did succeed in resuscitating the number of field goals attempted, stanching a free fall from 96.0 in 1947–48 to 75.4 per team per game in 1953–54. A major difference between 1946–48 and 1954–56 was the improved field goal and free-throw accuracy. The BAA scoring levels were very low. Even with all the concern over NBA stalling tactics, teams averaged roughly 80 points a game between 1948 and 1954, peaking in 1950–51 and then falling by 5 percent.

A more important issue revolves around the number of free throws attempted and the number of personal fouls. Personal fouls fell by more than 10 percent between the 1952–53 and 1953–54 seasons, before implementation of the shot clock. While personal fouls fell in 1954–55, they resumed the 1953–54 level thereafter. Probably because of the new limit on team fouls per quarter, free-throw attempts increased after the shot clock was implemented and reached levels higher than in pre–shot clock seasons.

Most players and coaches quickly adjusted to the shot clock. A few players found themselves in a predicament similar to silent movie stars who faced the advent of "talkies" with an unappealing voice. Players who were not fleet of feet might find themselves at a disadvantage under the new rules. George Mikan retired before the advent of the shot clock, although he came back briefly during the 1955–56 season. A number of players saw their points per game shrink (in most cases along with their minutes played). Billy Gabor, Paul Hoffman, Wally Osterkorn, George Ratkovicz, Al Roges, Fred Schaus, Don Sunderlage, and Paul Walther all lost three or more points per game and played at least one thousand fewer minutes in 1954–55 than in 1953–54. While Gabor, Hoffman, and Ratkovicz were in their thirties, the other players experiencing declines were not particularly large or old. Hoffman and Gabor were both guards. Ratkovicz might be the prototypical player who was out of sync with the new league; he was 6'-7" and weighed 225 pounds. Other players may have been cut during pre-season training or decided not to subject themselves to the rigors of the faster game. Since scoring increased throughout the league, players tallying fewer points per game in 1954–55 than in the previous season were definitely showing deterioration of their skills. Players such as Jim Baechtold, Clyde Lovellette, Ken Murray, and George Yardley saw significant increases in their playing time and in their points per game.

Another salient issue is whether the adoption of the shot clock coincided with a general improvement in the owners' fortunes. While Koppett and other observers believe the shot clock "saved" the NBA, the league's profit figures and home gate receipts present a more ambiguous situation. Owners collectively lost money in the last three seasons before the shot clock. In 1954–55 they collectively showed a modest profit, although readers are reminded of the Knicks' caveat of their profits being due to not paying explicit arena rental. The collective profits increased again in 1955–56, but part of this was because of the Hawks relocating to St. Louis. The teams in Minneapolis, Fort Wayne, and Rochester showed little improvement on the ledgers.

NBA attendance figures are notoriously unreliable during the 1940s and 1950s. However, looking at league attendance for the 1950s raises the intriguing possibility that the twenty-four-second shot clock's debut coincided with a further drop in attendance (see table 26).[37] Did Mikan's retirement outweigh the enthusiasm for the faster-paced game? One less team existed (and thus fewer games were played) in 1954–55 than in 1953–54, which accounts for part of the drop in attendance. On a per-game basis, attendance rose slightly, but the demise of the moribund Baltimore franchise probably accounted for this change, as the surviving teams may have collectively experienced a drop in per-game attendance. One could argue, though, that the introduction of the twenty-four-second shot clock prevented an even steeper decline. In the subsequent seasons, attendance climbed slowly. If the shot clock was a savior, salvation took some time.

Home gate receipts, too, demonstrate, at best, a lagged response to the new twenty-four-second rule (see table 21). Home gate receipts for the eight surviving teams were only $21,000 more between 1953–54 and 1954–55. The receipts had fallen by $170,000 between 1952–53 and 1953–54 (12.3 percent), surely a cause for concern. The 1954–55 figures, however, were less than the 1952–53 totals. The Philadelphia Warriors and St. Louis Bombers led a resurgence in home gate receipts in 1955–56, when every team showed an improvement in such receipts. The Boston Celtics and St. Louis Bombers showed significant increases in home game receipts in 1956–57. The league's improved condition, then, coincided not only with the new rule, but with the Hawks' franchise relocation and the Celtics' improvement in performance. Perhaps more importantly, the NBA crowned a new champion in 1954–55, as the Syracuse Nationals supplanted the now Mikan-less Lakers. The Lakers and the Nats showed no significant improvement in home game receipts after the shot clock was implemented, while the Pistons and the Royals showed only modest gains of $30,000-$40,000 each. Clearly the "shot-clock as savior" story applied to mainly teams in the larger cities.

The adoption of the twenty-four-second shot clock in 1954–55 also coincided with changes in directions of some franchises. In some respects the shot clock became a dividing point. The Lakers began to fade after the introduction of the shot clock and retirement of Mikan. Whether Mikan would have fared well under the clock is an interesting question. The Lakers tended to lead the league in field goal attempts during Mikan's last three full seasons, although the team was never among the leaders in free throws attempted. They might have played a faster tempo than some of their rivals, or they might have simply dominated the offensive boards and made a disproportionate number of tip-ins.

The Lakers' chief rivals, the Rochester Royals, also tailed off with the advent of the shot clock. If the Lakers' and Royals' downturns after 1954 weren't as dramatic as the teams shown in table 25, they were chronic. Not until the two teams reloaded with the likes of Baylor, Robertson, West, and Twyman did their records rebound for good.

Table 27 shows the immediate before and after records of teams with the twenty-four-second shot clock. The table also shows the 1953–54 records excluding games with the hapless Baltimore Bullets. The Bullets' terrible record boosted the other team's records.

Like Babe Ruth and the lively ball in baseball and the forward pass in the NFL, the shot clock transformed the game of basketball. For the next few decades, NBA basketball would be fundamentally different from college and high school ball. While some, perhaps even many, basketball fans disliked the faster-paced pro game, the shot clock created an appealing product that enthused many new fans in the years ahead.

The introduction of a second wave of African American players who were particularly talented may also help explain the increasingly frenetic pace of NBA games. Although there were too few black players around in 1954–55 to tell whether the shot clock helped them, it is intriguing that four of the five African American players saw improvement in their minutes played and points per game after the rule was put into effect. Ray Felix was the exception, and his statistical drop-off may have been the result of playing for a new team. The New York Knicks had more talent than Felix's original Baltimore team, so Felix may not have been required to bear as much of the scoring load. A sixth black player, Isaac Walthour, played sparingly in 1953–54 and did not play at all in 1954–55.

By 1959–60 NBA teams were attempting 25 percent more field goals than in the shot clock's inaugural season. The faster pace was matched by improved field goal accuracy (however, no similar improvement in free-throw accuracy occurred, and such accuracy has remained relatively constant at 75 percent over the decades).

The twenty-four-second shot clock has not, of course, eliminated defensive fouling late in the game by the trailing team. If the team with the lead is ahead by more than three or four points, the trailing team quickly fouls against them. The three-point shot from outside an arc has, to some degree, reduced the impetus to foul and has sped up the game, since, unlike before, trailing by three points means a team needs just one possession to tie the game. A collegiate official suggested this in 1954, but neither college nor pro officials endorsed the proposal. Surprisingly, the three-point shot was suggested by NBA observers only much later. Early adherents argued for a thirty-foot arc. NBL and NBA player and later college coach Bruce Hale said, "The good big man almost always whips the good little man. But if backcourt men could pop baskets from behind that 30-foot line, the importance of basketball giants would be somewhat minimized." The proposed rule had primitive aspects to it, as it would encourage the survival of two-hand set shots. NBA coach Alex Hannum claimed, "The two-handed set [shot] going for three points would not hurt the game's character and fans would love it."[38]

Sportswriter Jeremiah Tax pointed out that pro basketball's success in the latter part of the 1950s emanated from a general public attitude "toward all sports[,] which rates highest the most spectacular bit of action that each game offers." He surmised that basketball's ever-increasing scoring led to the "popular myth . . . that the pros simply trade baskets, paying scant attention to the defensive aspects of the game." He later attributed rising attendance to the twenty-four-second rule.[39]

Years later the NBA's success in pepping up the game proved too successful in the eyes of some critics. As scores began to leap by bounds, some observers thought scoring was becoming too easy, thereby cheapening the game. Maurice Podoloff admitted, "We have gone far enough in scoring and I definitely do not want to think of 200-point affairs." In the same interview, he urged changing the backcourt foul rule to eliminate the free throw and the ensuing "dreary tramp the length of the court."[40] Sportswriter Dick Young defended the twenty-four-second rule by saying it encouraged even teams with the lead to put up shots quickly in order to avoid being forced to take a poor shot as the shot clock expired. He also attributed the improvement in scoring to the growing prevalence of the jump shot: "You don't stop the jump shot. You just hope it misses."[41] Ultimately basketball team owners never seriously considered jettisoning the twenty-four-second rule.

The NBA's success with the twenty-four-second shot clock prompted a renewal of agitation for a similar rule in college and high school games. Some college coaches, undoubtedly knowing that talent disparities were wider in amateur ball than in the pros, worried about the shot clock's effects upon competitive balance. Concerns about the zone defense accompanied those surrounding the twenty-four-second rule. Although his methods were unscientific, *Sports Illustrated* columnist Jimmy Jemail surveyed eight college observers' opinions on the rule. Some of the coaches suggested that unless the zone defense was eliminated, the rule wouldn't work. In other articles, coaches suggested a limit on how long an individual player could possess the ball, such as a five-second limit before passing, shooting, or dribbling the ball. One reporter claimed that only one-seventh of the college coaches surveyed in 1951—years before the pros instituted their rule—supported some form of a shot clock rule (typically for thirty seconds instead of the pros' twenty-four seconds). Other collegiate observers were more sanguine about the shot clock's prospects in college basketball, with Joe Lapchick predicting that colleges would soon implement the rule. Lapchick's forecast proved premature, as college coaches were able to keep the shot clock out of their game for decades.[42] Coach Ken Loeffler worried that the shot clock tilted the balance toward too much scoring. "The worst thing that can happen to technique and tactics and consequent fan interest will occur if the colleges adopt the time limitation and no-zone defense rules. If they do, the tactics of coaching will receive a death blow and the coaches' time will be spent in chasing about the country recruiting shooters and runners." He then argued that such chasing would result in magnified abuses in recruiting when "the possibility of winning with defensive tactics is limited."[43]

Television

Most readers of this book, including me, cannot remember a time when television and televised sporting events were not ubiquitous. Major League Baseball had a long history of adapting with new technologies, ranging from cheap newspapers, radio, electric lighting, and television (this book does not span the Internet era, of course). The NBA's beginning coincided with television.

Although some baseball games had been telecast before World War II, clearly the war delayed diffusion of television technology. The northeast quadrant of the country began regular telecasts shortly after the war, but the diffusion took much of the 1950s to become nationwide. Because professional basketball was concentrated in the northeast region of the country, it was tailor-made to fill the hours of television schedules.

Major League Baseball struggled with adapting to radio broadcasts of games during the 1930s. The New York City clubs resisted radio broadcasts until the 1939 season, when Brooklyn Dodger official Larry MacPhail eagerly embraced radio broadcasts of home games (in return for suitable compensation). Baseball owners feared that radio broadcasts of home games were too close a substitute for attendance in person. The early broadcasts of baseball games overlapped with the general economic downturn. Some owners attributed the attendance doldrums of the 1930s, perhaps incorrectly, to radio broadcasts. In a volte-face, the baseball owners quickly agreed to televise their games, at home and on the road, after World War II. However, by the mid-1950s, with baseball's decline in attendance from the postwar boom, several owners had decided to reduce or eliminate telecasts of home games although they maintained telecasts of games on the road.[44]

Basketball owners, too, were ambivalent about televising games. According to Marty Glickman, a New York Knicks radio announcer, television sought out basketball and not the other way around. Glickman recalled a meeting at Toots Shor's, a famous hangout for professional athletes, with Knicks president Ned Irish and a few others. They were discussing radio broadcasts when Burt Lee, program director of WHN, suggested telecasting Knicks games. Irish asked, "How much would it cost me?" Lee apparently surprised Irish when he said, "Not only will it cost you nothing, but we'll pay you $250 per game."[45] (Glickman added that the price eventually went to $1,750 per game.) At $250 per game and thirty home games, the Knicks stood to make $7,500, enough to pay a starting player. By 1948 the Knicks arranged with the American Broadcasting Company to televise their entire 1948–49 basketball schedule in Madison Square Garden, as well as playoff games. The article in the *New York Times* did not specify whether the Knicks' home games at the 69th Regiment Armory would also be televised. The Knicks agreed to telecast all eighteen of their home games from Madison Square Garden over stations WPIX and WABD.[46] As table 11 shows, the Knicks' net home per-game receipts fell from $7,943 to $6,542 between the 1949–50 and 1950–51 seasons. R. C. Embry, president of the Baltimore team, believed that a 25 percent decline in attendance was attributable to telecasts of the team's games and ordered the practice halted, although he added that such a halt was contingent upon future attendance. The team's win-loss record deteriorated in the latter season, but not precipitously.[47]

While some baseball owners acquiesced to radio broadcasts only after they began receiving payment from radio stations, NBA owners had reason to worry about the effects of televising games upon home attendance. They received payment from the television stations for telecast rights, but such payments were hardly munificent. Even a minor decrease in attendance would wipe out any dollar gains from selling telecasting rights. Walter Brown, owner of the Boston Celtics, was hesitant to admit to Marty Glickman what his team was receiving for telecast rights. When Glickman asked Brown about it, Brown replied, "It's embarrassing." Glickman pressed Brown, "who mentioned $5,000. 'That's pretty good,' I said. Brown retorted, 'For the season?'"[48]

Researcher Jerry Jordan attempted to ascertain the effects of telecasts upon attendance at sporting events during the late 1940s. He reported mixed findings, with some evidence that people who attended games were more likely to own televisions and to watch games on television. Given the complexity of the problem, though, he didn't provide convincing evidence either way. The basketball team owners' persistence in televising home games suggests that many of them had reached a favorable estimation of the medium's effects.[49]

The owners approved a deal with the DuMont Network, which ceased broadcasting in 1956, to televise thirteen games during the 1952–53 season. League official Haskell Cohen reminisced that the league received $3,000 per game, which went to the home team. "They were so anxious to get that $3,000 that they said, 'Let's try it.'" Perhaps more prescient than the owners, league president Maurice Podoloff mused that someday "proceeds [from television] may supplement gate receipts to the point where the latter lose their importance."[50] Although owners wanted the $3,000, they remained suspicious of television. Rochester Royals owner Les Harrison admitted to Terry Pluto that the league failed to "sell stars" as the modern league does. "In fact, we put our worst games on because we feared that if we broadcast the best games, no one would buy a ticket. They'd all stay home and watch it for free. So what the public saw was the worst of pro basketball."[51] Harrison's observation had some truth as, during the 1953–54 season, *Basketball's Best* showed the tail-ender Milwaukee Hawks and Baltimore Bullets hosting four of the fourteen games (see table 28).

As would frequently happen, television's needs and desires sometimes clashed with those of team owners. Leonard Koppett pointed out that the television networks wanted Saturday afternoon games, while the owners preferred Saturday evenings. The Knicks certainly didn't seem eager to get a lot of games on national television, appearing just once on TV during the 1953–54 season.[52]

The DuMont Network renewed its contract with the NBA for the 1953–54 season and agreed to up the ante to $5,000 per Saturday afternoon game. Eventually the league upgraded to the National Broadcasting Company (NBC) for $100,000 per season.[53] League president Podoloff testified before the 1957 congressional hearings that the national broadcasting contract with NBC meant that each time a team hosted a televised game, it got $7,500. The league now attempted to rotate the exposures on television across seasons; however, some congressional investigators were slow to understand this concept during the hearings. In a typical year each team was on national television three times, with either one or two of these being home games. The money from the national television contract was not evenly divided in any given year, but over a two-year period it was equalized.[54]

Given the NBA's sluggish style of play before adopting the twenty-four-second shot clock, the league might have been better off not televising games nationally until the mid-1950s. With the shot clock and faster-paced games, the NBA provided excellent television drama. As Podoloff described it, television would help at the box office and in spreading the game: "[It will furnish] the personnel for our future teams. Because of TV, the game now goes into areas that never had seen basketball, much less the best basketball in the world. It's bound to have an effect on the kids watching. Every kid with an inch or two over the next fellow is thinking in terms of basketball, not baseball or football. We'll never have to worry about top-notch talent no matter how many teams we bring into the league."[55] Rosenthal also thought national telecasts of NBA games "[took] a lot of the gloss off some of the big oil company teams [who played in AAU and industrial ball leagues]." He concluded that good players, seeing the national publicity from playing in the NBA, would be more likely to eschew the AAU teams.[56] Unlike Major League Baseball, which relied upon extensive farm systems, the NBA and the NFL benefited from highly touted and publicized collegiate stars entering their leagues. These players retained their legions of fans as they entered the professional ranks. With nationally televised games, fans could, at least occasionally, continue to see their heroes. University of Kansas fans, thus, could watch Wilt Chamberlain dominate his pro opponents even though they lived nowhere near an NBA franchise.

Sportswriter Harold Rosenthal was enthusiastic about television's effect upon the NBA: "Within the short span of three years, Saturday afternoon network TV has boosted the NBA's attendance 30 per cent and has elevated the cage sport to No. 3 eminence behind baseball and football in the electronic picture." Rosenthal also lauded Podoloff and thought the president's idea of Saturday night telecasts of NBA basketball was a splendid idea.[57]

As network television revenues steadily increased, the players began demanding a share. They thought the television revenue would be a dandy way to fund their proposed pension, citing the National Hockey League's approach to funding a pension. In addition to the television revenues, the players hoped owners would attach a surcharge of twenty-five cents to the ticket price for the NBA All-Star Game and play-offs. Arthur Daley reported that a "man high in the N.B.A. councils" told him the cost of staging the 1964 All-Star Game "will eat up most of the TV money." By this time the NBA had to scramble to find a network that was willing to telecast its games nationally. Although the players used the threat of a walkout of the January 1964 All-Star Game to force the owners to negotiate, the resulting player pension was not directly funded by all-star or championship series television money. The proposed plan consisted of equal player and owner contributions.[58]

NBC continued to broadcast Saturday or Sunday afternoon games into the 1960s. By 1960 more than 90 percent of American households had a television, so professional basketball could be seen in almost every town in the country.[59] Sportswriter Joe King examined the lingering notion that television siphoned off attendance at pro basketball games, or at least in New York City: "A total of 31,138 for two events [NHL and NBA games at Madison Square Garden] on the same day—yet both games were televised in New York City, as well as nationally! That's what you might term, at first glance, living happily with TV sports." Ned Irish still demurred, claiming that blackouts of home games were still necessary to ensure good attendance figures. He pointed out that Madison Square Garden was not sold out for all Knicks' games, especially in the side balcony. Irish claimed, "If we had played on our usual Sunday night [instead of Saturday afternoon,] we would have taken in $10,000 to $12,000 more than we derived from the Saturday receipts plus TV." Irish's promotion man, Fred Podestra, summed up, saying, "We have suffered substantially more loss in gate revenue than we have taken in TV payments. It now becomes a question of looking ahead to estimate what the steadily rising loss will be next season, and either receive that amount from TV or consider other measures."[60] Irish was of two minds about television. "Whether we televised or not, we were sure to be hurt. It was a case of joining it, since we could not lick it. By televising, we at least have been able to win wider attention for our events. I feel sure that we also have helped develop many new sports fans who eventually will come to the Garden."[61]

Haskell Cohen of the league office stated: "The contests which were televised live over the NBC-TV network, reaching 170 stations on Sunday afternoons, were viewed by approximately 15,000,000 followers each week. The current season will see the television audience double this figure by virtue of the fact that NBA games will be featured by NBC-TV on both Saturday and Sunday afternoons. A total of 39 regular-season games are carded with eight playoff games slated for video viewers."[62]

The NBA's experience with network telecasting seemed to differ from that of Major League Baseball. The New York Yankees appeared so often on the MLB's weekly telecast that some wits thought the telecast should be dubbed "The Yankee Game of the Week." Since the home team kept the telecast revenue, the Yankees' advantage in market size was exacerbated by the television contract.[63] As table 28 shows, between the 1956–57 and 1957–58 seasons, every NBA team had exactly three home games shown on national television. The equal sharing of revenue from a national television contract was revolutionary, years ahead of those of the American Football League and National Football League. Because NBA owners apportioned home appearances on television on an equal basis, revenue from the national television contract was unlikely to affect any team's marginal revenue product, meaning the increased revenue from winning more games. While the television revenue may have increased owners' overall revenues, the lump-sum nature of the revenue and its lack of effect upon the marginal revenue product of each individual team meant there was little incentive to bid more for talented players, so the national television money was not likely to affect player salaries or competitive balance. In a sense, the equal-shares aspect kept owners from falling into a "prisoners' dilemma," whereby increased marginal revenue product would spur owners to bid more for players, thereby dissipating much of their revenue gains.[64]

By the 1958–59 and 1959–60 seasons, NBC telecast Sunday afternoon games during the entire season. In the latter season, the network also telecast a few Saturday games at 5:00 P.M. The network cut back to showing only Saturday games for the 1961–62 season. In 1961 only the Chicago Packers and St. Louis Hawks reported televising games locally. The following year, just the Los Angeles Lakers and St. Louis Hawks reported doing so. Several teams also had radio broadcasts of home games.[65]

Television also induced the owners to approve relocation of teams in smaller cities to larger cities. The owners approved the Rochester Royals' relocation to Cincinnati partly out of fear that a major television contract might be dropped, as the "sponsors supposedly want the games coming from 'major league cities' and they do not rate Rochester as 'major.'"[66]

Not all observers were pleased with television's effects on sports. Sportswriter Dick Young waxed indignant about the outrage of the birth of the television time-out. "The anger here involves television's influence on the outcome of athletic events—the seeming disregard for the desirability of an honest result when weighed against the prospects of a 'good show.'"[67] Despite Young's grousing, television became a permanent fixture of NBA life.

Conclusion

The eight NBA teams that survived the upheavals of the early 1950s enjoyed stability and revenue growth as the 1950s progressed. Rising franchise values reflected the better situation facing the owners. Mikan's retirement and the decline of the Rochester Royals allowed the Syracuse Nationals and Fort Wayne Pistons briefly and, eventually, the St. Louis Hawks to become contenders. New stars like Bill Russell and Bob Pettit changed the balance of power.

The owners' decision to implement the twenty-four-second shot clock helped transform the pro game into something quite distinct from other basketball games and would eventually prove popular and enduring. The new rule, if not immediately a panacea, stanched the ugliness of many NBA games' waning moments and created a product better suited for television. It is difficult to overrate the importance of the rule in eventually enhancing the league's image and popularity. Although big men would dominate the game, smaller but faster players also found their own niche. The era of the plodding (but deadly) set shooter was closing.

The league, though, still suffered from having franchises in smaller cities. While fans in Syracuse, Fort Wayne, and Rochester might have been enthusiastic and loyal, there certainly weren't enough of them to enable their teams to plausibly compete with teams in larger cities over the long run. Although the New York Knicks were declining, teams in the NBA Finals were shifting to those in the larger cities, such as St. Louis and Boston. Until owners of teams in smaller cities opted to relocate, they would operate at a disadvantage and retard the league's acceptance as a true major league sports entity. With professional hockey experiencing a decline during the mid-1950s, though, the NBA was poised to become America's third "major league."

6

Moving to Major League Status (1957–62)

Although some of the eight franchises were still struggling to earn sufficient revenues, the NBA's stability and the success of its twenty-four-second shot clock encouraged NBA owners. Some began considering relocating their teams to larger cities. Their improved product on the court and growing prosperity spurred other businesspeople to begin seeking teams of their own, leading to increases in franchise values and demands for expansion teams. NBA owners now had to decide whether to relocate existing franchises and whether to expand.

Attendance

As the 1950s waned, the NBA enjoyed improved attendance. Teams in the smaller cities transferred to Detroit, St. Louis, and Cincinnati. Along with exciting new collegiate players entering the league on a yearly basis, the league's eight clubs gradually saw attendance rise. *Basketball's Best* review for the upcoming 1961–62 season showed attendance figures for the previous season. While every one of the eight teams drew more than 100,000 attendees, the league's total of 1.7 million was dwarfed by attendance at Los Angeles Dodgers baseball games, and the World Series–winning Pittsburgh Pirates attracted more fans than did the entire NBA.[1] Haskell Cohen of the NBA office offered similar attendance figures for the 1959–60 season, with the Knicks leading the league with 332,578 fans. The Philadelphia Warriors were the best road draw with 405,212.[2] *Sports Illustrated* columnist Jeremiah

Tax had claimed that the NBA surpassed the two million mark in attendance during its 1957–58 season (a gain of 7 percent over the previous season), but it is possible that his figures include people attending with complimentary tickets, a claim echoed by Haskell Cohen for the 1958–59 season.[3]

When the Minneapolis Lakers moved to Los Angeles for the 1960–61 season, NBA owners might have hoped to see an explosion in attendance, similar to the experience the Brooklyn Dodgers had after relocating to the West Coast. The early indications were favorable, as the Lakers' ticket sales before the season started were four times higher than their best sales in Minneapolis. The club sold 1,600 season tickets at $100, which was just 400 fewer than the number sold by the world champion Boston Celtics.[4] Although baseball's Dodgers had a gratifying welcome, the Lakers struggled at first, despite having the electrifying Elgin Baylor and rookie Jerry West. The Lakers opened their home schedule with two games versus the New York Knicks, but the games had a combined attendance of less than 7,500. Granted the Knicks had the league's worst record the previous season, but the tepid response was very disappointing, as club officials had hoped for a gate of 200,000 for the season.[5] Fortunately, things eventually worked out for the Lakers, especially once the football season ended.

Some teams still struggled, however. Eddie Gottlieb desperately sought to sign Wilt Chamberlain. Some observers thought Chamberlain was NBA-ready even as a teenager, but, of course, league rules prohibited such an occurrence as signing high school players until a more enlightened era. During a year playing for the Harlem Globetrotters, Chamberlain proved a box office hit, and he apparently boosted attendance at Globetrotter games by 25 percent early in the 1958–59 season. During the 1959–60 season, Chamberlain's NBA debut proved equally exciting as he generated larger-than-average crowds throughout the league. According to sportswriter Art Morrow, the Philadelphia Warriors set an attendance record for their home games of 159,467, with ten games remaining on their home schedule. Another sportswriter claimed that Chamberlain "drew 500,000 new fans into NBA arenas around the country singlehandedly. . . . He is as valuable to this sport as Babe Ruth was to baseball."[6] His predecessor Bill Russell, already well known for leading the University of San Francisco to two NCAA titles and the U.S. Olympic team to a gold medal, also proved popular at the gate, drawing season-high numbers in various arenas, including more than 14,000 in St. Louis.[7]

Oscar Robertson proved yet another strong drawing card. As with Chamberlain, the "Big O" was a territorial draft pick, but for Cincinnati. The Royals had relocated from Rochester to Cincinnati a few years earlier, and the team coveted Robertson. He quickly attracted a record crowd of 8,176 to Cincinnati Gardens. A reporter for the *Sporting News* stated, "Most fans were there to see Robertson, and were a delight to the Royals' owners, who had only kept the franchise floating through two lean last-place years until they could put the Big O on display in their livery."[8] Sportswriter William Leggett reported that Cincinnati drew just 58,000 fans in the entire season before the Royals drafted Robertson but had attracted 35,000 in the team's first five home games with him. Robertson's debut at the Boston Garden also attracted a large crowd of 13,250, close to a sellout.[9]

Although pundits would discuss the fact that NBA crowds were overwhelmingly Caucasian, most of the new star players were African American. Regardless of whether the crowds embraced these stars, they were certainly curious about them. The Royals had employed Maurice Stokes, a highly talented African American player, on their roster. Robertson was a much-publicized player from his high school days at Crispus Attucks High School in Indianapolis, through his collegiate career at the University of Cincinnati, and to his performance with the 1960 U.S. Olympics team. Basketball and football held an advantage over Major League Baseball in that many of their stars were already well known before joining the league.

Rising Franchise Prices

Franchise sale prices are another indication of profitability. Changes in franchise values are based on current profitability and expected future profitability.[10] Although economists James Quirk and Rodney Fort show that during the 1960s and 1980s NBA franchises had more rapid appreciation in franchise values than did Major League Baseball teams, the trend during the 1950s was difficult to ascertain.[11] One of their appendixes shows franchise sales. Unfortunately for researchers, there were relatively few sales between 1946 and 1961. Instead there was one expansion team (the Baltimore Bullets) and a slew of folded franchises. Owning a BAA, NBL, or NBA franchise was fraught with risk. While the long-term trend was toward franchise appreciation (franchises could be had for tens of thousands of dollars during the first half of the 1946–61 period and for hundreds of thousands or even millions of dollars during the second half), getting to the time of appreciation was a harrowing ride. Most teams that folded after 1950 were in smaller cities, but even teams in large cities (Chicago, Baltimore, and Washington, D.C.) were not immune to financial distress. Those owners of teams that survived to be sold in the late 1950s for apparently healthy rates of appreciation endured seasons of losses.

Table 29 shows the sales histories of the eight NBA teams that survived the upheavals of the early 1950s.

The original owners of the Philadelphia Warriors, the Philadelphia Arena Corporation, were tiring of losing money and considered folding the franchise. Eddie Gottlieb, longtime Warriors coach and official, bought the team from them for $25,000. He paid $15,000 of his own money and borrowed the remainder; Abe Saperstein became a part owner in the team. Sportswriter Terry Pluto reported that ten years later Gottlieb sold the team for $875,000, amounting to a nominal rate of return of 42.7 percent per year.[12] Gottlieb's apparent gains from holding the Warriors must be adjusted for three factors: inflation, early losses, and risk. Between 1952 and 1962, the Consumer Price Index was remarkably stable and increased by just 14 percent. Gottlieb's handsome rate of appreciation would be adjusted somewhat (to 40.8 percent per annum). A more important factor was the financial losses he incurred early in his ownership tenure. While the Warriors' profit/loss figure for 1951–52 isn't available, the team's middling record probably meant losses were similar to that incurred in 1952–53: $34,000. The team began reporting profits only in 1955–56. Suppose Gottlieb suffered losses of $100,000 during his first four years of running the club; this would have been similar to having invested $125,000 in 1952 and watching it disappear. Even losing just $50,000 up front would have trimmed his per annum appreciation considerably. Finally, given the fact that two teams folded after he bought the club, he incurred a significant amount of risk. Gottlieb himself pleaded financial difficulties when he persuaded his fellow owners to award him territorial draft rights to Wilt Chamberlain.

Ben Kerner bought the ailing Tri-Cities Blackhawks for $30,000 in October 1951.[13] He retained the team until 1968, when he sold it for $3.5 million. A similar tale of early losses would also temper the apparently rapid rate of appreciation in his franchise's value.

The Harrison brothers decided to sell their Cincinnati Royals in the late 1950s. At first they hoped to sell the team to Norman Shapiro of Rochester for $200,000, but the other owners in the league eventually disallowed the sale because Shapiro hoped to return the team to Rochester. Instead they approved a sale to Frank Wood, a major stockholder in Cincinnati Gardens. Podoloff said Wood's group paid a $50,000 deposit. The league returned Shapiro's $50,000 deposit. The reported selling price was around $225,000. The league owners preferred Wood's group because it would maintain the franchise in Cincinnati.[14]

The Minneapolis Lakers' owner, Ben Berger, provisionally sold his team to a group headed by baseball's Marty Marion.[15] To keep the team in Minneapolis, a group of local businessmen purchased it. Eventually Bob Short gained control and later moved the team to Los Angeles. Once the team proved a success in Los Angeles, he later sold it to Jack Kent Cooke for millions of dollars.

Increased attendance and profits from relocating teams to larger cities, more lucrative national television contracts, and an influx of more exciting players better fitted to the twenty-four-second shot clock undoubtedly contributed to the appreciation in the value of surviving franchises. But unless an investor in the early 1950s had a strong stomach and faith in professional basketball, there were probably better ways to gain capital appreciation.

Salaries

As the league stabilized and revenues increased, owners began paying more in salaries. A sign of the league's growing prosperity was the rise in salaries received by rookies. The Philadelphia Warriors signed Tom Gola for roughly $12,000 for 1955–56, while Bill Russell signed with the Boston Celtics for $20,000 the following season.[16]

As the 1950s continued, disparities between teams' abilities to pay big stars became pronounced. Bill Russell declared that he would not sign with the Rochester Royals, who had the first pick in the draft, because it was a small-city team. Whether Russell's declaration was motivated by his suspicion that the Royals could not pay as well as teams in the larger cities or he was concerned about the racial atmosphere in a smaller city was not clear. He was able to use the threat of signing with the Harlem Globetrotters to dissuade Royals owner Les Harrison from drafting him.[17]

Ben Kerner's Hawks, whether in the Tri-Cities, Milwaukee, or St. Louis, were among the lowest-paid players in the league (see table 30). Part of this may have stemmed from the team's lackluster records until Bob Pettit joined. Kerner was a Jekyll-and-Hyde style of owner. He could be ruthless when negotiating salaries; as Rudy LaRusso remembered: "We heard that Kerner would tell you, 'Either you take this or you work at the car wash. Now make up your mind.'" He apparently tried to ameliorate his image by being generous in other ways. Zelmo Beaty recalled that Kerner would take the players to fine restaurants while on the road. Each year, he also bought one veteran player a new car. In fact, even though he had traded Beaty, he still bought him a Cadillac because it was the player's turn to get a car. Beaty echoed LaRusso's remarks about negotiating with Kerner: "I won't trade you. You'll just sit and get nothing." Clyde Lovellette remarked that Kerner implicitly used the St. Louis team's smaller revenue potential to hammer down salaries. "Ben told me, 'You might be an $18,000 or $20,000 player [elsewhere], but this is what you're worth to me ($12,000).'"[18]

Wilt Chamberlain not only rewrote the basketball record book, but he also rewrote the salary ledger. Despite the fact that because of the draft rules Chamberlain's only NBA option was with Philadelphia, he still had considerable bargaining power. After deciding to forego his senior year at the University of Kansas, he signed with the Harlem Globetrotters for a reported $65,000. The NBA had a rule prohibiting signing and using players whose college class had yet to graduate.[19]

If Chamberlain was making anywhere close to $65,000 with the Globetrotters, he might, in fact, have taken a pay cut to perform with Gottlieb's Warriors. The press estimated his contract with the team paid him around $30,000 or more. He might have received a signing bonus, too.[20] Chamberlain claimed that Saperstein offered him $100,000 for a second season with the Globetrotters. He also believed he could have landed a "$40,000-a-year desk job with a big company if he chose to play AAU ball." Chamberlain said he used his earnings to buy a house for his mother and allow her to quit her job as a cleaning woman. He also offered to finance his father's retirement, but his father chose to continue his $60-a-week job as a handyman.[21] During his brief retirement from the NBA because of what had become rough play, Chamberlain played a game with the Globetrotters in Chicago Stadium. More than 20,000 fans attended the game. Whether or not his retirement was intended to force Gottlieb to upgrade his contract, Chamberlain signed a three-year deal with the Warriors in August 1960. Gottlieb boasted that the contract made Chamberlain the highest-paid player in all of professional sports. At this point, sports reporters cited him as earning $60,000 from the Warriors the previous season.[22]

The press reports of Chamberlain earning $30,000 as a rookie, making him the game's highest-paid player, raised hackles. The Celtics' Walter Brown quickly countered that his star Bob Cousy made more than $30,000.[23]

Signing big-name college stars could boost a team's revenue considerably. The Minneapolis Lakers, moribund since George Mikan's retirement, signed Elgin Baylor for a $20,000 salary. The team's performance improved, and revenue jumped by more than $130,000. Oscar Robertson had a similar effect upon Cincinnati's fortunes. "Before Oscar had finished his college year, the Royals were $40,000 above previous seasons in advance sales, fired by the anticipation of The Big O romping in Royal pantaloons."[24]

Players' abilities to obtain salary increases could still border on the futile. Sportswriter Bill Furlong wrote about Walt Bellamy: "How does a man who wins Rookie of the Year and scores over 30 points a game while pulling down 18–19 rebounds a game fare in salary negotiations? His rookie salary of $22,500 was supplemented by a $1,500 bonus. As the 1962–63 campaign neared, he demanded a $10,000 raise. He didn't get it. Instead, the [Chicago] Zephyrs offered him $82,500 for a three-year contract . . . [and] finally signed him for $27,500."[25]

TEAM PAYROLL INFORMATION

Table 30 shows the team payroll information from the U.S House subcommittee's *Organized Professional Team Sports*. The teams did not uniformly report their player payroll information, with differences for player bonuses and coaches' salaries. Between the 1951–52 and 1956–57 seasons the payrolls rose. Since the general price level was fairly stable during this period, the increase signaled a rise in real salaries.[26]

The Minneapolis Lakers, despite being league champions for the first three years listed, boasted the highest payroll only in 1953–54. The team included coach John Kundla's salary in the figure, though, so its advantage versus the Boston Celtics or the New York Knicks might have been modest. The team's payroll fell by $13,000 after George Mikan retired but rose in 1955–56 when he "unretired" before it fell again. New York typically ranked near the league lead in payrolls. Despite the Rochester Royals' being a perennial contender, Les Harrison was able to keep the team's payroll below the league average. Indeed, the stability of the Royals' payroll is impressive. The Hawks' payroll began to increase toward the league average only after the team moved to St. Louis.

Table 30 also shows measures of the distribution of team payrolls. Only in 1951–52 did the team with the highest payroll double the smallest payroll. In comparison with Major League Baseball of the same period, the ratio of highest to lowest payroll was similar between the two sports.[27]

Philadelphia Warriors owner Eddie Gottlieb bemoaned the high salaries. "There's only one reason why we've got to struggle to put across basketball. It could be so easy. But our trouble is player salaries. Generally, the players are exorbitantly overpaid. No sport can apportion more than 25 per cent of its income for salaries and still survive. What do we in basketball do? We give up anywhere from 50 to 60 per cent of our 'take' to cover our payrolls." Major League Baseball owners during the mid-1950s paid roughly 17–21 percent of their total income (gate revenue from home and road games, exhibition games, media, concessions, and other sources) in player salaries.[28] Contrary to Gottlieb's claim, the NBA owners paid 40 percent of their gross receipts, which comprised the bulk of most teams' revenues, as player salaries. The ratio peaked in 1953–54 and fell off thereafter, coincidentally with the introduction of the twenty-four-second rule.

By 1957 league president Podoloff could testify to Congress that the average salary paid to NBA players was between $7,000 and $8,000, while the top players earned in excess of $20,000. He admitted that there was no minimum salary.[29]

Player Relations and Unions

How did the owners' treatment of players affect any underlying momentum to create a players' union? Basketball players, as with their hockey, baseball, and football brethren, were not aggressive in asserting their legal rights. All professional team sports players endured a reserve clause or something akin to it during their playing careers. The clause stipulated that a team could renew a player's contract in perpetuity. In essence, the team owners' interpretation meant that an owner controlled the player throughout his professional career unless he were traded, sold, or released. Often a player could be released with scant compensation.

Some players, though, were not passive about their contracts. George Mikan ended up on the Chicago American Gears and later claimed that the Gears did not fulfill their obligations. He asked the circuit court of Cook County to nullify his five-year contract calling for $7,000 per season. In addition, he was promised a five-year bonus of $25,000, which he claimed the team failed to pay. Mikan also chafed at what he termed was a one-sided contract under which he could be terminated at any point. Mikan quit the team on December 12, 1946. The team counter-filed and asked for damages of $100,000 to cover the losses that would be incurred by Mikan's breaking the contract. The team claimed to have spent large sums to promote him, as well as to have lost revenue at games for which the star sat out. Circuit judge Harry Fisher told reporters that the key issue was whether the eligibility phase of the contract, the phrase that governed releasing a player, was divisible from the rest of the contract. The reporter noted that Major League Baseball had recently revised its ten-day release clause to allow for a thirty-day notice or severance pay. Mikan and the Gears eventually worked out a compromise that brought him back on the court by the end of January, although neither party dropped its suit.[30]

Some owners and league officials used the reserve clause as an overt threat. Ed Macauley recalled that after his team, the St. Louis Bombers, folded, the league assigned the rights to him to the Boston Celtics. Macauley received an offer from a team in the American (Basketball) League. While he was discussing the situation with Celtics owner Walter Brown, league president Podoloff called and said, "Put Macauley on the phone. If you so much as think of going to the other league you'll be sued, you'll be out of basketball, and your career will come to an end." Macauley was naturally aggrieved by Podoloff's needless outburst and retorted, "Mr. Podoloff, do me a favor. You sue me. Let's go to court. Let's find out whether such things as the reserve clause are legal." Podoloff and the owners certainly didn't want a court test of the reserve clause, and nothing came of the commissioner's bluster. In any event, Macauley and Brown had come pretty close to finalizing a deal.[31]

Another star player, Bob Cousy, became an integral part of the players' efforts to create a player union. At first the players were seeking an organization similar to the rather ineffectual one then operating in Major League Baseball (this was a decade before Marvin Miller raised baseball players' consciousness about their economic exploitation by the owners). A modern reader might be shocked to see how modest the players' goals were: better scheduling of games to reduce the number of Saturday night/Sunday afternoon road trips; limits on the number of exhibition games; and protection for players whose team folded during the season. While the last goal was becoming moot as the league stabilized, players could easily recall the collapse of the Washington Capitols during the 1950–51 season. The Indianapolis and Baltimore teams also folded after subsequent seasons.

Player representatives from seven teams helped organize a committee to "work for the betterment of basketball in the NBA to the mutual benefit of the owners and the players." Players with the Fort Wayne Pistons declined to join the committee, in deference to team owner Fred Zollner, who disliked unions and told his players so.[32] Because of the frequent doubleheaders that brought half of the league's teams together, players had convenient communication among themselves.

The owners and Maurice Podoloff employed their own stalling tactics for resolving player requests. They did, after all, have the whip hand. Podoloff complacently remarked: "I and most of the NBA owners have no great opposition to the players' committee. After all, if they have any grievances or suggestions they may be quite helpful. But it is not necessary to form a 'union' to receive an appointment with me. What I do really want to know is this: Is it necessary to hire a lawyer who apparently is unfamiliar with basketball to air some complaints? Why is it necessary to have a businessman from Worcester act as secretary-treasurer? Is it possible that they are trying to capitalize on some free advertising?" Podoloff continued by saying players were making an average of $7,500 a season.[33] He conveniently forgot that he knew very little, if anything, about basketball, when the owners anointed him as president. Chances are that Podoloff was sincere, however, when he repeatedly proclaimed that players could come to him with grievances, and perhaps he would have treated them in an even-handed manner.

NBA owners, though, were dealing with a more sophisticated group of athletes than their baseball peers. Almost all of the basketball players had attended and graduated from four-year colleges or universities. Several players had lucrative outside jobs. Although baseball owners rigged their players association during the 1950s with their own hired gun as the players' counsel, basketball owners never committed such gaucheries. One is entitled to wonder, though, whether owner acquiescence to most of the players' rather modest demands might have forestalled a more militant player union in the 1960s.

In early 1956 the players again issued a set of demands, including limits on the number of exhibition games, an arbitration board to adjudicate player-management disputes, severance pay for released players, moving expenses for traded players, and limits on the number of personal appearances at the team's behest.[34] When Podoloff and the owners did nothing, Cousy and the NBA players began to consider affiliating with the AFL-CIO. In response, Podoloff asked the players to give him three months to set up some sort of grievance process. He claimed that the owners were considering discussing the matter with the players.[35] The efforts of Cousy and the other player representatives were also hampered by the lukewarm support of their fellow players. By 1958 Cousy was ready to step down as the spokesman, citing insufficient enthusiasm among the players. "Considering all the gains made by the Players' Association last spring, there should be more interest and co-operation," he said. "If there is not a healthy sign at the All-Star get-together, I'm ready to step down." Cousy claimed that only forty-one players had paid their annual dues of $10 for 1957.[36]

Three players testified before a congressional hearing in 1957: Bob Cousy, Ed Macauley, and Bob Pettit. They all saluted the reserve clause and the reverse-order draft, although Cousy mentioned the desirability of tinkering with the draft. All three thought the two institutions promoted competitive balance and prevented chaos. Macauley said some interesting things about the state of affairs when the NBL and BAA competed for players:

> As a result [of the NBL/BAA bidding war] the contract I received that first year was probably substantially greater than I would have received had it not been for that particular attention. Now, this proved disastrous for me because of the financial setup and, because of this bidding. Most ballplayers, myself in particular, with the [St. Louis] Bombers, were pushed up into an income bracket that the owners possibly could not afford. As a result, I think the salary they paid me in the first year contributed somewhat to the fact that the ball club at the end of the season ended financially. They couldn't continue.[37]

Although the players did not wish to upset the basic institutions of the league, they did express a desire for a pension; they also admitted that the owners acceded to their requests to limit exhibition games and to increase the travel money.[38] Macauley again took a conciliatory stance, saying: "I believe that the basketball players eventually should have the advantages of a pension program. . . . At the present time, though we have 80 ballplayers in the league, it is just on the basis of funding a thing like that just for 80 ballplayers. If you take the normal retirement age of 65 and provide $100 a month for the ballplayers on the basis of 80 ballplayers, it would take about $1,200,000 to fund that. I think it is not practical to say that the NBA has at this date $1,200,000 to put into that fund."[39]

While an outside observer might find Macauley and other players to be naïve, many players recalled that a more informal attitude permeated the league. The owners and the players were probably closer than they are today. Macauley requested to be traded from Boston to St. Louis because of an ill child, and Celtics owner Walter Brown acceded to the request. Podoloff believed that owners might oblige any player who had a reasonable location preference.

The league's national television contract for Saturday afternoon telecasts also created a rift between players and owners. The Major League Baseball players' pension was funded by all-star game and television revenue, and the basketball players hoped owners would devote television money to a similar pension fund. Baseball team owners used the player pension to keep players in line and to forestall formation of new leagues by threatening to withdraw their pensions. Basketball players developed a plan that was similar to that enjoyed by National Hockey League players, although Bob Cousy was doubtful that any such pension would benefit his contemporaries, a prescient belief on his part. Decades later, pioneering NBA players would still be petitioning the league for some modest pension for themselves.[40]

The basketball players were not alone in agitating for better treatment from team owners. Hockey players decided to form a players association in response to the NHL's television deal. These players, too, wanted the television revenue to fund a pension plan, similar to the one baseball owners had initiated in the late 1940s. When the owners balked, the hockey players filed a civil lawsuit charging the owners with antitrust violations. Given hockey's interlocking ownerships of franchises, the antitrust charges were plausible.[41]

In public the owners naturally claimed they could not afford to fund a player pension. One league official, unnamed by *New York Times* columnist Arthur Daley, echoed Eddie Gottlieb's claim that "the cost of our payrolls in relation to receipts is close to 60 per cent. [*sic*; he was exaggerating], while both baseball and football will run 25 to 30 per cent. They also make huge amounts of money from television. We have none. We formed our own TV network for the All-Star game, mainly as a promotional gimmick to project our image." This official continued by stating: "The owners in this league are not wealthy men and I guess only Fred Zollner of Detroit could be classified as a tycoon. The rest of them amaze me. Why do they take this financial beating, year after year? There's only one answer: They're basketball nuts."[42] The NBA owners clearly hoped to deflect pressure to create a player pension by pleading penury and insanity.

Eventually, though, Podoloff's dilatory responses and the owners' intransigence would culminate in a famous standoff before the 1964 NBA All-Star Game that was to be telecast before a national audience. The players wanted definite action on creating a pension plan and issued an ultimatum: a promise on moving forward on the pension or no game. At that point new president Walter Kennedy begged the players not to scuttle the game with the ensuing publicity disaster.[43] He promised that he would share the players' concerns with the owners and come up with solutions. He apparently retained sufficient credibility and goodwill to persuade the players to trust him.

Competitive Balance

The deterioration of the Minneapolis Lakers and the Rochester Royals opened the door to new basketball champions. The Philadelphia Warriors and the Syracuse Nationals won titles after Mikan retired for the first time. Other teams became ascendant as well.

The St. Louis Hawks had drafted Bob Pettit a couple of years before making their playoff run in 1957 (battling the Celtics through seven games). The Hawks actually had a losing regular-season record that season. Flush with cash, Hawks owner Ben Kerner strengthened the team's bench and acquired Clyde Lovellette as third wheel behind stars Pettit and Cliff Hagan.

The owners' decision to integrate began to pay huge dividends. The entry of great African American players also altered the balance of power during the second half of the 1950s, starting with Bill Russell of the Celtics. The Minneapolis Lakers gained from drafting Elgin Baylor in 1958 and Jerry West, who was white, in 1960. These two greats transformed the Lakers into perennial contenders. The Los Angeles Lakers became the NBA's version of the Brooklyn Dodgers, seemingly forever chasing the Boston Celtics (in the role of the New York Yankees). The Cincinnati Royals accomplished a similar, albeit more modest, rise by drafting Oscar Robertson to add with Jack Twyman and Wayne Embry. (Robertson never got to play with budding star Maurice Stokes before the latter fell victim to a terrible injury.) Wilt Chamberlain lifted the Philadelphia Warriors in the early 1960s to league power.

THE IMPACT OF GREAT ROOKIES

Between the territorial picks and regular drafts, a team could aspire to improve its record pretty quickly if it acquired a top-flight rookie. While baseball rookies rarely led the American or National League in major statistical categories such as home runs, batting average, wins, or earned run average, professional basketball rookies sometimes vaulted to the top of statistical categories. Wilt Chamberlain led the NBA in scoring and rebounding during his rookie season while Oscar Robertson led the league in assists as a rookie.

Although George Mikan's retirement heralded a shift in the league's balance of power, talented rookies such as Pettit, Russell, Baylor, Chamberlain, Robertson, and West became the league stars who remain in the public's consciousness. (Really, how many modern fans know of George Mikan, Bob Cousy, Dolph Schayes, Bob Davies, and a host of other early NBA stars?) Table 31 shows the change in win-loss records for selected NBA teams after they added a particular talented rookie. While it is unlikely that a team's change in record was solely the effect of adding one player, the table is suggestive. In addition to some of the better-known rookies, Tom Gola is included because his Warriors improved during his rookie season. Gola was the team's fifth-highest scorer, although he ranked sixth in the league in assists.

Readers might be surprised by the relatively small changes in Pettit's and Russell's teams' records. Pettit broke in finishing fourth in scoring and third in rebounding, but even he could not single-handedly lift the Hawks to a winning record. Russell joined the Celtics mid-season. The club had been an established winner for several seasons and had added Tommy Heinsohn. Russell's effects can be seen in subsequent seasons, as a good Celtics team began winning more than 75 percent of its regular-season games. Of course, Russell proved his value in leading his team to so many championships.

As a comparison, table 31 also includes the rookie season of more recent players. Few players have transformed a team as significantly as Lew Alcindor/ Kareem Abdul-Jabbar did. The Milwaukee Bucks were an expansion team in 1969–70. The Phoenix Suns, another expansion team, and the Bucks were involved in perhaps the most famous coin flip in NBA history. The Bucks won the toss and got Alcindor. The Suns got Neal Walk. The Suns' record also improved dramatically in 1970–71, but Connie Hawkins was the real impetus for that team's improvement.[44]

Although Chamberlain, Baylor, and Robertson clearly improved their teams' records, none transformed a team as dramatically as did Larry Bird, Tim Duncan (who was fortunate enough to join a temporarily down-on-its-luck San Antonio Spurs team), and Abdul-Jabbar. While these three players may not have been the sole reasons for their teams' improvements, they were certainly catalysts for the improvements.[45] The NBA of the late 1950s might have featured teams that were too evenly matched for any rookie to assist his team in improving its win-loss record by much more than .200.

GETTING A DOMINANT CENTER

In the NBA you almost had to have one of three players on your team to win the championship series: George Mikan, Bill Russell, or Wilt Chamberlain. Between the 1949 and 1969 finals, only four teams without one of these centers won the title. In two of these cases, the Rochester Royals in 1951 and the St. Louis Hawks in 1958, Mikan and Russell were injured during the playoff series. The Syracuse Nationals (1955) and the Philadelphia Warriors (1956) won during the interregnum between Mikan and Russell.

The Chicago American Gears signed George Mikan out of DePaul before the 1946–47 season. After that team folded, the NBL assigned Mikan to the Minneapolis Lakers, since in their original incarnation as the Detroit Gems they had been such an inept team (4–40). Mikan and Jim Pollard transformed the Lakers into NBL champions. Mikan-led teams won titles every season he played, except 1950–51, when he was injured in the playoffs (seven in eight seasons, aside from his brief "un-retirement" during the 1955–56 season). Mikan first retired after the Lakers won yet another championship, saying, "I want to leave basketball while Mikan is still Mikan."[46]

Unlike Mikan, NBA owners and Harlem Globetrotters owner Abe Saperstein tussled over the rights to Bill Russell and Wilt Chamberlain. Russell led the University of San Francisco to two NCAA titles, while Chamberlain continued the University of Kansas' legacy as a basketball powerhouse. Both men knew their market value and leveraged this power during negotiations. The Globetrotters allegedly offered Russell $50,000, which, if accurate, was much more than several NBA owners were willing to pay. Russell also made it known that he did not wish to play for teams in smaller cities, such as Rochester. The Royals had the first pick in the 1956 draft.

Boston coach Red Auerbach learned that Russell preferred to play in the NBA instead of with the Globetrotters and was willing to play for less than $50,000. The wily Celtics coach and general manager had exercised the team's territorial pick in the draft by selecting Tommy Heinsohn, so the team had no first-round pick. He figured that the Royals would not use their pick to tab Russell, leaving the St. Louis Hawks with the second pick. Auerbach paid a heavy price to get Russell, giving up all-star center Ed Macauley and rookie draftee Cliff Hagan (the third pick in the 1953 draft). The legend surrounding the situation says that in order to ensure that the Royals would not select Russell, Celtics owner Walter Brown told Royals owner Les Harrison, "If you pass on Russell, I'll help you get the Ice Capades." Harrison later denied this version of the story, maintaining that his club never intended to draft Russell because of his high salary demands and that the Ice Capades booking was just an example of ice arena owners helping each other out. Harrison complained, "I was cheated out of Russell, who played poorly at the [college] All-Star Game because he didn't want to play in a small city like Rochester. We weren't drawing well in Rochester, and it looked to me as if Russell couldn't play. . . . We had Maurice Stokes at center."[47] Instead of Russell, Harrison chose . . . (insert drum roll here) . . . Sihugo Green.

Ben Kerner used Macauley, who was popular with St. Louis fans because of his days with the St. Louis Bombers years earlier, and Hagan to support Bob Pettit. His Hawks gave the Celtics some tough championship series battles (four times in five years), so one can't argue that Kerner made a huge mistake. Kerner explained his decision this way: "I heard that [Russell] had turned down $50,000 from the Globetrotters. I heard he wanted $25,000 or $50,000—it didn't matter because to me, it may as well have been a million.

We didn't have the money. I had been in St. Louis for only one year and I needed immediate help."[48]

Kerner indeed became the model owner in the NBA. He had finally moved his team to a viable site and had good talent with which to draw adequate crowds. While Auerbach lucked out in getting Bob Cousy and shrewdly recognized Russell's unique fit with the Celtics' existing talent and acquired the center, Kerner used clever trades to build his team. Aside from Bob Pettit and Bob Ferry, most of the Hawks were acquired via trades and purchases, as recounted by sportswriter Lowell Reidenbaugh. One of Kerner's deals was so successful that the Celtics complained about it to Podoloff. Similar to how the New York Yankees complained about the Boston Red Sox' purchases of and trades for what talented players the St. Louis Browns possessed during the late 1940s (and the American League's chorus of complaints regarding the Yankees and Kansas City Athletics' series of transactions in the late 1950s), Boston whined about the St. Louis Hawks getting veterans Clyde Lovellette and Sihugo Green from the moribund Cincinnati Royals. Podoloff declared, "I have no right to single out a particular deal for disapproval until I am ready to charge and prove fraud. The new owners in Cincinnati paid $200,000 for the franchise and they have given every assurance that they will operate next year. I could see nothing out of the way in their sale of the two players."[49] Kerner began acting like baseball's New York Yankees in acquiring veterans for the 1959–60 playoff run. He bought veteran Larry Foust from the woebegone Minneapolis Lakers for $20,000 and three players, including two on the "farm-out" list. Kerner told reporter Gilbert Rogin, "The cheapest thing you can buy is talent."[50] Unlike St. Louis, Reidenbaugh believed that the Celtics and the Philadelphia Warriors (another powerhouse in 1960) were mainly built by draft.[51]

Bill Russell began playing with the Celtics in December 1956 after completing competition in the Olympics. Some sportswriters were skeptical about his abilities. Arthur Daley wrote, "When he begins performing for the Boston Celtics he won't necessarily be the tallest player, the best rebounder, best defender or even the highest scorer. . . . If he gets his head over the basket in the pro league, some helpful rival will probably push it through the hoop. He has much to learn. . . . The pros will show him tricks under the boards he never suspected could exist. . . . Russell won't be able to do much goaltending because these guys are, in the main, as big as he is. They'll fake him out of his shoes and they'll disdainfully refuse to fall for his fakes."[52]

Russell did not transform the Celtics into regular-season giants. They already had a solid core of players with Bob Cousy and Bill Sharman while adding Tommy Heinsohn, who became NBA Rookie of the Year. The Celtics won five more games during 1956–57 than in 1955–56, but they were a winning team with or without Russell. Where he made a difference was in the playoffs. The Celtics had never been in the league championship series, and now they would miss only one championship series as long as Russell played.

Fans flocked to Celtics games, and sportswriters admitted that Russell was worth the reported $24,000 salary he received, the most ever for a rookie (the veteran Cousy reportedly made $25,000). Russell's Boston Garden debut attracted eleven thousand fans, despite the game's being televised. Some fifteen thousand turned out to Madison Square Garden to watch him. Arthur Daley now practically gushed about Russell: "A pro talent scout ordinarily would bypass a shot-maker of Russell's limited range. But Russell also is as tremendous a defensive player as has been around in ages. Not only is he extraordinary in capturing enemy rebounds off the backboards, he's fast enough to race from one backboard to the other and is agile as a goal-tender. . . . Actually, it's difficult to measure Bill's defensive value because much of it is psychological—a shooter hurrying a shot he shouldn't take in order to avoid him or not taking one he should take."[53] As Auerbach and others pointed out, Russell didn't merely block shots, sending the basketball into the stands as an "in your face" gesture, but he used blocked shots to trigger the team's vaunted fast break. In a sense, he complemented Cousy's ability as a playmaker.

If Russell transformed the defensive aspect of the game, Wilt Chamberlain left NBA officials, coaches, and players slack-jawed with his athletic abilities. Even as a junior high and high school player, Chamberlain invited comparison with pro players. If an athlete could be called "Superman," Wilt probably had as good a claim on that name as any. Sportswriter Jeremiah Tax recounted Chamberlain's physical abilities: "He has run the quarter mile in 49 seconds flat, bettered 6 feet 7 in the high jump, put the shot 51 feet, can lift 265 pounds in the clean-and-jerk and 210 in the military press."[54] While today's centers might be able to lift more, given their time in the weight room, it is hard to come up with another big man possessing the same set of physical skills. Remember, too, that Chamberlain ran for the University of Kansas track team and later played professional volleyball.

Philadelphia owner Eddie Gottlieb viewed Chamberlain as a potential savior for his shoestring operation. He boldly claimed Chamberlain as his territorial pick while the youngster was still in high school. The league initially rebuffed Gottlieb's claim, but he declared, "Why not? Listen, I guarantee that Wilt will be our first-round pick after his senior year in college and I'm taking him now. If he breaks a leg, if he can't play—I still get him. I'm taking a gamble on the guy." The territorial rule applied to where a player attended college, but Gottlieb wanted to bend the rule so that it applied to Wilt's Philadelphia Overbrook High School. Red Auerbach later claimed that the Celtics considered trying to get Chamberlain to play for "basketball powerhouse" Harvard University so as to be able to claim him (Russell and Chamberlain as teammates boggles the mind). The owners acquiesced to Gottlieb's demand, and Auerbach uncharitably said, "The league felt sorry for Eddie, so they made a provision for him. We didn't like it in Boston, but back then deals were made all the time." Even as early as 1957, league president Podoloff told a congressional committee that Chamberlain was destined for the Philadelphia team. Chamberlain declined to play his senior year at Kansas and instead played for the Harlem Globetrotters for a salary reported in excess of $50,000.[55]

These factors—pruning weak teams, the twenty-four-second shot clock, and the debut of talented African American superstars—greatly affected competitive balance in the NBA. The improvement arising from eliminating weak teams had reached its maximum by the mid-1950s. The debut of African American superstars upset the parity reached during the 1955–57 seasons. Had the reverse-order draft been effective in redressing competitive balance, and had these new superstars been distributed evenly across teams, the parity might have persisted. Then again, the dominance of Russell and Chamberlain might have been too much for even the reverse-order draft to overcome.

Relocation

By the 1954–55 season, with the contraction of teams described previously, the NBA settled into a stable, eight-team league. The league still operated in such smaller cities as Rochester, Fort Wayne, and Syracuse. The National Football League and the All-American Football League had operated teams in Los Angeles and San Francisco since World War II. Football, of course, played a schedule conducive to cross-country travel, even by train. Baseball and basketball, with their multi-game weekly schedules, would have to depend on express trains and reliable air travel. For the taller basketball players, overnight travel by train was less comfortable than for the rank-and-file baseball player.

Geography affected attempts to relocate existing franchises. All professional team sports leagues have stringent rules pertaining to relocating franchises. As law professor Jeffrey Glick pointed out, an owner relocating his team in search of greater profits might create "serious hardships for the other league members both in terms of travel schedules and costs. . . . by balancing the interests of all teams in site selection, a legitimate restraint can promote on-field competition in locations acceptable to both participants, create a marketable product and thereby promote economic competition."[56] In public, at least, owners frequently bemoaned transportation costs. Baseball's Walter O'Malley of the Brooklyn Dodgers and his sidekick Horace Stoneham of the New York Giants had to convince their fellow National League owners that the visiting teams' share of enlarged gate receipts in Los Angeles and San Francisco would offset the increased transportation costs.[57] To forestall such actions, leagues normally require super-majorities of owners to approve such relocation.

NBA owners individually decided to relocate, pending approval from their peers. The NBA's lack of gate sharing also affected owners' willingness to countenance a fellow owner's desire to relocate. When baseball's Boston Braves moved to Milwaukee, all of the owners gained from the attendance and revenue bonanza. The Braves' home gate receipts soared between 1952 and 1953, and, thanks to the league's gate-sharing rules, all of the owners received much larger payouts from playing in Milwaukee instead of Boston. The owners were so impressed that they voted to increase the per-attendee gate share for the 1954 season.[58] Unless the NBA owners voted to implement a gate-sharing plan, an individual owner desiring greener pastures would garner all of the potential gains while possibly raising costs for his peers. Of course, such a roaming owner would face increased travel costs, too, but he would have potentially higher revenues to offset such an increase. An NBA owner eyeing the potentially lucrative Los Angeles market might have considerable reason to persuade his fellow owners with side payments to cover any additional transportation costs.

While NBA teams were used to flying between cities in the northeast quadrant of the United States, coast-to-coast flights or train travel promised to be both time-consuming and more expensive. Baseball's National League proved amenable to the Dodgers and Giants relocating to the West Coast in part because two teams were relocating instead of just one. The American League expanded to Los Angeles in 1961, but incumbent owners complained about the long trip to the West Coast to play just one team. When Charles O. Finley moved his Athletics from Kansas City to Oakland, he mitigated his fellow owners' transportation complaints.

The BAA and NBA, of course, had experienced frequent franchise turmoil in the 1940s and 1950s, with a reduction from seventeen to eight teams within a span of six seasons. Even before the BAA started play, the Indianapolis franchise shifted to Detroit, ostensibly for just one season while the owners obtained the materials needed to convert their arena floors from ice hockey to basketball.[59] When the BAA absorbed the remaining NBL teams for the 1949–50 season, it inherited a fairly new Denver Nuggets team (not to be confused with the American Basketball Association Denver Nuggets team that eventually joined the NBA in the 1970s).[60] The league's vagabonds, the Tri-Cities/Milwaukee/St. Louis (Black)Hawks, settled down for about a decade. The Rochester Royals and the Fort Wayne Pistons transferred to Cincinnati and Detroit respectively for the 1957–58 season. These relocations actually improved the transportation situation for league members, as players no longer had to endure the adventure of getting to Fort Wayne. The Minneapolis Lakers moved to Los Angeles before the 1960–61 season, and the Philadelphia Warriors transferred to San Francisco for the 1962–63. A year later the Syracuse Nationals moved into Philadelphia. Basketball, like baseball, sometimes resorted to a kind of musical chairs, reoccupying cities once vacated (Milwaukee, Chicago, and Baltimore would also get new teams before the end of the 1960s).

Although owners would not gain gate receipts when a fellow owner relocated, a certain benefit was accruing to all of them. As long as owners relocated their teams to more desirable television markets, all owners could aspire to a better national television deal. The major television networks scorned games emanating from small cities. Getting out of Rochester, Fort Wayne, and Syracuse undoubtedly helped give the NBA a "big-league" cachet in the eyes of television executives. Larger television revenues were an offset to the increased transportation costs. Today, of course, increased television revenues dwarf any fears of transportation cost increases.

Not all of the relocations worked out. The St. Louis Bombers failed after four seasons, and the Milwaukee Hawks' shift to St. Louis went poorly the first season or two. The Hawks had been perennial cellar-dwellers while in Milwaukee and, in fact, played very few home games there. Although St. Louis businessmen had assured Hawks owner Ben Kerner of the potential for selling many season tickets, the team sputtered.

One bright spot appeared at about the same time Kerner's Hawks moved to St. Louis. Morris Fox, who headed a group of investors wanting to obtain a franchise for Washington, D.C., accused the league of reneging on a promise of a franchise. He threatened legal action unless the league honored the letter he supposedly possessed stating such a promise. Later, Morris threatened to start his own league. The league could at least take solace in the fact that NBA franchises were now worth suing for.[61]

Fred Zollner of the Fort Wayne Pistons and Les Harrison of the Rochester Royals were the next owners to eye greener pastures. Zollner wanted to relocate his team to Detroit, where there was a larger population and where he had piston-manufacturing facilities. As with St. Louis, Detroit previously had a franchise in the league. Zollner figured that his team could draw better playing in Detroit's Olympia Stadium, which had a capacity of 13,000 for basketball. He also hoped to play a few home games in Fort Wayne to satisfy his team's original fans. Zollner's biggest hurdle proved to be the rental fee for the Olympia. Stadium owner Jim Norris, of the hockey Norris family, wanted $3,000 per game, a figure that probably made playing in Detroit untenable, but Zollner eventually negotiated a mutually acceptable rental fee.[62] For Zollner and Detroit fans, the problem was that the Pistons were in decline after playing in the 1955–56 championship series, going fourteen consecutive seasons without a winning record. One sportswriter quoted a Detroiter as saying, "Piston games were known as a place where you could take your girl and sit upstairs for fifty-cents and neck in privacy."[63]

Zollner found Detroit a mixed blessing. Two professional basketball teams had played in Detroit during the late 1940s, one in the BAA and the other in the NBL, but both teams quickly folded. Sportswriter Tommy Devine said that although the city had a reputation for being a "bad basketball town," he believed that reputation was unwarranted. He placed the blame on inept promotion. Zollner's first year in Detroit did not replicate the success of baseball's relocations. Devine thought Zollner should have arranged to play Pistons games in the University of Detroit Memorial Building, built for basketball but with a seating capacity of just nine thousand. The Olympia lacked the Memorial Building's convenience and parking. Devine said some observers estimated that Zollner would lose more than $100,000 for the season. Detroit's lukewarm response to the Pistons continued during the team's second season there.[64] Because Zollner's principal business—manufacturing pistons—was lucrative, he had sufficient capital to weather some losses, unlike his rival Harrison.

Les Harrison blamed declining attendance in Rochester for forcing his Royals to move to Cincinnati. Apparently attendance had slumped to 2,500 per game, which Harrison said was inadequate to maintain the club.[65] Historian Donald Fisher cited Cincinnati's larger population base (36.6 percent more in the city and 50.3 percent more in the metropolitan area) as one of the reasons for Harrison's decision. Cincinnati also boasted a much larger arena, but even more important was the surfeit of collegiate playing talent within its territory (including the University of Cincinnati and Ohio State University). Harrison could look forward to claiming Oscar Robertson in a couple of seasons under the territorial draft rule. Although Harrison hoped to hang on long enough to acquire Robertson, he was dogged by bad luck. One of his star players, Maurice Stokes, was grievously injured in a playoff game and never played again. The Royals drew poorly with a losing record during the 1957–58 season, and Rochester businessmen sought to reacquire the team. According to Fisher, Harrison had a buyer, Norman Shapiro, who was willing to pay $200,000 for the team. The league voted against the transfer, ostensibly because it did not want to jeopardize a national television contract that insisted on having teams from just "big-league" cities in the league (although the Syracuse Nationals were still in the league). Harrison eventually sold the franchise for $225,000 to Frank E. Wood Jr., a part owner of Cincinnati Gardens, where the Royals played.[66]

While the league undoubtedly gained some credibility by shifting the Tri-Cities, Fort Wayne, and Rochester teams to Milwaukee/St. Louis, Detroit, and Cincinnati, respectively, none of these transfers generated the gains in attendance, revenues, and profits the owners expected.

About the time Harrison and Zollner were being disappointed with their teams' relocations, baseball again witnessed a marvelous transformation. The National League Brooklyn Dodgers and San Francisco Giants moved to the West Coast for the 1958 season. While the Giants drew more fans in San Francisco than they did in the final year at New York's Polo Grounds, the Dodgers saw a much more dramatic increase in attendance in Los Angeles. The National Football League's Los Angeles Rams had drawn well for years. These experiences made NBA owners covetous of the West Coast.

As early as 1958, Maurice Podoloff was hoping to overcome owners' concerns regarding transportation costs and to plant an NBA franchise in California. The NBA had to wait until a suitable basketball auditorium was finished.[67]

Although the Lakers had begun rebuilding by drafting the wondrous Elgin Baylor (basketball's equivalent to Mickey Mantle in possessing outstanding talent but being limited by bum legs), the team's fortunes ebbed in Minneapolis. Economists James Quirk and Rodney Fort wrote that the league put the Lakers on probation, requiring the team to average $6,600 in gate receipts or else the league could exercise its option of buying it for $150,000 and relocating. The Lakers reportedly lost more than $100,000 during the 1957–58 season while averaging just 2,000 spectators per game. Although the picture brightened during the next season with Baylor's debut, new owner Bob Short began casting an eye toward more profitable venues.[68]

As part of the NBA's efforts to drum up publicity on the West Coast, the Celtics played the Lakers at San Francisco's Cow Palace. The game was attended by more than 13,000 people. Short chortled, "There is every possibility we'll move to San Francisco." By "we" he meant the league via expansion, but he didn't rule out the possibility of the Lakers moving there. He amended his statement to say that he thought some existing teams should be given first right to move to the West Coast. Mixing self-interest with pragmatism, Short pointed out that although he could have moved his team to Chicago, he chose not to, saying, "It would ruin pro basketball to have taken the kind of a team we had at that time [sans Baylor] into Chicago."[69] Given the fate of the expansion Chicago team in the early 1960s, Short's assessment proved accurate. Fans were not likely to support a new basketball team in town if it were inept.

Baylor transformed the Lakers, pushing the team into the playoffs and helping to increase gate revenue by over $130,000. The transformation temporarily stopped any thought of relocating the franchise, and Minneapolis businessmen jumped on the bandwagon. Bob Short candidly stated, "If [Baylor] had turned me down [to play another year of college ball], I'd have been out of business. The club would have gone bankrupt."[70] Sportswriter Jeremiah Tax unctuously reported that "the cure for pro basketball's weaker franchises does not necessarily involve moving them to other cities but, rather, concentrating on building better, winning teams and trusting to fans to respond to this effort." Tax claimed that the only two teams in the league that would not show a profit for the 1958–59 season were the Pistons and the Royals, teams with lousy records in relatively new locations. He admitted that Chicago was a more likely location for an expansion team than either of California's two largest cities because of transportation and scheduling difficulties.[71]

To gauge interest, NBA teams played some more games in Los Angeles. The Philadelphia Warriors played the Minneapolis Lakers, with a preliminary game "between a navy team from Los Alamitos versus 'The Vagabonds,' an All-Negro All-Star Team." The game attracted just over 10,000 fans, presumably to watch the Lakers and Warriors. Two other games drew much smaller crowds.[72] These results offered no guarantees that any NBA team in Los Angeles would repeat the success of baseball's Dodgers. Indeed, the Dodgers' success might have worked against any basketball team's prospects by siphoning off some of the potential patrons for NBA basketball.

When Bob Short sought approval to move his Lakers to Los Angeles, Ned Irish of the New York Knicks dissented. His ostensible concern was the increased travel costs, but Short parried this by offering to pay any extra cost. Baseball's Walter O'Malley of the Dodgers and Horace Stoneham of the San Francisco Giants had made similar offers. However, because of the success of their transfers, such payments were probably quickly discontinued. Sportswriter Leonard Koppett believes Irish's real motive in trying to stymie Short's proposal was to force the Lakers into selling Elgin Baylor to the Knicks.[73] At least for public consumption, the NBA announced on April 27, 1960, that the owners had voted unanimously to approve Short's relocation of his Lakers pending a suitable schedule.[74]

Short obtained exclusive pro basketball rights to the Memorial Sports Arena in Los Angeles (capacity 14,000), but he had to pay $2,800 a game plus $800 for ticket sellers, ushers, and cleaners.[75] When the arena was already occupied, the team would play in the Los Angeles State College gymnasium (capacity 6,000).

The league scheduled two-game series in Los Angeles to save on travel costs. As former Lakers' player Rodney "Hot Rod" Hundley recalled, "When teams came to L.A., we played them twice, say, Friday and Saturday—to cut the travel. Then we'd head east on these long trips for two to three weeks at a time."[76]

Unlike the Los Angeles Dodgers, the Lakers did not get immediate validation of their decision to relocate. Early crowds came nowhere close to filling the Memorial Sports Arena. Bobby "Slick" Leonard, another former Lakers player, remembered that only 4,000 people showed up for the opener. "The Sports Arena had all these neat things—escalators, a fan that blew wind through the flag during the National Anthem, and an attendance counter. In the corner of the arena was a scoreboard that showed the attendance. Every time someone came through the turnstile, it kept count on the board. Early in the season, the crowds were 2,500–3,000. The fans sat and watched, like it was a game on a neutral court. By playoff time, we were close to selling out."[77]

The Lakers reached 81,000 in attendance after a game with the Cincinnati Royals; there were still eleven home games left. While 81,000 did not excite most owners, it matched the franchise's attendance during its last season in Minneapolis. Lakers assistant general manager Lou Mohs explained, "If we average 6,000 per game, we'll not only wipe out last year's $100,000 deficit, but have some money in the bank." The Lakers were also able to get additional gate receipts by charging four dollars for choice seats, the second-highest ticket price in the league, and collected $50,000 or more in television money. The team had to draw a couple of thousand fans per game just to cover the Los Angeles Coliseum rental fee of $2,000 and the cleanup costs of $600 to

$800 per game.[78] The team sold one thousand season tickets at $100 each to help maintain the gate. As a comparison, the Boston Celtics sold about fourteen hundred season tickets. Mohs thought that football hurt the team in the early going.[79]

Philadelphia Warriors owner Eddie Gottlieb hoped to sell his franchise to a group of San Francisco investors. The league initially rebuffed Gottlieb's request to approve the sale, because it wanted to maintain a presence in Philadelphia and, ironically, because a Philadelphia departure would leave just three "eastern" clubs and six "western clubs," triggering scheduling difficulties. Desperate to sell his Warriors, Gottlieb sounded out owners of the Syracuse, Detroit, and Chicago franchises to see if they would sell. He then planned to move his new team to Philadelphia. The league eventually agreed to the San Francisco sale, with the Knicks and Celtics voting against it because they feared diminished gate receipts from fewer games with the Wilt Chamberlain–led Warriors; the Syracuse owners successfully petitioned to move their team to Philadelphia (becoming the 76ers). Moving a franchise was not a simple exercise in the NBA.[80]

These relocations gave the NBA an all-big-city roster of teams, fulfilling Ned Irish's vision (again). If the relocations didn't fill the owners' coffers, they did at least bolster the NBA's image as big league.

Expansion

After several seasons of relative stability, albeit with relocating franchises to larger cities, the eight-team NBA pondered expansion. The improving profitability of NBA teams created a desire by other investors for their own teams. By the mid-1950s NBA owners and sportswriters were discussing expansion. League president Maurice Podoloff announced that interested parties were seeking franchises for Des Moines, Dallas, Pittsburgh, and Indianapolis. Since Pittsburgh and Indianapolis had been the sites of failed franchises and Des Moines was a small city, basketball fans were entitled to be skeptical of Podoloff's announcement. At least Des Moines had a new arena.[81]

A key issue concerning expansion was how to stock the nascent teams with players. The league certainly had experience in reassigning players with the franchises that folded, as discussed earlier. The existing teams typically did not want to part with their best players, although they could be induced to surrender marginal players, especially for a price. In Major League Baseball owners of existing teams offered the dregs of their rosters to the four expansion teams of 1961–62: journeymen players, aging stars, or unpromising youngsters. The owners charged the newcomers hundreds of thousands of dollars for these fringe players rather than charge an overt entry fee. However, this was not all bad for the new owners, as the fees for players established a convenient item for depreciation under a favorable ruling by the Internal Revenue Service.[82]

Owners frequently bemoaned the lack of good players, but when expansion beckoned, they changed their tune. One NBA coach raised an interesting point. As mentioned in the earlier discussion on relative quality, during the 1950s the NBA certainly did not corral all of the best players in the country. A dwindling few performed with the Harlem Globetrotters. Some played for AAU teams while working for their sponsoring company. Other players slipped through the NBA teams' porous scouting efforts. Al Cervi pointed out, "There's a load of players in this country who never get a chance with the pros because it's impossible to scout them all. I'd sure like to have the time to look at some of the small college players you never get a chance to see. All of us get leads on players. Some we see, but for most of the others, it becomes impossible." The sportswriter concluded that Cervi indicated that he'll "never [again] make a No. 1 draft pick without seeing the guy."[83] Given the stories recounted by players and coaches in Isaacs, Pluto, and Salzberg's collections of reminiscences, Cervi's description of scouting rings true.

Near the end of the 1956–57 basketball season, rumors swirled around Marty Marion, star shortstop of the St. Louis Cardinals. Marion and his associates wanted to place a franchise in Kansas City, where an auditorium seated 10,500. Sportswriter Jeremiah Tax said the plan was for Marion's group to pay $100,000. In return, each of the eight existing teams would offer three players from its roster. Marion's group could select one player from each team. In addition, his team would receive additional draft picks of amateur players (after incumbent teams exercised any territorial selections). Tax probably overestimated the incumbent's generosity. He surmised that "self-interest would demand that [incumbent owners] offer at least some of their best players. When Marion brings his team into Boston next year . . . who will come out to watch if he can't provide solid competition?" He admitted, though, that some owners had already indicated they would make available only mediocre talent, quoting an anonymous owner as saying, "Why should I help him by hurting myself? I've spent years, and lost money too, trying to build a winning team." Marion did not get his team.[84]

Ned Irish was lukewarm about expansion, fearing that undercapitalized owners would flounder. "I estimate that a new franchise would have to be backed by $200,000 to $300,000 for the first three years, before there would be good hope to expect returns on the investment."[85] Maurice Podoloff later echoed Irish's remarks during his testimony to Congress in 1957. He pointed out that while incumbent owners didn't mind if a newcomer lost money for years owning an existing team, an expansion team likely cost everyone money. A new weak team often hurt the gates of the incumbent teams. "If you want to lose your own money, that is your privilege, but you will cost the league as a whole anywhere from $50,000 to $60,000 a year in loss of gate receipts." Podoloff testified that he explained this to a set of potential investors in a new Washington, D.C., team. "Morris, we'll take you in, provided you are not a shoestring operator, and providing you are not a fly-by-night. If you want to come in here for 1 year and lose us $50,000, we don't want you. We can't afford to lose it. But if you will have enough money, unencumbered cash, in money realized from the sale of common stock, which cannot be withdrawn, if you have $200,000, I'll be quite sure that you have enough money."[86]

After Marion's failure to obtain a team, investors petitioned the NBA for franchises almost on a yearly basis: from Cincinnati and Washington, D.C., in 1956 and several groups in 1958. The NBA Board of Governors told interested Washington investors that the league was not considering expansion for the 1956–57 season but would possibly do so thereafter. A league spokesman said, "We would prefer to accept two new teams rather than one when we are ready to [expand] as to keep the league balanced." The spokesman identified other cities, such as Pittsburgh, Baltimore, Portland, Cincinnati, Los Angeles, and Chicago, as being interested in hosting NBA franchises. A Washington group hadn't been willing to accept a "no" answer and filed suit, charging that the league had earlier denied them permission to buy the bankrupt Baltimore Bullets.[87] Given the league's precarious state when the Bullets folded, that denial might have been an act of financial mercy.

By 1958 the clamor for an NBA franchise climaxed. Twelve groups requested franchises for San Francisco or Los Angeles, while groups in Pittsburgh, Baltimore, Cleveland, Chicago, and Houston also expressed interest. An NBA spokesman stated that these groups were more interested in expansion teams rather than existing teams.[88]

Major League Baseball owners responded to threats of the Continental League and congressional scrutiny of their antitrust exemption by expanding by four teams between 1961 and 1962. The expansion into four of the territories being considered by the Continental League effectively preempted that entity. The NBA had absorbed the National Basketball League and was never seriously threatened by the one or two short-lived rival leagues in the early 1950s. Erstwhile ally Abe Saperstein, frustrated in his bid for an NBA franchise, eventually began threatening to form his own league. Saperstein was interested in obtaining a franchise for Chicago, and as he pointed out, Chicago Stadium remained available for basketball. The two Chicago teams of the 1940s had folded, but Saperstein downplayed the previous failures, saying, "The interest is here. The Stags flopped because they didn't have any men with promotional ability in the organization."[89] Although Saperstein proved to be a shrewd promoter of a barnstorming team (the Harlem Globetrotters), whether his promotional acumen was sufficient to repeatedly attract audiences to the same venue was unproven.

The NBA owners continued to debate the merits of expansion, with Chicago remaining the front-runner over Los Angeles, San Francisco, and Seattle. Podoloff announced, "[Chicago] is a major league city and we feel that it's ready for pro basketball this time." He claimed the league had received thirty-two applications from Los Angeles and San Francisco, as well as from Houston and Portland. According to Podoloff, three-fourths of the owners had to approve any expansion. "The stumbling blocks are travel and personnel. To make it feasible we would have to have four or five teams on the West coast in an intra-divisional setup. . . . Although the colleges are turning out a constant stream of talent, it's hard to say whether there would be enough good players to go around."[90] Today's fans might consider whether there are sufficient players talented enough to fill out the rosters of the current thirty teams.

Before the 1959–60 season the NBA owners unanimously approved a new franchise for Chicago owned by Max Winter and Dave Trager. Winter was a former official with the Minneapolis Lakers. Leonard Koppett believes the league owners charged the new group $500,000, a figure that probably would have appeared fantastic to owners ten years earlier.[91]

The new franchise, named the Chicago Packers, had difficulty getting started as their owners sought to use Chicago Stadium. Oddly enough, the incumbent owners proved generous in setting up the team. The Packers would get the first choice of the regular draft after the Cincinnati Royals exercised their territorial pick and took Oscar Robertson. The Boston Celtics, Philadelphia Warriors, and St. Louis Hawks agreed to waive their first-round draft picks and allow the Packers three more first-round selections. In addition, the incumbent teams would offer three players each, of which the Chicago team could select one player from each team.[92] When the Packers failed to negotiate for the use of Chicago Stadium, thereby delaying their entry into the league, this offer of first-round draft picks vanished. For the record, the Hawks took Lenny Wilkens; the Warriors took Al Bunge; and the Celtics selected Tom Sanders.

After arranging to play in the Chicago Amphitheater, which was located near the stockyards (hence the Packers moniker), the team received the very first pick in the spring 1961 draft. The New York Knickerbockers had the league's worst record and normally would have the first pick, but the other owners voted to let Chicago have it. Leonard Koppett believes these owners' action was retaliation for all the years of Ned Irish's arrogance. Koppett, a New York City writer, thought the league undoubtedly would have been better off letting the Knicks develop a strong team, but the owners apparently chose to disregard their collective self-interest.[93] Even with Walter Bellamy and six second-round draft picks (including longtime NBA and ABA players Don Kojis and Doug Moe), the Packers' baptismal season was terrible, ending with a record of 18-62. The team's .225 win-loss percentage was worse than baseball's New York Mets' initial season win-loss mark of .250. As sportswriter Phil Elderkin pointed out, "The right to be last often costs heavily in sports." He listed costs of $500,000 to field the team, including the franchise cost.[94] After just two seasons in Chicago, the Packers (renamed Zephyrs for the 1962–63 season) would relocate to Baltimore to become the Bullets (now Wizards). The NBA, similar to baseball's American League, was a remarkably forgiving league in replacing teams in cities that had hosted previous failures.

Podoloff disclosed that the NBA had ambitious plans to expand. In late 1959 he claimed the league wanted to expand to twelve teams in 1961 and eventually to fifteen, with three five-team divisions. Five of the new teams would be in a West Coast division. His prediction proved too optimistic, as the league would not expand to a tenth team until the 1966–67 season, when it would yet again place a team in Chicago. In the *Official Basketball Guide* he proclaimed that Pittsburgh and Baltimore would soon be candidates for franchises, given the new stadiums being completed in those cities. He also forecast San Francisco as a future member. Pittsburgh would never receive an NBA franchise, however, and its ABA franchise would not fare well.[95]

Integration

While racial integration of all NBA teams occurred by the mid-1950s, there was plenty of room for progress. Some African American players wondered whether there was a quota on the number of black players a team would have; if so, any such quota appeared to have disappeared within a decade. The

1958–59 season was the first in which every team had an African American player. As Ron Thomas points out, there were now nineteen black players out of ninety-two, or 21 percent of the league. During the 1960–61 season every team had at least two black players, and by 1964–65 Thomas shows that blacks made up almost half of the league's rosters.[96]

Bill Russell became the NBA's first black coach in 1966–67, although many historians cite John McLendon as the first black coach in a professional basketball league when he coached the Cleveland Pipers of the short-lived American Basketball League in 1961–62 (McLendon came close to being the first coach-manager to be fired by later New York Yankees owner George Steinbrenner). However, William "Pop" Gates preceded both of them when he was player-coach of the Dayton Rens during the NBL's swan song season of 1948–49. Wayne Embry became the first African American general manager when he assumed the position with the Milwaukee Bucks in 1971.

Despite these milestones, black players continued to face unpleasant situations. As late as 1959, Elgin Baylor faced discriminatory behavior in Cincinnati and in Charlotte, North Carolina. In the former case, Baylor and his teammates walked out of a midtown hotel when he and two black teammates were denied rooms. The three black players had to register at a nearby hotel run by blacks. "They told us there we couldn't even get in a halfway decent restaurant and we had to buy some things at a grocery store and make sandwiches for dinner," Baylor said. Bill Russell, too, found that playing in Charlotte, North Carolina was an unpleasant experience, as he was barred from staying at the same hotel as his teammates.[97]

A few weeks later the Lakers agreed to transfer a game with the Cincinnati Royals from the Ohio city to Charleston, West Virginia. Cincinnati Royal's officials assured the Lakers that there would be no problems in Charleston, but Baylor and his black teammates were again told, "The three colored boys cannot stay here. They'll have to go somewhere else."[98] Charleston mayor John T. Copenhaver tried to shift the blame, saying, "Charleston, as a municipality, has nothing for which to apologize. The incident was something over which our city has no control. Solutions to all of the problems arising out of the demand and rapid advancement of the Negro race are not yet at hand. Until the task has been completed, the best course for all to pursue is the one of wisdom and common sense."[99] The Charleston Businessmen's Club even had the temerity to demand compensation for Baylor's refusal to play under such conditions, "since it jeopardize[d] possible future NBA attractions there." The club was willing to accept league punishment of Baylor, but, of course, Podoloff did not act on their behalf.[100] Podoloff instead retorted,

"Somebody slipped at Charleston. The league had every assurance against any indignity. . . . I know Elgin's failure to play cost us the game but he was under great emotional strain because of his attitude toward segregation." Lakers owner Bob Short said, in Baylor's support, "If he had failed to play for any other reason, no matter how big a star he is, certainly he would have been punished." For good measure, Short added, "The segregation problem would make it difficult for an NBA team to place a franchise there [in Texas, which was being considered for a team], in my opinion."[101] Podoloff's final edict was that the teams would insist on a clause for any commitment to play a game in a neutral city that would "adequately protect the club and player against any type of embarrassment."[102]

Things weren't much better up north. According to an issue of the "NBA Bulletin," Podoloff identified the various hotels used in 1950. For each hotel, he indicated whether black players were allowed to stay there. The ironically named Hotel Lincoln in Indianapolis "agrees to house Negro players in the hotel, but requests that arrangements be made so that they would not use the hotel restaurants and dining rooms."[103]

Years later *Sport* magazine reporter John Devaney wrote an explosive article concerning the NBA and race. His article opened with the following exchange between Howard Cosell (whose nasal voice the reader is invited to recall) and Wilt Chamberlain:

> COSELL: "Bluntly put to you, a Negro player, are we reaching the point . . . where perhaps there are too many Negro players in the National Basketball Association for box-office appeal?"
>
> CHAMBERLAIN: "I definitely think that probably we have. I think that [there] has been sort of like a stagnant box-office attraction due to the fact that we are somewhat overpopulated with . . . first-class and star Negro players."

Devaney continued by pointing out that the league had gone from six black players (out of eighty players) to forty-seven (out of ninety-nine) between 1955–56 and 1965–66. Three-quarters of the all-stars were black. He also described how the league's attendance had increased by 50 percent since 1960 (although he did not specify how much of this was due to the creation of an additional team). The Boston Celtics' average attendance rose from 7,448 per game in 1960–61 to 8,779 in 1964–65, despite the monotony of their championships and their use of a large number of black players. The league's television revenues rose substantially, too. An unidentified NBA observer said, "Up to 1960 or so, you kept a colored player as your ninth or tenth man. You had to pay him only $6500 or so, a lot less than you had to pay a white boy. But not any more. Now the tenth and eleventh players are white boys, to balance off the squad."[104]

There was no "white flight" of fans from the NBA's changing complexion. All things considered, the NBA did a credible job in integrating, especially in comparison with Major League Baseball and the National Football League.

Conclusion

By the late 1950s, NBA owners were gradually shifting their teams to larger cities. These shifts did not always result in prosperity, but the league's image was burnished. The shifts also held the promise of increasing attendance and gate receipts, given the new cities' greater population bases and larger stadiums. The roster of all big cities also made the league's national television contract more attractive to the networks.

Concurrent with the relocation of franchises, wondrous new players meshed with the use of the twenty-four-second shot clock to create an exciting, appealing game. As a measure of how great this wave of players was, the names Chamberlain, Russell, Robertson, Baylor, and West still appear on many fans' top five players of all time. The league's general stability and incipient prosperity bolstered player salaries and emboldened players to seek more rights. Owners, too, enjoyed rising franchise values, so much so that other businesspeople wanted teams of their own.

NBA owners struggled to successfully expand their league. However, their attempt to stock the new expansion team, the Chicago Packers, with a respectable roster was not entirely successful. Thus, Chicago once again proved a difficult market for the NBA. Nevertheless, the NBA's expansion efforts were not significantly less successful than baseball's American League's expansion with its new Washington Senators or the National Football League's horrendous Dallas Cowboys and Minnesota Vikings debuts.

The NBA Becomes "Major League"

Why did the NBA survive and eventually prosper? A series of events and decisions helped improve the league's prospects. Ned Irish's high hopes aside, the BAA/NBA's early history was written in red ink. The attrition of teams during the league's first decade buttressed the owners' claims of losses, and the demand for pro basketball did not prove sufficient to ensure many teams' survival, much less success. The merger with the NBL led to chaos, but out of the chaotic 1949–50 season the league winnowed many of its weak franchises. By the mid-1950s the surviving eight teams were still shaky, but improving bottom lines encouraged prospective owners to raise their bids for franchises.

The BAA/NBA was hampered by constraints of stadium capacities in several of the smaller cities and by a lack of interest in the larger cities, such as Philadelphia. The sparse attendance and attendant meager gate receipts left precious little after paying stadium rentals and travel expenses. Until the NBA owners could entice greater numbers of *paying* fans into their arenas, they would continue to bathe in red ink.

BAA owners also struggled to convince fans that they were offering a quality product. The absorption of NBL teams helped raise the quality of players in what was now the NBA while lessening the competition for players. As with all owners of professional sports teams, NBA owners looked to slashing payrolls to remain solvent, but they had difficulty wielding the scalpel. The owners had a well-educated workforce and faced competition from AAU teams and Abe Saperstein, as well as from the attractive possibilities of outside employment for their players. Nevertheless, NBA salaries were barely above Major League Baseball's minimum salary. Only when revenues began to rise significantly did NBA players begin receiving larger salaries, well in excess of what the AAU teams and Saperstein were willing to pay. The NBA owners therefore began cornering the market on the best players. By the late 1950s the NBA had established itself as the pinnacle of basketball. The Harlem Globetrotters dropped any pretense of superiority once Wilt Chamberlain signed with the Philadelphia Warriors. However, the increased salaries also brought forth more aggressive demands from the players, who, sensing the financial stability, began organizing a union to further their interests.

The league surmounted some ugly gambling incidents without the fans doubting the honesty of the games. Whether the college betting scandal boosted NBA attendance is difficult to ascertain, but certainly the league avoided any attendance backlash associated with allegations of crooked games.

The NBA's competitive imbalance, as measured by the ratio of actual standard deviation to idealized standard deviation in win-loss percentages, shrank during the mid-1950s. The Minneapolis Lakers and later the Boston Celtics dominated championships, but all teams experienced ups and downs. The reserve clause and reverse-order draft did little to foster competitive balance. The NBL assigned George Mikan to the Lakers while the Celtics acquired Bill Russell in a trade (after using a territorial draft pick). In Mikan's case the NBL was trying to redress Detroit's chances for its relocation to Minneapolis. This, at least, was redressing competitive balance with a vengeance. The winnowing of teams that thinned out the most unstable owners also fostered competitive balance. Mikan's retirement dulled the Lakers' edge.

Part of the league's earlier imbalance stemmed from the skewed home/away schedules of many teams. Since the home team had a marked advantage in winning games, the owners must have believed the increased revenue from staging the doubleheaders that created the disparity in home/away games was worth the resulting "unfairness." Just as the league appeared to have reached an ideal state of balance in 1956–57, a wave of talented rookies upset the balance of power.

Due to the nature of the NBA's schedule and because the ability to generate crowds on the road was positively related to the visiting teams' record, gate sharing was unlikely to shift large amounts of revenue from teams in the largest cities to teams in smaller cities. The New York Knicks devoutly desired the demise of teams from small cities such as Waterloo, Anderson, Sheboygan, Tri-Cities, and others. The owners' decision not to implement gate-sharing rules probably hastened the demise of weak franchises while preventing greater losses for teams in larger cities.

By the late 1950s the NBA had transformed its product from a stodgy, rough-hewed game into a more exciting, fluid contest—one quite different from its college competitor. The owners' decision to implement a twenty-four-second shot clock created "product differentiation" with a vengeance. However, the new rule did not immediately boost attendance and gate receipts. To achieve its promise as an audience pleaser, the rule needed better athletes and better venues. Fortunately for the owners, a wave of players with the requisite abilities to exploit the faster-paced game was imminent. With brilliant incoming African American players like Elgin Baylor and Oscar Robertson, the game entered a new era of high-flying acrobatics and grace. The exciting product gradually enthralled fans and increased the league's popularity, boosting both attendance and gate receipts.

Although geography was not destiny, the league owners were cognizant of the consequences of its effects. As in Major League Baseball, a better way to improve revenue parity was to induce teams in smaller cities (or sharing cities) to relocate. The NBA would mimic its older peers in the game of franchise musical chairs. The five NBA teams remaining in the smallest cities after the shake-up of the early 1950s eventually relocated to larger cities.

Ned Irish ultimately saw his dream of the NBA being a true big-league circuit with these moves into larger cities. While moving into Cincinnati, Detroit, and St. Louis may not have saved much in transportation costs or generated significantly greater crowds, they were much more convenient locations than Rochester, Fort Wayne, and the Tri-Cities and gave the league a "major league" aura. NBA personnel would endure no more Green Parrot Cafés.

Rather than move to the West Coast during the 1950s, the NBA owners opted to relocate ailing franchises to large cities in the Northeast. By not expanding, the NBA risked encouraging an interloper league that would fill the vacant cities. The short-lived American Basketball League of 1961–62 was such an interloper that filled the vacancies by fielding teams in Chicago, Hawaii, Los Angeles, Kansas City, Pittsburgh, San Francisco, Washington, and Cleveland. The ABA would prove a more formidable challenger later in the 1960s when the NBA hesitated to expand beyond nine teams. When the NBA expanded to a tenth city, Chicago would yet again be the league's choice.

The NBA did not exist in a cultural vacuum. While the owners were hardly social revolutionaries, their relatively rapid racial integration after a hesitant start did them credit. Once they recognized how talented many African American players were, the owners quickly signed the top ones. Fans did not avoid games with African American players, and white players appeared to have largely accepted black players as both teammates and opponents. Whatever discrimination occurred seemed to be aimed at the black players who were not among the elite. Owners, too, were not quick to hire African American coaches and general managers, although the NBA's record was better than those of Major League Baseball and the National Football League.

As with Major League Baseball owners, NBA owners were slightly befuddled by television. Here their acumen proved inadequate. The owners did not realize at first that exciting, fast-paced basketball was tailor-made for television. Perhaps fortunately for the owners, the viewing audience for the league's early forays into telecasts was small, given the ugly style of ball that was all too often being played. They also did not recognize that fans wanted to see the best teams and players on television, nor did they seem to understand that electrifying players like Bob Cousy could generate new fans with their inimitable style of play. The owners created a national television contract with equal sharing of revenues years before baseball and football did. Eventually the NBA reached a beneficial accommodation with both integration and with television and just in time to showcase the exciting new generation of players coming into the league exploiting the shot clock to its fullest potential by the late 1950s.

The owners' decisions to absorb NBL teams, ruthlessly pare weak teams, tamper with playing rules, introduce African American players, relocate to larger cities, and develop a relationship with television all proved beneficial, although sometimes with a lag. The owners' attempts to succor teams in Washington, D.C., Baltimore, and Chicago proved less useful. The BAA owners' failure to pursue George Mikan when his Chicago team folded, though, was possibly a major blunder.

The league's survival, frequently precarious, was a testimony to a group of owners' determination and their willingness to absorb losses. Walter Brown, Fred Zollner, Les Harrison, Eddie Gottlieb, Ned Irish, Ben Kerner, and Maurice Podoloff could justly feel proud of their efforts.

Estimating Factors Affecting Net Gate Receipts

Economists have difficulty estimating demand for professional sporting events. Most teams offer multiple ticket prices, so deciding which ticket price to use as an independent variable presents challenges.

Because BAA/NBA teams funded the league office by paying 5 percent of their net gate receipts to the league, its president, Maurice Podoloff, had access to game-by-game net gate receipts. The collection at the Joseph M. O'Brien Historical Research Center contains such information for all but the final two weeks of the 1949–50 and 1950–51 seasons.

By employing fixed-effects regression analysis, it was possible to ascertain what factors were important in determining net gate receipts. Unfortunately, I was unable to find ticket prices for all of the teams for these seasons, but, even with the knowledge of such prices, deciding which price to use in the estimation would have remained troubling.

Regression analysis sorts out the variables' effects upon gate receipts. For instance, Sunday games may have attracted the largest crowds, but if owners tried to schedule the "most attractive" rival for Sunday games, the two effects can best be isolated by using regression analysis.

The model for 1950–51 was estimated using a standard fixed-effects panel regression with robust standard errors. I did this for two reasons. First, I used a fixed-effects model because it is very likely that for each team a unique and unobserved time-constant factor will exist that affects that team's net gate receipts. For example, one team may have an unusually loyal fan base. Ignoring these unobserved effects and using ordinary least squares regression would yield biased and inconsistent estimates of the model coefficients when this unobserved effect is correlated with any of the independent variables in the model.[1] Although researchers cannot measure such a variable directly, the fixed-effects panel regression allows them to deal with these unobserved effects appropriately. Second, researchers use robust standard errors to deal with any potential heteroskedasticity in the cross-section as well as potential serial correlation within panels.

The fixed-effects regression equation includes the visiting teams' win-loss records. Because the home teams' win-loss records, populations, and population-squared variables do not vary within a team, these variables were not used. In addition, I used dummy variables for Opening Day, Holiday, Saturday, Sunday, Doubleheader, Globetrotter, and Madison Square Garden games (1 if the game had the characteristic; 0 otherwise).

Tables 32 and 33 show that the visiting teams' records positively affected the gate receipts. For the handful of games where the Harlem Globetrotters appeared as part of a doubleheader, or where four NBA teams played two games at the same venue (Doubleheader dummy), the gate receipts were higher. If you were visiting New York, you played before more people at Madison Square Garden than if you played at the Knicks' alternative home site, the 69th Regiment Armory. Saturday and Sunday games had similar effects on net gate receipts, which was somewhat of a surprise. The Opening Day dummy variable was not statistically significant.

Table 32 shows the fixed-effects regression estimate, and table 33 shows a regular regression estimate. The latter model incorporates population variables that proved not to be statistically significant.

Tables

Table 1. National Economic Indicators, 1945–61

	($000,000,000s)			(000,000s of nominal $s)		
	GNP	REAL GNP	CPI	Sp.Rec.	Movies	Sports
1945	211.9	355.2	53.9	6,139	1,450	116
1946	208.5	312.6	58.5	8,539	1,692	200
1947	231.3	309.9	66.9	9,249	1,594	222
1948	257.6	323.7	72.1	9,692	1,506	232
1949	256.5	324.1	71.4	10,010	1,451	239
1950	284.8	355.3	72.1	11,147	1,376	222
1951	328.4	383.4	77.8	11,564	1,310	220
1952	345.5	395.1	79.5	12,102	1,246	220
1953	364.6	412.8	80.1	12,720	1,187	221
1954	364.8	407.0	80.5	13,077	1,228	224
1955	398.0	438.0	80.2	14,078	1,326	230
1956	419.2	446.1	81.4	14,979	1,394	237
1957	441.1	452.5	84.3	15,333	1,126	242
1958	447.3	447.3	86.6	15,817	992	249
1959	483.7	475.9	87.3	17,381	958	269
1960	503.7	487.7	88.7	18,295	951	290
1961	520.1	497.2	89.6	19,506	921	306

Note: Gross National Product/Real Gross National Product (GNP Deflated by the Implicit Price index 1958 = 100); Sp. Rec. (Spending on Recreation); Movies; Sports (Spectator).

Source: U.S. Department of Commerce, Bureau of the Census, *Historical Statistics of the United States: Colonial Times to 1970,* 2 vols. (Washington, DC: U.S. Government Printing Office, 1975), GNP/Real GNP on 224; CPI (Consumer Price Index "All Items") on 210; Sp. Rec. on 401, Movies and Spectator Sports, 401.

Table 2. Cities with BAA and NBA Franchises, 1946–64

	1950 Pop. (000s)	1960 Pop. (000s)	1950 Baseball[1]	1950 Football[2]	Fate of BAA/ NBA Team[3]
Basketball Association of America (1946–47)					
Eastern Division					
Boston (Celtics)	801	697	MLB(2)	None	—
New York (Knickerbockers)	7,892	7,782	MLB(3)	NFL(2)	—
Philadelphia (Warriors)	2,072	2,003	MLB(2)	NFL(1)	1963[4]
Providence (Steamrollers)	249	207	—[5]	None	1949
Toronto (Huskies)	673	672	AAA	None	1947
Washington (Capitols)	802	763	MLB(1)	NFL(1)	1951
Western Division					
Chicago (Stags)	3,620	3,550	MLB(2)	NFL(2)	1950
Cleveland (Rebels)	915	876	MLB(1)	NFL(1)	1947
Detroit (Falcons)	1,850	1,670	MLB(1)	NFL(1)	1947
Pittsburgh (Ironmen)	677	604	MLB(1)	NFL(1)	1947
St. Louis (Bombers)	857	750	MLB(2)	None	1950
National Basketball League (1946–47)					
Eastern Division					
Fort Wayne (Pistons)	134	162	—[6]	None	1957[4]
Rochester (Royals)	332	319	AAA	None	1957[4]
Syracuse (Nationals)	221	216	AAA	None	1964[4]
Toledo (Jeeps)	304	318	AAA	None	1948
Tri-Cities (Blackhawks)[7]	161	184	B/C	None	1951
Youngstown (Bears)	168	167	C	None	1947
Western Division					
Anderson (Packers)	47	49	None	None	1950
Chicago (American Gears)	3,620	3,550	MLB(2)	NFL(2)	1947
Detroit (Gems)	1,850	1,670	MLB(1)	NFL(1)	1947
Indianapolis (Kautskys)[8]	427	476	AAA	None	1949
Oshkosh (All Stars)	41	45	D	None	1949
Sheboygan (Red Skins)	42	46	D	None	1950
Other Cities Hosting NBL or NBA Teams					
Baltimore (Bullets)	950	939	AAA	NFL	1955
Chicago (Packers/Zephyrs)	3,620	3,550	MLB(2)	NFL(2)	1963[4]
Cincinnati (Royals)	504	503	MLB(1)	None	—
Denver (Nuggets)	416	494	A	None	1950
Los Angeles (Lakers)	1,970	2,479	AAA	NFL(1)	—
Milwaukee (Hawks)	637	741	AAA	None	1952[4]
Minneapolis (Lakers)	833	796	AAA	None	1961[4]
San Francisco (Warriors)	775	740	AAA	NFL(1)	—
Waterloo (Hawks)	65	72	B	None	1950

Table 2. (cont.)

1. For "Baseball" and "Football," number in parenthesis is number of teams in Major League Baseball (MLB) or the National Football League (NFL).

2. For "Baseball": cities with Minor League Baseball are shown with Minor League classification. Baltimore, Los Angeles, Milwaukee, Minneapolis, and San Francisco would get Major League Baseball franchises by 1961.

3. Fate: 1949 means folded after 1948–49 season, unless denoted otherwise (see note 4).

4. Relocated after season.

5. Had Class B Minor League team in 1946–49.

6. Had Class A Minor League team in 1948.

7. Buffalo team transferred to Tri-Cities in mid-season (1946–47).

8. Indianapolis Kautskys later named Jets when the team joined the NBA.

Sources: City population from U.S. Department of Commerce, *Census of Population,* Vol. I, *Characteristics of Population,* pt. A, Number of Inhabitants (Washington, DC: U.S. Government Printing Office, 1961), 1–69 to 1–99; Craig Carter and Rob Reheuser, eds., *The Sporting News Official NBA Guide, 2002–2003 Edition* (St. Louis, MO: Sporting News, 2002), 714; Nelson, *National Basketball League,* 237. Toronto population figures (1949 and 1961) from Kieran, *Information Please Almanac, 1952,* 614, and Golenpaul, *Information Please Almanac, 1966,* 614. Minor League status from Lloyd Johnson and Miles Wolff, *The Encyclopedia of Minor League Baseball* (Durham, NC: Baseball America, 1993), 47–66. National Football League status from Tod Maher and Bob Gill, *The Pro Football Encyclopedia: The Complete and Definitive Record of Professional Football* (New York: Macmillan, 1997), 260–61.

Table 3. BAA/NBA Teams' Attendance for Selected Years

	Comp. Tickets	Paid Tickets	Total Tickets	Net Receipts	Average Per Seat[1]
1946–47					
Boston	44,541	50,454	94,995	57,875	1.15
Chicago	83,952	70,474	154,426	93,951	1.33
Cleveland	0	67,778	67,778	64,683	0.95
Detroit	25,690	37,195	62,885	48,236	1.30
New York	26,626	103,703	129,329	204,043	1.97
Philadelphia	5,882	128,950	134,832	191,117	1.48
Pittsburgh	9,956	40,970	50,926	56,005	1.37
Providence	3,828	77,883	81,711	117,740	1.51
St. Louis	21,266	93,601	114,887	113,808	1.22
Toronto	10,816	64,056	74,872	43,590	0.68
Washington	7,734	65,693	73,427	98,901	1.51
LEAGUE	239,291	800,757	1,040,068	1,089,949	1.36
1947–48					
Baltimore	2,741	74,326	77,067	110,405	1.49
Boston	35,597	51,654	87,251	46,372	0.90
Chicago	34,717	89,561	124,278	138,137	1.54
New York	56,537	108,618	165,155	182,970	1.68
Philadelphia	4,048	103,029	107,077	160,173	1.55
Providence	2,547	38,440	40,987	46,796	1.22
St. Louis	21,937	79,101	101,038	102,636	1.30
Washington	4,512	65,908	70,420	97,986	1.49
LEAGUE	162,636	610,637	773,273	885,475	1.45

	Season Attendance	Playoffs	Pre-Season
1956–57			
Boston	288,998	74,904	17,000
Fort Wayne	108,054	2,200	7,000
Minneapolis	82,211	3,113	10,419
New York	288,998	0	29,384
Philadelphia	154,004	4,575	32,000
Rochester	122,502	0	17,000
St. Louis	217,310	46,715	23,546
Syracuse	118,883	10,007	12,500
LEAGUE	1,367,866[2]	141,514	148,849

1. Average per seat is the average net receipts divided by the number of paid tickets.

2. For 1956–57, league season attendance was listed as 1,365,866, but the team figures sum to 1,367,866.

Sources: JMOHRC, Professional Men, Basketball Association of America, loose page (January 1947–May 1947) for 1946–47; "Bulletins" (January 1948–June 1948), "BAA Bulletins #50," April 26, 1948; "Attendance" folder for 1956–57 figures.

Table 4. BAA/NBA Arena Sizes

	Arena	Capacity
1946–47		
Boston Celtics	Boston Garden	13,900
Chicago Stags	Chicago Stadium	22,000
Cleveland Rebels	Cleveland Arena	12,500
Detroit Falcons	Olympia Stadium	14,000
New York Knickerbockers	Madison Square Garden	18,000[1]
Philadelphia Warriors	Philadelphia Arena	6,000
Pittsburgh Ironmen	Duquesne Gardens	7,000
Providence Steamrollers	Rhode Island Auditorium	7,000
St. Louis Bombers	St. Louis Arena	20,000
Toronto Huskies	Maple Leaf Gardens	14,000
Washington Capitols	Uline Arena	7,000
1948–49		
Baltimore Bullets	Baltimore Coliseum	4,000
Fort Wayne Pistons	North Side High School	4,000
Minneapolis Lakers	Minneapolis Auditorium	10,000
Indianapolis Jets	Butler Fieldhouse	14,000
Rochester Royals	Edgerton Park	4,200
1961		
Boston Celtics	Boston Garden	13,909
Chicago Packers	Chicago Amphitheater	11,000
Cincinnati Royals	Cincinnati Gardens	14,000
Detroit Pistons	Convention Arena	10,939
Los Angeles Lakers	L.A. Sports Arena	14,871
New York Knickerbockers	Madison Square Garden	18,000
Philadelphia Warriors	Convention Hall	9,200
St. Louis Hawks	Kiel Auditorium	10,000
	St. Louis Arena	15,000
Syracuse Nationals	Onondaga War Memorial	7,500

1. New York also played at 69th Regiment Armory, capacity 5,200.

Sources: Boston Celtics program, November 16, 1946; New York Knickerbockers program, November 20, 1948, 11; Mokray, *1961 Official NBA Guide*, 3–5.

Table 5. New York Professional Team Sports Ticket Prices, 1946–62

	NY Giants[1]	NY Yankees[2]	NY Knicks[3]
1946	$3.00–$4.00	n/a[4]	DNP[5]
1947	n/a	n/a	$3.50–$5.00
1948	n/a	n/a	$2.50–$4.00
1949	n/a	n/a	n/a
1950	n/a	$1.75–$3.00	$2.50–$3.50
1951	n/a	$1.75–$3.00	$2.50–$3.50
1952	$3.00–$4.00	$1.75–$3.00	$2.50–$3.50
1953	$3.60–$4.80	$1.75–$3.00	$2.50–$3.50
1954	$3.50–$4.50	$2.00–$3.00	$2.50–$3.50
1955	$3.50–$4.50	$2.10–$3.15	$3.00–$4.00
1956	$4.00–$5.00	$2.10–$3.15	$3.00–$4.00
1957	$4.00–$5.00	$2.10–$3.15	n/a
1958	n/a	$2.10–$3.15	n/a
1959	$4.00–$5.00	$2.50–$3.50	$2.50–$4.50
1960	n/a	$2.50–$3.50	$3.00–$5.00
1961	$4.00–$5.00	$2.50–$3.50	n/a
1962	n/a	$2.50–$3.50	$3.00–$5.00

1. NFL New York Giants reserved and box seats prices.

2. Reserved grandstand and box prices.

3. Madison Square Garden Side, End Loge, and Mezzanine. Prices for 1946–47 season shown in 1947.

4. n/a: not available.

5. DNP: did not play.

Sources: New York Giants media guides and programs, various years, Joyce Sports Collection, Notre Dame University and Pro Football Hall of Fame, Canton; Yankees prices from *The Sporting News*, April Opening Season issue, various years; Knicks prices from their newsletter and programs; *Official NBA Guide, 1958–59*, 3; Mokray, *1961 Official NBA Guide*, 3–5.

Table 6. BAA/NBA Teams' Ticket Prices, 1946–62

	1946–47	1958–59	1961–62
Boston Celtics	$1.25–$2.75	$1.50–$3.00	$1.75–$3.50
Chicago Packers	n/a[1]	n/a	$1.50–$4.00
Roch./Cin. Royals	n/a	$0.90–$3.00	$1.00–$3.00
Ft. Wayne/Det. Pistons	$1.25–$1.75[2]	$0.75–$3.00	$1.00–$4.00
Minn./L.A. Lakers	n/a	$1.50–$3.30	$2.00–$4.00
New York Knicks[3]	$1.00–$5.00	$1.50–$4.50	$1.50–$5.00
Philadelphia Warriors	$1.35–$2.60	$1.50–$2.50	$1.25–$3.00[4]
Tri-C./Mil./StL. Hawks	$1.00–$2.50[5]	$1.50–$2.75	$1.50–$3.50
Syracuse Nationals	$1.20–$2.40[6]	$0.90–$2.75	$0.90–$3.00

1. n/a: not available.

2. Price for 1948–49.

3. For games at the 69th Regiment Armory, New York charged slightly less for the best tickets.

4. Philadelphia charged $1.25–$3.00 in 1958–59 and $1.75 to $3.75 for doubleheaders in 1961–62.

5. Price for 1951–52.

6. Price for 1947–48.

Sources: For 1946–48, see various team programs; *Official NBA Guide, 1958–59*, 3; Mokray, *1961 Official NBA Guide*, 3–5.

Table 7. Possible Effects of BAA/NBA Gate Sharing, 1946–48

	Net Home Receipts	Share	33% Share	Post-Share Receipts[1]	Revised Share
1946–47					
Boston	57,875	0.053	19,292	71,611	0.066
Chicago	93,951	0.086	31,317	95,661	0.088
Cleveland	64,638	0.059	21,546	76,119	0.070
Detroit	48,236	0.044	16,079	65,185	0.060
New York	204,043	0.187	68,014	169,056	0.155
Philadelphia	191,117	0.175	63,706	160,439	0.147
Pittsburgh	56,005	0.051	18,668	70,364	0.065
Providence	117,740	0.108	39,247	111,521	0.102
St. Louis	113,808	0.104	37,936	108,899	0.100
Toronto	43,590	0.040	14,530	62,087	0.057
Washington	98,901	0.091	32,967	98,961	0.091
LEAGUE	1,089,904	1.000	363,301	1,089,904	1.000
Std. Dev.		0.051			0.034
1947–48					
Baltimore	110,405	0.125	36,798	110,498	0.125
Boston	46,372	0.052	15,456	67,807	0.077
Chicago	138,137	0.156	46,041	128,987	0.146
New York	182,970	0.207	60,984	158,877	0.179
Philadelphia	160,173	0.181	53,386	143,678	0.162
Providence	46,796	0.053	15,597	68,090	0.077
St. Louis	102,636	0.116	34,209	105,319	0.119
Washington	97,986	0.111	32,659	102,218	0.115
LEAGUE	885,475	1.000	295,129	885,475	1.000
St. Dev.		0.055			0.037

1. Post-Share Receipts = Net Home Receipts – 33% Share + Share of Common Visitors Pool (1/11 in 1946–47 and 1/9 in 1947–48).

Sources: JMOHRC, Professional Men, Basketball Association of America, loose page (January 1947–May 1947) for 1946–47; "Bulletins," (January 1948–June 1948), "BAA Bulletin #50," April 26, 1948.

Table 8. Characteristics of BAA/NBA Players, 1946–47, 1950–51, and 1954–55 Seasons

	1946–47	1950–51	1954–55
Number of Teams in League	11	11	8[1]
Number of Players in League	161	135	105
Number of Players per Team[2]	16.6	14.7	13.9
Number without College	9	4	4
Number Playing One Year	66	9	19
Number Playing Two Years	29	21	9
Number Playing Six+ Years	13	52	58
Average Years Played	2.68	5.44	6.13
Standard Deviation	2.05	3.26	3.99
Average Age as of 12/31	25.41	25.83	25.83
Standard Deviation	2.49	2.81	3.12
Age 30+	13	12	16
Prior NBL Experience	23	38	12

1. Baltimore folded early in the season, leaving eight teams.

2. Some players played for more than one team during season.

Sources: Zander Hollander, *The Modern Encyclopedia*, 2nd ed. (Garden City, NY: Dolphin Books, 1979), 476–574; Davis S. Neft and Richard M. Cohen, *The Sports Encyclopedia: Pro Basketball,* 5th ed. (New York: St. Martin's, 1992), 47–56 and 111–25.

Table 9. The Game on the Court: BAA/NBA Team Averages, 1946–60

Season	FGPct[1]	FGA/G[2]	FTPct[3]	FTA/G[4]	PF/G[5]	PPG[6]
1946–47	0.279	92.9	0.641	24.8	20.8	67.7
1947–48	0.284	96.0	0.675	27.0	22.2	72.6
1948–49	0.327	88.7	0.703	31.3	25.6	80.0
1949–50	0.340	83.1	0.715	33.0	27.0	80.0
1950–51	0.357	83.5	0.732	33.4	27.0	84.0
1951–52	0.367	80.8	0.735	33.2	26.9	83.7
1952–53	0.370	77.1	0.715	35.9	28.8	82.7
1953–54	0.372	75.4	0.709	33.0	25.4	79.5
1954–55[7]	0.385	86.4	0.738	35.9	24.8	93.1
1955–56	0.387	91.4	0.745	38.0	26.4	99.0
1956–57	0.380	94.6	0.751	36.9	25.1	99.6
1957–58	0.383	101.8	0.746	38.3	25.5	106.6
1958–59	0.395	102.3	0.756	36.3	26.0	108.3
1959–60	0.410	108.7	0.734	35.8	25.6	115.3

1. FGPct: field goals made/field goals attempted.

2. FGA/G: field goal attempts per game.

3. FTPct: free throws made/free throws attempted.

4. FTA/G: free throws attempted per game.

5. PF/G: personal fouls per game.

6. PPG: Points per game.

7. Twenty-four-second shot clock introduced for 1954–55 season.

Source: Carter and Reheuser, *Sporting News Official NBA Guide, 2002–2003 Edition,* 656–710.

Table 10. NBA Teams' Attendance and Receipts, 1950–51

	Home Games	Comp. Tickets	Paid Tickets	Total Tickets	Gross Receipts ($000s)	Tax[1] ($000s)	Net Receipts[2] ($000s)	Average per Seat[3] ($000s)
Balt.	33	2,551	52,823	55,374	95.2	9.3	85.9	1.63
Bos.	34	16,202	142,546	158,748	238.9	42.9	196.0	1.37
Ft.W.	34	7,097	99,922	107,019	144.7	13.0	131.6	1.32
Ind.	34	9,159	110,377	119,536	137.6	26.7	110.9	1.00
Minn.	34	11,643	160,767	172,410	291.5	57.3	234.3	1.46
N.Y.	27	30,235	116,112	146,347	219.2	43.3	175.9	1.51
Phila.	33	8,881	98,684	107,565	193.1	46.4	146.7	1.49
Roc.	34	8,280	73,592	81,872	143.3	24.8	118.5	1.61
Syr.	33	2,987	171,107	174,094	270.8	46.9	223.9	1.31
Tri-C.	35	7,837	93,494	101,331	141.0	27.0	114.0	1.22
Wash.	18	2,937	20,716	23,653	35.7	7.1	28.6	1.38
LEAGUE	349	107,809		1,247,949		344.7		1.37
			1,140,140		1,911.1		1,566.4	

1. Tax: tax paid.
2. Net Rec.: gross receipts – tax.
3. Avg. Seat: Net Rec./Paid Tickets
Source: JMOHRC, "NBA Bulletin #187B" (April 1951–July 1951 folder), June 19, 1951.

Table 11. NBA Teams' Prospective Revenue-Sharing Figures, 1949–51

	No. of Home Games	Net Home Receipts	No. of Road Games	Net Road Receipts	Average Net Home Record	Average Net Road Record	Difference[1]	W-L Pct.
1949–50								
Anderson	29	64,426	28	119,241	2,222	4,259	2,037	0.578
Baltimore	29	73,281	30	130,116	2,527	4,337	1,810	0.368
Boston	27	102,949	29	120,154	3,813	4,143	330	0.324
Chicago	20	106,842	33	136,193	5,342	4,127	−1,215	0.588
Denver	28	55,805	27	72,334	1,993	2,679	686	0.177
Fort Wayne	31	125,663	31	110,581	4,054	3,567	−487	0.588
Indianapolis	29	128,354	27	161,684	4,426	5,988	1,562	0.609
Minneapolis	29	245,880	33	174,876	8,479	5,299	−3,179	0.750
New York	28	222,397	29	126,054	7,943	4,347	−3,596	0.588
Philadelphia	28	79,681	31	124,458	2,846	4,015	1,169	0.382
Rochester	28	154,659	33	165,756	5,524	5,023	−501	0.750
St. Louis	30	76,483	29	123,234	2,549	4,249	1,700	0.382
Sheboygan	28	75,646	23	67,749	2,702	2,946	244	0.355
Syracuse	30	190,922	28	131,433	6,364	4,694	−1,670	0.797
Tri-Cities	33	150,652	25	75,817	4,565	3,033	−1,533	0.453
Washington	31	86,224	28	98,925	2,781	3,533	752	0.471
Waterloo	29	73,171	23	74,430	2,523	3,236	713	0.306
LEAGUE	487	2,013,035	487	2,013,035	4,134	4,134	0	0.500
1950–51								
Baltimore	29	78,198	28	88,065	2,696	3,145	449	0.364
Boston	31	182,192	28	128,199	5,877	4,579	−1,299	0.565
Fort Wayne	28	107,319	30	134,783	3,833	4,493	660	0.471
Indianapolis	30	101,239	28	140,259	3,375	5,009	1,635	0.456
Minneapolis	31	212,245	28	167,356	6,847	5,977	−870	0.647
New York	26	170,094	31	166,799	6,542	5,381	−1,161	0.545
Philadelphia	29	124,472	29	132,543	4,292	4,570	278	0.606
Rochester	29	101,789	31	139,528	3,510	4,501	991	0.603
Syracuse	29	199,604	29	130,582	6,883	4,503	−2,380	0.485
Tri-Cities	29	97,177	30	117,049	3,351	3,902	551	0.368
Washington	18	28,592	17	57,758	1,588	3,398	1,809	0.286
LEAGUE	309	1,402,921	309	1,402,921	4,540	4,540	0	0.500

1. Difference: Average Net Road Receipts – Average Net Home Receipts. A positive number indicates the team would have been a net beneficiary of revenue sharing.

Note: The league office compiled gate-receipt figures on a weekly basis. For both years, the reports were compiled a week or two before the conclusion of the regular season, so some regular-season games are missing.

Source: JMOHRC, Box 5, Professional Men, National Basketball Association, "Gate Receipts."

Table 12. Attendance at New York Knicks Home Games, 1951–54

	69th Regiment Armory			Madison Square Garden			
	Games	Attendance	Average	Games	Attendance	Average	W-L Pct.
Balt.	3	8,000	2,667	4	39,475	9,869	0.250
Bos.	4	19,400	4,850	8	92,818	11,602	0.608
Ft.W.	5	20,000	4,000	2	18,574	9,287	0.507
Ind.	2[1]	4,500	4,500	2	23,607	11,804	0.453
Mil.	2	5,500	2,750	3	27,459	9,153	0.311
Minn.	0	—	—	9	110,445	12,272	0.644
Phila.	5[1]	14,500	3,625	6	56,901	9,484	0.357
Roc.	0	—	—	8	78,149	9,769	0.620
Syr.	2	9,200	4,600	10	91,926	9,193	0.617
	23	81,100	3,862	52	539,354	10,372	0.617

1. The *New York Times* did not report attendance at two games played at the Armory.
Sources: *New York Times* and *New York Herald.*

Table 13. Competitive Balance in the BAA/NBA, 1946–62

Season	Best W-L Pct.	Worst W-L Pct.	Actual StDev[1]	Ideal. StDev[2]	Ratio[3]
1946–47	.817	.250	.165	0.065	2.55
1947–48	.604	.125	.162	0.072	2.25
1948–49	.750	.200	.168	0.065	2.60
1949–50	.797	.177	.176	0.064	2.77
1950–51	.647	.286	.116	0.062	1.88
1951–52	.621	.258	.129	0.062	2.10
1952–53	.686	.174	.193	0.060	3.20
1953–54	.639	.222	.154	0.059	2.62
1954–55	.597	.361	.087	0.059	1.48
1955–56	.625	.431	.061	0.059	1.04
1956–57	.611	.431	.054	0.059	0.92
1957–58	.681	.264	.121	0.059	2.05
1958–59	.722	.264	.150	0.059	2.55
1959–60	.787	.253	.188	0.058	3.25
1960–61	.722	.266	.144	0.056	2.57
1961–62	.750	.225	.167	0.056	2.98

1. StDev.: Actual Standard Deviation of W-L Pct.
2. Ideal. StDev: Idealized Standard Deviation ($.5/\sqrt{N}$). In some seasons, teams played different numbers of games. I used the smallest common number of games (unless a team folded).
3. Ratio: Actual Standard Deviation/Idealized Standard Deviation
Source: Carter and Reheuser, *Sporting News Official NBA Guide, 2002–2003 Edition,* 648–742.

Table 14. NBA Team Records, 1949–50 and 1950–51

Team	1949–50 W-L Pct	1950–51 W-L Pct	Difference[1]
Boston Celtics	0.324	0.565	0.241
Philadelphia Warriors	0.382	0.606	0.224
Baltimore Bullets	0.368	0.364	−0.004
New York Knickerbockers	0.588	0.545	−0.043
Tri-Cities Blackhawks	0.453	0.368	−0.085
Minneapolis Lakers	0.750	0.647	−0.103
Fort Wayne Pistons	0.588	0.471	−0.117
Rochester Royals	0.750	0.603	−0.147
Indianapolis Olympians	0.609	0.456	−0.153
Washington Capitols	0.471	0.286	−0.185
Syracuse Nationals	0.797	0.485	−0.312

1. Numbers may not add up exactly due to rounding.
Source: Carter and Reheuser, *Sporting News Official NBA Guide, 2002–2003 Edition*, 122–46.

Table 15. Players on All-NBA Teams, 1946–62

	Original Team	Number of other teams played for during career (1946 on)[1]	Number of times All-NBA 1st-Team[2]	Number of times All-NBA 2nd-Team
Arizin, Paul	Philadelphia	0	3	1
Baumholtz, Frank[3]	Cleveland	0	0	1
Baylor, Elgin	Minneapolis	0	4	0
Beard, Ralph	Indianapolis[4]	0	1	1
Braun, Carl	New York	1 (last season)	0	2
Brian, Frank	Anderson	2	0	2
Calverley, Ernie	Providence	0	0	1
Cervi, Al[3]	Rochester	1	0	1
Chamberlain, Wilt	Philadelphia	2	3	0
Costello, Larry	Philadelphia	1	0	1
Cousy, Bob	Boston[5]	1 (last season)	10	1
Dallmar, Howie	Philadelphia	0	1	0
Davies, Bob	Rochester	0	4	1
Feerick, Bob[3]	Washington	0	2	1
Foust, Larry	Fort Wayne	2	1	1
Fulks, Joe	Philadelphia	0	3	1
Gallatin, Harry	New York	1 (last season)	1	1
Garmaker, Dick	Minneapolis	1	0	1
George, Jack	Philadelphia	1	0	1
Gola, Tom	Philadelphia	1	0	1
Groza, Alex	Indianapolis[4]	0	2	0
Guerin, Richie	New York	1	0	3
Hagan, Cliff	St. Louis	1	0	2
Halbert, Chuck	Chicago	5	0	1
Heinsohn, Tom	Boston	0	0	2
Jeannette, Buddy	Baltimore	0	0	1
Johnston, Neil	Philadelphia	0	4	1

Table 15. (cont.)

	Original Team	Number of other teams played for during career (1946 on)[1]	Number of times All-NBA 1st-Team[2]	Number of times All-NBA 2nd-Team
Logan, John	St. Louis	1 (last season)	0	3
Lovellette, Clyde	Minneapolis	3	0	1
Macauley, Ed	St. Louis	2	3	1
Martin, Slater	Minneapolis	2	0	5
McGuire, Dick	New York	1	0	1
McKinney, Bones	Washington	1 (last season)	1	1
Miasek, Stan	Detroit	3	1	1
Mikan, George	Chicago[6]	1	6	0
Mikkelsen, Vern	Minneapolis	0	0	4
Pettit, Bob	Milwaukee	0	8	0
Phillip, Andy	Chicago	3	0	2
Pollard, Jim	Minneapolis	0	2	2
Risen, Arnie[3]	Indianapolis[7]	2	0	1
Robertson, Oscar	Cincinnati	1	2	0
Russell, Bill	Boston	0	1	4
Sadowski, Ed[3]	Toronto	4	1	0
Sailors, Ken	Cleveland	4	0	1
Schaus, Fred	Fort Wayne	1 (last season)	0	1
Schayes, Dolph	Syracuse	0	6	6
Scolari, Fred	Washington	4	0	2
Seymour, Paul	Toronto	2	0	2
Sharman, Bill	Washington	1	4	3
Shue, Gene	Philadelphia	4	1	1
Stokes, Maurice	Rochester	0	0	3
Twyman, Jack	Rochester	0	0	2
Wanzer, Bob	Rochester	0	0	3
West, Jerry	Los Angeles	0	1	0
Yardley, George	Fort Wayne	1	1	1
Zaslofsky, Max	Chicago	4	4	0

Fifty-six different players were named either First-Team or Second-Team All-NBA. Twenty-two of these players (39.3%) spent their entire career with one team.

Twenty-two players were named to All-NBA teams three times or more. Thirteen of these players (59.1%) spent their entire career with one team.

1. Last season: Played all but last season of career with original team.

2. Six players selected for First Team in 1951–52 (still had five on Second Team).

3. Baumholtz, Cervi, Feerick, Risen, and Sadowski played prior to 1946–47 season.

4. Indianapolis Olympians of NBA.

5. Drafted by Tri-Cities Blackhawks and traded to Chicago Stags, but Chicago folded before Cousy played for them. Played seven games as player-coach for Cincinnati Royals 1969–70.

6. Chicago American Gears of NBL, folded. Mikan's rights were assigned to Minneapolis.

7. Indianapolis Kautskys of NBL.

Note: Several of these players would continue to be named to All-NBA teams during the 1960s and 1970s.

Sources: Carter and Reheuser, *Sporting News Official NBA Guide, 2002–2003 Edition*, 148–49; *Total Basketball*, various pages.

Table 16. NBA Teams' Experiences with Integration, 1949–56

	Year before Integration	W-L Pct.	Gate Receipts before Integration	Year of Integration	W-L Pct.	Gate Receipts after Integration
Bos.	1949–50	.324	102,949	1950–51	.565	182,192
Ft.W.	1954–55	.597	95,156	1955–56	.514	131,061
Min.	1954–55	.556	97,096	1955–56	.458	107,916
N.Y.	1949–50	.588	222,397	1950–51	.545	170,094
Phila.	1953–54	.403	99,771	1954–55	.458	121,157
Roc.	1954–55	.403	88,000	1955–56	.431	106,300
Syr.	1952–53	.662	150,484	1953–54	.583	135,958
Tri-C.	1948–49	.453	150,652	1949–50	.368	97,177
Wash.	1949–50	.471	86,224	1950–51	.286	28,592

Sources: JMOHRC, Box 5, Professional Men, National Basketball Association, "Gate Receipts;" U.S. House, *Organized Professional Team Sports*, 2928–35.

Table 17. Outcomes of BAA/NBA Home, Road, and Neutral Games, 1946–60

Season	Home Team Win-Loss	Home Pct.	Road Pct.	# Games Neutral[1]	% Games Neutral[2]
1946–47	202-129	0.610	0.390	0	0.00
1947–48	107-85	0.557	0.443	0	0.00
1948–49	212-132	0.616	0.384	16	4.44
1949–50	351-167	0.678	0.322	43	7.66
1950–51	254-85	0.749	0.251	15	4.24
1951–52	213-80	0.727	0.273	37	11.21
1952–53	195-83	0.701	0.299	73	20.80
1953–54	151-84	0.643	0.357	89	27.47
1954–55	139-59	0.702	0.298	90	31.25
1955–56	141-80	0.638	0.362	67	23.26
1956–57	172-76	0.694	0.306	40	13.89
1957–58	150-85	0.638	0.362	53	18.40
1958–59	148-80	0.649	0.351	60	20.83
1959–60	149-84	0.639	0.361	67	22.33
	2584-1309	0.664	0.336	650	14.31

1. # Games Neutral: number of games at neutral sites.
2. % Games Neutral: percentage of total games played at neutral sites.
Source: Carter and Reheuser, *Sporting News Official NBA Guide, 2002–2003 Edition.*

Table 18. NBA Teams' Home, Road, and Neutral Win-Loss Records by Team, 1950–56

	Home		Road		Neutral	
	Win-Loss	Pct.	Win-Loss	Pct.	Win-Loss	Pct.
Boston	125-34	.786	58-115	.335	58-32	.644
Fort Wayne	132-49	.729	49-118	.293	36-35	.507
Minneapolis	126-32	.797	70-105	.400	55-32	.632
New York	113-43	.724	75-107	.412	49-31	.613
Philadelphia	104-44	.703	38-127	.230	50-54	.481
Rochester	131-53	.712	60-111	.351	39-26	.600
Syracuse	157-38	.805	59-116	.337	23-26	.469
Tri-Cities[4]	75-69	.521	34-124	.215	40-79	.336
Baltimore	61-66	.480	6- 86	.065	9-46	.164
Indianapolis	63-32	.663	18- 71	.202	12- 9	.571
Washington	6-11	.353	4- 13	.235	0- 1	.000
League	1093-471	.699	471-1093	.301	371-371	.500

	Home – Road	Home – Neutral	Neutral – Road
	Win-Loss Pct.[1]	Win-Loss Pct.[2]	Win-Loss Pct.[3]
Boston	0.451	0.142	0.309
Fort Wayne	0.436	0.222	0.214
Minneapolis	0.397	0.165	0.232
New York	0.312	0.112	0.200
Philadelphia	0.472	0.222	0.250
Rochester	0.361	0.112	0.249
Syracuse	0.468	0.336	0.132
Tri-Cities[4]	0.306	0.185	0.121
Baltimore	0.415	0.317	0.098
Indianapolis	0.461	0.092	0.369
Washington	0.118	0.353	−0.235
League	0.398	0.199	0.199

1. Home – Road W-L Pct.: Home W-L Pct. – Road W-L Pct.

2. Home – Neutral W-L Pct.: Home W-L Pct. – Neutral W-L Pct.

3. Neutral – Road W-L Pct.: Neutral W-L Pct. – Road W-L Pct.

4. Tri Cities 1950–51; Milwaukee 1951–55; St. Louis 1955–56 (franchise relocated to different cities and presumably better prospects).

Source: Carter and Reheuser, *Sporting News Official NBA Guide, 2002–2003 Edition*, 672–93.

Table 19. NBA Teams' Profit and Losses, 1951–57 ($000s)[1]

	1951–52	1952–53	1953–54	1954–55	1955–56	1956–57	Total[2]
Boston	–64	–5	–53	33	35	47*	–6
Fort Wayne	–46	–71	–59	–25	–20	–24	–246
Minneapolis	–11*	6*	–18*	–36	–35	–66	–160
New York	46	92	78	114	120	87	536
Philadelphia	n/a	–33	–19	–7	56*	26	22
Rochester	–11	–30	–15	–35	–24	–18	–131
Mil./St.L.[3]	–11	0	–16	–30	7	–3	–53
Syracuse	–2	–12	1	–13*	–17	5	–38
Total	–99	–55	–102	2	123	55	–76

* Won NBA Championship
1. Does not include teams that folded 1951–54.
2. May not add up due to rounding.
3. The Hawks relocated from Milwaukee to St. Louis in 1955.
Source: U.S. House, *Organized Professional Team Sports*, 2928–35.

Table 20. NBA Teams' Gross Receipts, 1951–57 ($000s)[1]

	1951–52	1952–53	1953–54	1954–55	1955–56	1956–57	Total[2]
Boston	168	229	234	279	206	353	1,470
Fort Wayne	163	210	142	163	189	159	1,026
Minneapolis	366	306	324	217	186	134	1,533
New York	270	352	346	395	424	438	2,226
Philadelphia	n/a	119	129	145	330	257	980
Rochester	184	163	143	146	186	185	1,007
Mil./St.L.[3]	116	109	98	124	200	304	950
Syracuse	266	189	202	199	208	206	1,270
Total	1,533	1,677	1,619	1,669	1,929	2,035	10,462
Mean		210	202	209	241	254	
St. Dev.		85	93	90	88	105	

1. Does not include teams that folded 1951–54.
2. May not add up due to rounding.
3. The Hawks relocated from Milwaukee to St. Louis in 1955.
Source: U.S. House, *Organized Professional Team Sports*, 2928–35.

Table 21. NBA Teams' Home Game Receipts (Net of Admissions Taxes), 1951–57[1,2]

	1951–52	1952–53	1953–54	1954–55	1955–56	1956–57
Boston	167,927	229,056	234,316	279,429	306,084	519,928
Fort Wayne	n/a	181,218	97,690	95,156	131,061	120,351
Minneapolis	232,376	191,264	178,542	97,096	107,916	95,980
New York	242,959	320,150	303,704	340,022	392,267	403,842
Philadelphia	n/a	97,432	99,771	121,157	224,925	212,118
Rochester	140,600	120,400	91,800	88,000	106,300	112,000
Mil./St.L.[3]	75,387	88,339	66,564	77,073	175,817	267,987
Syracuse	219,712	150,484	135,958	131,491	139,807	n/a
Total		1,378,343	1,208,345	1,229,424	1,584,177	

1. Does not include teams that folded 1951–54.
2. Fort Wayne Pistons, Philadelphia Warriors, and Syracuse Nationals: net after arena rental, association share, and visiting teams' share (which should be zero, unless for doubleheaders). All others have not deducted for arena rental and association share.
3. The Hawks relocated from Milwaukee to St. Louis in 1955.
Source: U.S. House, *Organized Professional Team Sports*, 2928–35.

Table 22. NBA Teams' Media (Radio and Television) Revenue, 1951–57 ($000s)[1]

	1951–52	1952–53	1953–54	1954–55	1955–56	1956–57	Total[2]
Boston	0	7	15	28	23	18	90
Fort Wayne	n/a	2	3	13	11	17	46
Minneapolis	12	26	22	45	40	20	166
New York	62	69	58	80	49	61	379
Philadelphia	n/a	0	6	11	12	24	52
Rochester	9	4	24	3	9	15	63
Mil./St.L.[3]	33	33	36	4	55	44	205
Syracuse	6	6	14	24	14	n/a	63
Total	122	147	177	207	213	198	1,064

1. Does not include teams that folded 1951–54.
2. May not add up due to rounding.
3. The Hawks relocated from Milwaukee to St. Louis in 1955.
Source: U.S. House, *Organized Professional Team Sports*, 2928–35.

Table 23. NBA Teams' Exhibition Games Revenue, 1951–57 ($000s)[1]

	1951–52	1952–53	1953–54	1954–55	1955–56	1956–57	Total[2]
Boston	8	13	5	9	6	5	46
Fort Wayne	n/a	13	20	12	12	3	61
Minneapolis	42	59	64	48	26	9	248
New York	4	4	7	12	6	5	40
Philadelphia	n/a	12	19	11	9	9	60
Rochester	8	12	7	16	14	14	71
Mil./St.L.[3]	36	26	29	70	11	17	189
Syracuse	31	18	1	6	6	n/a	62
Total	129	158	153	185	90	62	78

1. Does not include teams that folded 1951–54.
2. May not add up due to rounding.
3. The Hawks relocated from Milwaukee to St. Louis in 1955.
Source: U.S. House, *Organized Professional Team Sports*, 2928–35.

Table 24. BAA/NBA Franchise Records, 1946–62

	Year[1]	Won[2]	Lost[3]	Pct.[4]	Titles[5]	Best[6]	Worst[7]
Active Franchises							
Boston Celtics	1946	651	457	.588	5	.787	.324
Syracuse Nationals	1949	528	405	.566	1	.797	.481
Minn./L.A. Lakers	1948	547	451	.548	5	.750	.264
Philadelphia Warriors	1946	558	545	.506	2	.653	.174
Roc./Cin. Royals	1948	504	494	.505	1	.750	.253
New York Knicks	1946	556	548	.504	0	.671	.266
Ft.W./Detroit Pistons	1948	475	522	.476	0	.597	.367
Tri-C./Mil./St.L. Hawks	1949	428	507	.458	1	.681	.258
Chicago Packers	1961	18	62	.225	0	.225	.225
		4265	3991	.517	15		
Defunct Franchises							
Anderson Packers	1949	37	27	.578	0	*	*
Baltimore Bullets	1947	158	292	.351	1	.583	.222
Chicago Stags	1946	145	92	.612	0	.639	.583
Cleveland Rebels	1946	30	30	.500	0	*	*
Denver Nuggets	1949	11	51	.177	0	*	*
Detroit Falcons	1946	20	40	.333	0	*	*
Indianapolis Jets	1948	18	42	.300	0	*	*
Indianapolis Olympians	1949	132	137	.491	0	.609	.394
Pittsburgh Ironmen	1946	15	45	.250	0	*	*
Providence Steamrollers	1946	46	122	.274	0	.467	.125
St. Louis Bombers	1946	122	115	.515	0	.623	.382
Sheboygan Red Skins	1949	22	40	.355	0	*	*
Toronto Huskies	1946	22	38	.367	0	*	*
Washington Capitols	1946	157	114	.579	0	.817	.286
Waterloo Hawks	1949	19	43	.306	0	*	*
		954	1228	.437	1		

*One season only.
1. Year: Year entered the BAA or NBA.
2. Won: Number of games won.
3. Lost: Number of games lost.
4. Pct.: W-L Pct.
5. Titles: Championship titles won.
6. Best: Best W-L Pct.
7. Worst: Worst W-L Pct.
Source: Carter and Reheuser, *Sporting News Official NBA Guide, 2002–2003 Edition*, 122–45 and 177.

Table 25. BAA/NBA Teams Experiencing Large Fluctuations in Win-Loss Pct.
between Seasons

Team	Season	Pct.	Season	Pct.	Change[1]
Minneapolis Lakers	1959–60	.333	1961–62	.675	.342*
Cincinnati Royals	1959–60	.253	1961–62	.538	.285*
Boston Celtics	1949–50	.324	1950–51	.565	.242
Philadelphia Warriors	1952–53	.174	1953–54	.403	.229
Philadelphia Warriors	1949–50	.382	1950–51	.606	.224
Fort Wayne Pistons	1948–49	.367	1949–50	.588	.221
St. Louis Hawks	1956–57	.472	1958–59	.681	.209*
Philadelphia Warriors	1958–59	.444	1959–60	.653	.209
Minneapolis Lakers	1957–58	.264	1958–59	.458	.194
Philadelphia Warriors	1950–51	.606	1952–53	.174	−.432*
Washington Capitols	1948–49	.633	1950–51	.286	−.347*
Syracuse Nationals	1949–50	.797	1950–51	.484	−.312
Washington Capitols	1946–47	.817	1947–48	.583	−.233
St. Louis Bombers	1947–48	.604	1949–50	.382	−.222*
Baltimore Bullets	1947–48	.583	1949–50	.368	−.215*
Minneapolis Lakers	1956–57	.472	1957–58	.264	−.208
Rochester Royals	1953–54	.611	1954–55	.403	−.208
New York Knicks	1958–59	.556	1959–60	.360	−.196
Roch./Cin. Royals	1957–58	.458	1958–59	.264	−.194

*Difference compiled over three seasons.
1. Change: Difference in the two percentages shown.
Source: Carter and Reheuser, *Sporting News Official NBA Guide, 2002–2003 Edition*, 122–46.

Table 26. NBA League Attendance, 1952–66

	No. of Games	Regular Season Attendance	Ave. per Game	No. of Playoff Games	Playoff Attendance	Total Attendance
1952–53	351	1,126,698	3,516	23	107,633	1,234,331
1953–54	324	981,606	3,257	15	73,769	1,055,375
1954–55	288	900,016	3,371	21	70,836	970,852
1955–56	288	1,101,897	4,298	21	136,033	1,237,930
1956–57	288	1,199,217	4,624	17	132,612	1,331,829
1957–58	288	1,167,462	4,550	21	143,024	1,310,486
1958–59	288	1,249,028	4,876	22	155,208	1,404,236
1959–60	300	1,296,973	5,071	25	224,329	1,521,302
1960–61	316	1,455,886	5,180	25	180,955	1,636,841
1961–62	360	1,433,878	4,626	29	231,457	1,665,335
1962–63	360	1,657,737	5,383	29	280,008	1,937,745
1963–64	360	1,795,665	5,691	27	252,999	2,048,664
1964–65	360	1,804,759	5,749	26	264,770	2,069,529
1965–66	360	2,022,436	6,430	27	292,201	2,314,637

Source: JMOHRC, Professional Men, National Basketball Association, "Attendance" Folder,
loose page.

Table 27. NBA Team Records Before and After Adoption of the Twenty-four-Second Shot Clock

	1953–54		1953–54 (excluding games with Baltimore)		1954–55		Gain/ Loss[1]
	W-L	Pct.	W-L	Pct.	W-L	Pct.	
Boston	42-30	.583	33-29	.532	36-36	.500	−.032
Fort Wayne	40-32	.556	32-32	.500	43-29	.597	.097
Milwaukee	21-51	.292	15-49	.234	26-46	.361	.127
Minneapolis	46-26	.639	40-24	.625	40-32	.556	−.069
New York	44-28	.611	37-25	.597	38-34	.528	−.069
Philadelphia	29-43	.403	23-39	.371	33-39	.458	.087
Rochester	44-28	.611	37-27	.578	29-43	.403	−.175
Syracuse	42-30	.583	35-27	.565	43-29	.597	.032
Baltimore[2]	16-56	.222					
	324-324	.500	252-252	.500			
w/o Baltimore	308-268	.535					

Note: Twenty-four second rule took effect for the 1954–55 season.

1. Gain/Loss = (1954–55 W-L Pct.) – (1953–54 W-L Pct. Without Baltimore).

2. The Baltimore Bullets folded after the 1953–54 season.

Source: Carter and Reheuser, *Sporting News Official NBA Guide, 2002–2003 Edition,* 676 and 680.

Table 28. NBA Teams' Televised Games, 1953–1958

	53–54 H-R[1,2]	55–56 H-R	56–57 H-R	57–58 H-R	Total H-R
Baltimore	2-1	0-0	0-0	0-0	2-1
Boston	1-1	1-2	1-2	2-1	5-6
Fort Wayne/Detroit	0-3	1-3	2-1	1-2	4-9
Milwaukee/St. Louis	2-1	2-1	1-3	2-1	7-6
Minneapolis	1-1	1-3	2-1	1-2	5-7
New York	1-0	2-2	1-2	2-1	6-5
Philadelphia	2-3	2-1	1-2	2-1	7-7
Rochester/Cincinnati	3-0	2-0	2-0	1-1	8-1
Syracuse	2-4	1-0	2-1	1-3	6-8
	14-14	12-12	12-12	12-12	50-50

1. H: Home Game.

2. R: Road Game.

Sources: *Basketball's Best: A Pictorial Review of the 1953–54 NBA,* 26; *Basketball's Best: A Pictorial Review of the 1955–56 NBA,* 36; *Basketball's Best: A Pictorial Review of the 1956–57 NBA,* inside back cover; *Basketball's Best: A Pictorial Review of the 1957–58 NBA,* inside back cover. Missing 1954–55 edition.

Table 29: Franchise Sales of Surviving Eight Original NBA Clubs

Franchise	Year of First Sale[1]	Amount	Year of Later Sale[2]	Amount
Celtics	1951	$2,500[3]	1965	$3,000,000
Pistons	No Sales			
Lakers	1947	$15,000[4]	1965	$5,000,000
Knicks	No Sales			
Warriors	1952	$25,000	1962	$850,000
Royals/Kings	1946	$25,000[5]	1958	$225,000
Nationals/76ers	1956	unknown	1963	$500,000
Hawks	1951	$30,000	1968	$3,500,000

1. First recorded sale.
2. Later recorded sale (not necessarily second sale).
3. Walter Brown purchased an 80 percent share in the Boston Celtics.
4. Half share.
5. Rochester Royals paid an entry fee to NBL.

Sources: Quirk and Fort, *Pay Dirt*, 446–59. Gottlieb purchase price for Philadelphia Warriors from Pluto, *Tall Tales*, 208, and Robert Teague, "NBA Bars $850,000 Deal to Shift Warriors to West Coast," *NYT*, May 5, 1962, 23.

Table 30. NBA Teams' Player Salaries and Bonuses, 1951–57 ($000s)

	1951–1952	1952–1953	1953–1954	1954–1955	1955–1956	1956–1957	Total
Boston	93	96	109	102	106	129	634
Ft. Wayne[1]	72	79	93	100	106	103	553
Minneapolis[2]	82	87	127	114	131	90	632
New York[1,3]	91	98	107	102	114	126	639
Philadelphia[4]	n/a	65	75	77	105	100	421
Rochester	73	71	74	74	76	75	443
Mil./St. Louis[5]	46	57	69	80	96	93	441
Syracuse[1]	73	78	71	90	90	79	481
Total	530	631	724	739	825	795	4,245
Mean	76	79	91	92	103	99	531
Total w/o Phila.	530	566	649	663	721	695	3,824
Mean w/o Phila.	76	81	93	95	103	99	546
High:Low[6]	1.99	1.69	1.84	1.55	1.72	1.71	1.45
St. Dev.[7]	15.6	14.5	21.7	14.5	16.3	19.6	
Gross Receipts	1533	1677	1619	1669	1929	2035	10,462
Salary/GR[8]	.346	.376	.448	.443	.428	.390	.406

1. Fort Wayne Pistons (1952–57), New York Knicks (1952–55), and Syracuse Nationals (1951–53) include bonus payments ranging from $500 to $9,750.

2. Minneapolis Lakers called "Salaries (players and coach)."

3. New York Knicks called "Team Compensation."

4. Philadelphia Warriors called "Team Payroll."

5. Milwaukee Hawks moved to St. Louis for 1955–56 season.

6. High:Low: Highest payroll/Lowest payroll.

7. St. Dev: Standard deviation (a measure of the distribution about the mean payroll) of the eight teams' payrolls (seven teams for 1951–52).

8. Salaries and Bonuses/Gross Receipts.

Source: U.S. House, *Organized Professional Team Sports*, 2928–35.

Table 31. Talented NBA Rookies' Effects on Teams' Win-Loss Records

Player	Team	Rookie Season	Previous Season W-L Pct.	Rookie Season W-L Pct.	Gain[1]
Bob Cousy	Celtics	1950–51	.324	.565	.242
Paul Arizin	Warriors	1950–51	.382	.606	.224
Bob Pettit	Hawks	1954–55	.292	.361	.069
Tom Gola	Warriors	1955–56	.458	.625	.167
Bill Russell	Celtics	1956–57	.542	.611	.069
Elgin Baylor	Lakers	1958–59	.264	.458	.194
Wilt Chamberlain	Warriors	1959–60	.444	.653	.209
Jerry West	Lakers	1960–61	.333	.456	.122
Oscar Robertson	Royals	1960–61	.253	.418	.164
Wes Unseld	Bullets	1968–69	.439	.695	.256
Lew Alcindor[2]	Bucks	1969–70	.329	.683	.354
Bill Walton	Blazers	1974–75	.329	.463	.134
Larry Bird	Celtics	1979–80	.354	.744	.390
Magic Johnson	Lakers	1979–80	.573	.732	.159
Michael Jordan	Bulls	1984–85	.329	.463	.134
Hakeem Olajuwon	Rockets	1984–85	.354	.585	.232
Patrick Ewing	Knicks	1985–86	.293	.280	−.012
Tim Duncan	Spurs	1997–98	.244	.683	.439

1. Gain: Post W-L Pct. – Previous W-L Pct.; numbers may be off due to rounding.
2. Known as Kareem Abdul-Jabbar in later years.
Source: Carter and Reheuser, *Sporting News Official NBA Guide, 2002–2003 Edition*, 122–45.

Table 32. Fixed-Effects Regression Equation for NBA Gate Receipts, 1950–51

Dependent Variable: Gate Receipts (Game-by-Game) Independent Variables	Coefficient	t-statistic
Intercept	286	0.72
Opening Day Dummy	299	0.70
Madison Square Garden Dummy	3,907***	6.62
Visiting Team W-L Pct.	6,626***	8.56
Holiday Dummy	1,988***	5.21
Saturday Dummy	1,095***	4.65
Sunday Dummy	1,000***	4.39
Globetrotters Dummy	15,339***	15.14
Doubleheader Dummy	4,639***	6.16

***Significant at 1% level.
N = 309
R-squared: 0.757
Adjusted R-squared: 0.742
Source: JMOHRC, Box 5, Professional Men, National Basketball Association, "Gate Receipts" (through March 4, 1951).

Table 33: Ordinary Least Squares Regression Equation for NBA Gate Receipts, 1950–51

Dependent Variable: Gate Receipts (Game-by-Game) Independent Variables	Coefficient	t-statistic
Intercept	−4,727	−6.55
Opening Day Dummy	280	0.53
Madison Square Garden Dummy	3,621***	5.03
Home Team W-L Pct.	10,373***	10.33
Visiting Team W-L Pct.	7,002***	7.43
Holiday Dummy	2,159***	4.68
Saturday Dummy	401	1.56
Sunday Dummy	1,643***	6.41
Population	−0	−1.54
Population Squared	0	0.95
Globetrotters Dummy	15,549***	12.91
Doubleheader Dummy	4,469***	4.85

***Significant at 1% level.

N = 309

R-squared: 0.627

Adjusted R-squared: 0.613

Source: JMOHRC, Box 5, Professional Men, National Basketball Association, "Gate Receipts" (through March 4, 1951).

Notes

Materials from the Joseph M. O'Brien Historical Resource Center, Naismith Memorial Basketball Hall of Fame are denoted as (JMOHRC). Minutes from BAA meetings are denoted as BAA, "League Minutes." Other abbreviations used are *NYT* (*New York Times*), *TSN* (*The Sporting News*), and *SI* (*Sports Illustrated*).

Introduction

1. *Philadelphia Warriors Arena News*, Nov. 9, 1955, 3, lists such games at Lincoln High School.

2. James Murray, "A Trip for Ten Tall Men," *SI*, Jan. 30, 1961, 53.

3. Charles Salzberg, *From Set Shot to Slam Dunk: The Glory Days of Basketball in the Words of Those Played It* (1987; Lincoln: University of Nebraska Press, 1998), 212. The league has, to paraphrase an old Virginia Slims cigarette ad, "come a long way, baby!" Perhaps we could get Dick Vitale to intone this, since he is adept at infusing phrases with enthusiasm.

4. Of course, Mikan had the fortune—or the foresight, perhaps—of retiring just as the twenty-four-second rule debuted. He retired before the 1954–55 season (when the rule took effect) and then "un-retired" (just like later-day superman Michael Jordan) briefly for the 1955–56 season. The Minneapolis Lakers considered launching a children's television show that would feature Mikan (JMOHRC, "NBA Bulletin #183," May 7, 1951, Sid Hartman to Maurice Podoloff).

5. Norman Katkov, "Mr. Basketball, George Mikan," *Sport*, March 1959, 48–49, 76–79. When dressed in civilian clothes, he looked more like Clark Kent, as personified by George Reeves, than Superman.

6. The NBA's formative years occurred during a period of social ferment. Viewing the NBA from fifty or sixty years ago requires a different prism. America in the

postwar era differed greatly from today. Americans were concerned about the Soviet Union, atomic weapons, teenage delinquents, and buying a house in the suburbs. The problems of a fledgling band of basketball players and owners probably didn't "amount to a hill of beans in this crazy world," as Humphrey Bogart intoned in *Casablanca*. Cold War tension affected sports. The Amateur Athletic Union and its Russian counterpart, hoping to stage a home-and-home set of basketball contests, faced bureaucratic scrutiny and obstruction. Sometimes, though, basketball transcended politics, as when a Russian coach asked visiting Americans to send film of Bob Cousy in action. People around the world wanted to see the Cooz. Since basketball was not America's "national pastime," it avoided much of the hyperbole surrounding baseball during the Cold War ("Russians' Tour Barred," *NYT*, Oct. 22, 1955, 17; "Ferris Disclaims Bid," *NYT*, Oct. 8, 1955, 17; Ed Linn, "The Wonderful Wizard of Boston," *Sport*, Jan. 1960, 52–60).

7. In the America of 1949, a New York Knickerbockers program could show a cartoon Baltimore Bullets player, decked with bandoliers, simultaneously dribbling a basketball while firing a shot at a cowardly opponent (not identified as a member of the Knicks, however). In the wake of the 2009 Gilbert Arenas incident (in which it was found that Arenas had unloaded firearms in his locker), such a program cover would render NBA officials aghast. On another Knickerbockers program cover, the cartoon showed a scantily clad young woman on the court, under the heading, "Freeze!" The two players and referee shown on the cover are perspiring, but the young lass appears to be shivering. Aside from the cultural gulf presented by the two programs, the BAA's relative lack of popularity is reflected by the fact that both games were part of a doubleheader, with high school games filling the twin bill (New York Knickerbockers programs, Dec. 3, 1949, and Nov. 11, 1950). If you chose to lend your innocence, the 1950s was a poor time to do so, as the decade appears to have been filled with several "loss of innocence" events: college basketball point shaving, rock 'n' roll payola, game show rigging, and U-2 (the spy plane, not Bono as a gleam in his father's eye).

Chapter 1. Economics of Sports Leagues

1. U.S. House, Antitrust Subcommittee, Committee on the Judiciary, *Organized Professional Team Sports: Hearings before the Antitrust Subcommittee of the Committee on the Judiciary*, serial no. 8, 85th Congress (Washington, DC: U.S. Government Printing Office, 1957), 2896.

2. David Surdam, "What Brings Fans to the Ball Parks: Evidence from New York Yankees' and Philadelphia Phillies' Financial Records," *Journal of Economics* 35 (2009): 41.

3. The standard deviation is $.5/\sqrt{N}$, where N is the number of games. The standard deviation is greatest for the 16-game National Football League schedule and smallest for the 162-game Major League Baseball schedule.

4. James Quirk and Rodney D. Fort, *Pay Dirt: The Business of Professional Team Sports* (Princeton, NJ: Princeton University Press, 1992), 244–68.

5. Ronald Coase, "The Problem of Social Cost," *Journal of Law and Economics* 3 (1960): 1–44; Simon Rottenberg, "The Baseball Players' Labor Market," *Journal of Political Economy* 64 (1956): 242–58.

Chapter 2. The Beginnings

1. Murry Nelson, *The National Basketball League: A History, 1935–1949* (Jefferson, NC: McFarland, 2009), 226–32.

2. The National League had teams in six of the eight largest cities, with Brooklyn (third largest) and Baltimore (sixth largest) being the exceptions. Louisville, Kentucky, ranked fourteenth in population, and Hartford, Connecticut, ranked well below any of these, with only 37,180 people (Donald Dodd, *Historical Statistics of the States of the United States: Two Centuries of the Census, 1790–1990* [Westport, CT: Greenwood Press, 1993], 443–62).

3. The Sheboygan, Wisconsin, basketball team, in fact, modeled itself after the Green Bay Packers, with local citizens owning stock in the team and organizing as a nonprofit entity. The Tri-Cities Blackhawks (Davenport, Rock Island, and Moline) was another team organized on a similar basis until Ben Kerner bought a controlling share (Neil Isaacs, *Vintage NBA: The Pioneer Era, 1946–1956* [Indianapolis: Masters Press, 1996], 67). These locally owned teams frequently lacked the reservoirs of capital needed to compete with wealthy owners of BAA teams (Donald M. Fisher, "The Rochester Royals and the Transformation of Professional Basketball, 1945–57," *International Journal of the History of Sport* 10 [1993]: 23). In addition to the winnowing of teams in small cities, NBA owners shared other traits with their football brethren. Craig Coenen's history of the early National Football League bears an uncanny resemblance to the NBA's early history, as owners struggled to establish the league as having the best quality; granted a high proportion of free tickets; rigged the schedule to save a few dollars; played doubleheaders with high school games; bought failing franchises to get a star player; adjusted the rules to inject more offense and excitement; eventually induced wealthier owners to join the league; loaned players between teams; barnstormed; and enticed top collegiate players to sign up instead of playing semi-pro ball or working in non-sports jobs (Craig R. Coenen, *From Sandlots to the Super Bowl: The National Football League* [Knoxville: University of Tennessee Press, 2005], 15, 24, 58–59, 61, 77, 82–85, 91–92, 95, and 105).

4. BAA, "League Minutes," June 6, 1946, and Oct. 3, 1946; Robert W. Peterson, *Cages to Jump Shots: Pro Basketball's Early Years* (New York: Oxford University Press, 1990), 152. The territorial protection was later expanded to seventy-five miles (JMOHRC, League Information, "Constitution and Bylaws of the NBA, 1951").

5. U.S. House, *Organized Professional Team Sports*, 2854. Podoloff identified the teams in New York, St. Louis, Chicago, Boston, and Detroit as being well funded,

while those in Philadelphia, Toronto, and Pittsburgh were not. In the end, though, the owners of teams in St. Louis, Chicago, and Detroit decided to pull the plug after losing money for several seasons. Despite its capital shortage and subsequent sale, the Philadelphia team remained in the league.

6. Leonard Koppett, 24 Seconds to Shoot (1968; Kingston, NY: Total Sports Illustrated Classics, 1999), 17–19; BAA, "League Minutes," June 6, 1946; see also Arthur Daley, "Pro Basketball Is In!" Sport, Jan. 1947, 14–15 and 89–91.

7. Koppett, 24 Seconds to Shoot, 18.

8. Irish and Madison Square Garden had competition from Max Kase. Kase, a New York sports editor, had the idea to form a professional basketball league based on teams in large cities. The other BAA owners selected Irish (BAA, "League Minutes," June 6, 1946, and Dec. 5, 1946). The BAA undoubtedly made the correct choice, as the "deep pockets" of Irish and Madison Square Garden were crucial to the league's survival. Kase and the BAA owners reached an amicable agreement (Koppett, 24 Seconds to Shoot, 15).

9. Fisher, "Rochester Royals," 22; Koppett, 24 Seconds to Shoot, 15–43; "$84,600 in Prizes for Pro Quintets," NYT, Oct. 24, 1946, 38. The BAA owners might have also desired to avoid the situation that plagued early National League baseball teams that lost a surprising number of games to non-league teams: were the league's players really the best? I will discuss the BAA's struggle to achieve supremacy on the court in a subsequent chapter.

10. "$84,600 in Prizes for Pro Quintets," 38; BAA, "League Minutes," Oct. 3, 1946, and Dec. 5, 1946. Owners later debated cutting games to forty minutes, but seven of nine teams voted to retain the forty-eight-minute length (BAA, "League Minutes," May 21, 1947, and June 9, 1947). Owners continued to consider reducing games to forty minutes as late as May 1948 (BAA, "League Minutes," May 10, 1948). One owner suggested sixty-minute games, but the other owners overruled him (JMOHRC, "NBA Bulletin #58," Dec. 17, 1946).

11. Fisher, "Rochester Royals," 24.

12. "Basketball Tie-Up Is Set," NYT, Oct. 22, 1946.

13. "$84,600 in Prizes for Pro Quintets," 38.

14. Advertisements, NYT, Nov. 10, 1946, sec. V, 2, and Nov. 11, 1946, 40. Ticket prices were $1.50 to $3.50 at the 69th Regiment Armory.

15. "Knicks to Make Debut in Garden," NYT, Nov. 11, 1946, 40.

16. Advertisements, NYT, Nov. 10, 1946, sec. 2, 6, and Nov. 11, 1946, 42.

17. RCA Victor television advertisement, NYT, Nov. 4, 1946, 5.

18. Louis Effrat, "17,205 See Chicago Five Beat Knickerbockers in Garden," NYT, Nov. 12, 1946, 43; BAA, "League Minutes," Dec. 5, 1946.

19. Koppett, 24 Seconds to Shoot, 28–29.

20. BAA, "League Minutes," Dec. 5, 1946.

21. Isaacs, Vintage NBA, 1, 27, and 111.

22. "Celtics' Future Periled," NYT, Dec. 3, 1951, 36.

23. JMOHRC, "NBA Bulletin #39a," Nov. 9, 1949; "NBA Bulletin #52," Dec. 12, 1949.

24. Ed Linn, "Is the N.B.A. Big League?" *Sport*, Jan. 1957, 10–11 and 82–85.

25. JMOHRC, "NBA Bulletin #28," Dec. 2, 1949; Al Hirshberg, "The Celtics' Cinderella Star," *Sport*, Jan. 1962, 51–52 and 70–71.

26. Terry Pluto, *Tall Tales: The Glory Years of the NBA* (New York: Simon and Schuster, 1992), 22; JMOHRC, "NBA Bulletin #154," Jan. 29, 1951.

27. Al Ruck, "Hitting the Hoop: Old Celtic on Game Today and Yesterday," *TSN*, Feb. 11, 1948, sec. 2, 8.

28. U.S. House, *Organized Professional Team Sports*, 2945.

29. JMOHRC, "NBA Bulletin #39," Nov. 4, 1949; "NBA Bulletin #63," Jan. 27, 1950. The National Hockey League's policy of not sharing regular-season gate revenue also meant that hockey attendance figures were suspect. Sportswriter Dan Parker described discrepancies between reported New York Rangers attendance figures at Madison Square Garden and the league's official figures. According to Parker, the team announced higher attendance to the public than it did to the league office. Much of the discrepancy may have resulted from counting as attendees those spectators with complimentary tickets. Baseball's National League had a detailed set of rules for maintaining turnstiles and counting attendance (Dan Parker, "The Hockey Rebellion," *SI*, Oct. 28, 1957, 21; U.S. House, *Organized Baseball: Hearings before the Subcommittee on Study of Monopoly Power of the Committee on the Judiciary,* serial no. 1, pt. 6, 82nd Cong., 1st sess. [Washington, DC: U.S. Government Printing Office, 1952], 1107).

30. Joseph Sheehan, "Knicks Top Pistons after Warriors Halt Celtics before 18,255 at Garden," *NYT*, Dec. 28, 1957, 12. The staging of the 2010 NBA All-Star Game in the new Dallas Cowboys football stadium with 108,000 in attendance would have seemed miraculous to the early NBA owners.

31. JMOHRC, "BAA Bulletin #58," Dec. 17, 1946.

32. JMOHRC, "BAA Bulletin #20," Sept. 19, 1946.

33. Peterson, *Cages to Jump Shots*, 158 and 162; Jack Barry, "Pro Basketball's Future Promising," *Boston Garden Arena Sports News* 20, no. 5 (1947–48): 11; JMOHRC, Professional Men, Basketball Association of America, "Attendance Figures, 1946–47"; "BAA Bulletin #50," April 26, 1948.

34. Dave Farrell, "Crowded Schedule Blamed for Slump in NHL Attendance," *TSN*, Jan. 4, 1950, sec. 2, 2.

35. Bolstered by strong attendance during the late 1940s, the NHL owners decided to expand their season, voting to increase the season from sixty to seventy games beginning with the 1949–50 season.

36. Joseph M. Sheehan, "Garden Figures Indicate a Halt in Downward Attendance Trend," *NYT*, Jan. 14, 1955, 25.

37. Louis Effrat, "Knicks Set Back Syracuse, 85 to 77," *NYT*, Jan. 4, 1953, S1. As 1952 ended, the Knicks had attracted crowds of more than 14,000 four times, although these may have included children paying half price, while the collegians' best attendance was 12,756.

38. Joe King, "Pros Steal Garden Show from Colleges," *TSN*, Jan. 25, 1956, sec. 2, 2; Jack Orr, "Irish Still Picking Garden Lettuce," *TSN*, Dec. 17, 1952, sec. 2, 6; Dan Daniel, "Basketball Regains Favor in Gotham," *TSN*, Jan. 19, 1955, sec. 2, 10.

39. Koppett, *24 Seconds to Shoot*, 20; "Knicks List Home Dates," *NYT*, Sept. 17, 1952, 41. A year later the Knicks staged eleven games at the Garden, although three were afternoon games ("Knicks Schedule 3 Matinee Games," *NYT*, Oct. 9, 1947, 36). By the third season, 1948–49, Madison Square Garden hosted nineteen games versus eleven at the Armory ("30 Games at Home Slated for Knicks," *NYT*, Sept. 21, 1948, 37). According to New York Knickerbockers programs, during the early 1950s the team played most of its November and December games at the Garden and most of its February and March games at the Armory. By the 1959–60 season, the Knicks staged just one game at the Armory. This also happened to be a nationally televised game with the Cincinnati Royals. Irish probably figured television couldn't do much harm to the attendance for such a game with the lackluster Royals ("Knicks Schedule 31 Home Games," *NYT*, Sept. 17, 1959, 49).

40. Bill Reddy, "Syracuse Cage Pros Spin Gate on Promotions," *TSN*, Feb. 6, 1952, sec. 2, 5; Jack Durkin, "Boys from Syracuse Win 30 of First 36 Games," *TSN*, Jan. 25, 1950, sec. 2, 5; U.S. House, *Organized Professional Team Sports*, 2930.

41. Fisher, "Rochester Royals," 28.

42. Rich Westcott, *The Mogul: Eddie Gottlieb, Philadelphia Sports Legend and Pro Basketball Pioneer* (Philadelphia: Temple University Press, 2008), 178.

43. The top price for games at Madison Square Garden had been $4.50 in 1946–47 (Advertisement, *NYT*, Feb. 10, 1948, 30).

44. During the BAA's inaugural season, the Chicago Stags charged between $1.00 and $3.00 for tickets, while the Providence Steamrollers had prices of $1.25 up to $2.50 (JMOHRC, Professional Men, Basketball Association of America, Box 1, Chicago Stags Programs and Providence Steamroller Programs).

45. Bob Broeg, "Cage Pros Plan 2 Doses for 1 Ducat," *TSN*, Feb. 16, 1949, sec. 2, 2.

46. Team owners occasionally ran afoul of the lingering price controls introduced during World War II. United States Attorney Edmund Port charged the Syracuse Nationals for charging more than the ceiling prices allowed by the Office of Price Stabilization ("U.S. Sues Syracuse Five," *NYT*, Oct. 21, 1952, 39).

47. See David Surdam, "A Tale of Two Gate-Sharing Plans: The National Football League and the National League, 1952–1956," *Southern Economic Journal* 73 (April 2007): 944–45; David Surdam, *The Postwar Yankees: Baseball's Golden Age Revisited* (Lincoln: University of Nebraska Press, 2008), 173–74.

48. BAA, "League Minutes," June 6, 1946; JMOHRC, "NBA Bulletin #87B," June 19, 1951; U.S. House, *Organized Professional Team Sports*, 2945.

49. Richard F. Triptow, *The Dynasty That Never Was: Chicago's First Professional Basketball Champions—The American Gears* (n.p.: Richard F. Triptow, 1996), 5. Murry Nelson described how the NBL split revenue from doubleheaders among the four

participating teams. Each team received a share of the gate receipts (Nelson, *National Basketball League*, 179–80).

50. U.S. House, *Organized Professional Team Sports*, 2885.

51. Bob Broeg, "Unwieldy Basket Loop Sags at Gate," *TSN*, Feb. 8, 1950, sec. 2, 1; Broeg, "Cage Pros Plan 2 Doses," sec. 2, 2.

52. Joe Ives, "Lack of Split Hurts Cagers," *TSN*, Jan. 17, 1951, sec. 2, 2.

53. Ray Kennedy and Nancy Williamson, "Money: The Monster Threatening Sports," *SI*, July 17, 1978, 82.

54. U.S. House, Antitrust Subcommittee, Committee on the Judiciary, *A Bill to Allow the Merger of Two or More Professional Basketball Leagues*, 92nd Congress (Washington, DC: U.S. Government Printing Office, 1972), 21–22.

55. Pluto, *Tall Tales*, 216.

56. Koppett, *24 Seconds to Shoot*, 49.

57. David Surdam, "The American 'Not-So-Socialist' League in the Postwar Era: The Limitations of Gate Sharing in Reducing Revenue Disparity in Baseball," *Journal of Sports Economics* 3 (Aug. 2002): 270; Surdam, "Two Gate-Sharing Plans," 934.

58. The reality of gate sharing is that even though such worthies as New York Yankees general managers Ed Barrow and George Weiss and Brooklyn Dodgers general manager Branch Rickey and owner Walter O'Malley bemoaned "socialism in baseball," these gentlemen were primary beneficiaries of baseball's revenue-sharing policies during much of the mid-twentieth century. There is scant evidence that revenue sharing promoted competitive balance (if so, ask a St. Louis Browns fan) and only modest evidence that it mimicked Robin Hood in transferring money from the "rich" to the "poor." At least the NBA owners avoided the hypocrisy inherent in Yankees' and Dodgers' complaints about revenue sharing.

59. Surdam, "Two Gate-Sharing Plans," 934.

60. Surdam, "'Not-So-Socialist' League," 287–88; Surdam, "Two Gate-Sharing Plans," 944–45.

61. Peterson, *Cages to Jump Shots*, 153.

62. For a thorough look at the AAU Tournament, which pitted top amateur company teams, see Adolph H. Grundman's *The Golden Age of Amateur Basketball: The AAU Tournament, 1921–1968* (Lincoln: University of Nebraska Press, 2004). As a point of trivia, Morris Udall, later an Arizona congressman, played for the Denver Nuggets.

63. Red Auerbach and John Feinstein, *Let Me Tell You a Story: A Lifetime in the Game* (New York: Little, Brown, 2004), 45–48. As Auerbach recounts the story, the whole thing smacks of a Judy Garland/Mickey Rooney musical: "Hey, kids, let's get together and put on a professional basketball game!"

64. Pluto, *Tall Tales*, 117.

65. Ray Gillespie, "Bomber Fans Sing Praises of Great Big Masterful Doll," *TSN*, Dec. 24, 1947, sec. 2, 6. The same article described how Doll might have been involved

in one of the potentially weirdest trades ever. The St. Louis businessman owned both a hockey team and a basketball team. A fellow owner suggested trading his high-scoring hockey wingman for Doll, but Bombers coach Ken Loeffler nixed the trade.

66. John Wray, "Pro Cagers Too Tough for Colleges—Loeffler," *TSN*, Jan. 28, 1948, sec. 2, 7. In this same article Loeffler also remarked that the Bombers paid $1,000 for movies of their opponents, which he studied closely.

67. Stan Baumgartner, "Could Top College Cagers Defeat Best Pros?" *TSN*, Dec. 31, 1947, sec. 2, 4. See also "Pro Champions Defeat the Great Kentuckians," *Life*, Dec. 5, 1949, 150–52.

68. Bill Carlson, "Kundla Is Coach 'Nobody Knows,'" *TSN*, Jan. 30, 1952, sec. 2, 8.

69. Stew Thornley, "Minneapolis Lakers vs. Harlem Globetrotters," 1989, http://stewthornley.net/mplslakers_trotters.html, viewed Jan. 23, 2010.

70. For a good description of the first game, see Michael Schumacher, *Mr. Basketball: George Mikan, The Minneapolis Lakers, and the Birth of the NBA* (New York: Bloomsbury USA, 2007), 114–18. The Des Moines newspaper listed the score but no details of the second game, held on February 28, 1949. See also Maurice Shevlin, "Trotters Meet Lakers on Stag Card Tonight," *Chicago Tribune*, Feb. 19, 1948, sec. 3, 1; "Trotters Top Lakers with Rally, 61–59," *Chicago Tribune*, Feb. 20, 1948, sec. 3, 1; Robert Cromie, "20,046 See Lakers Lose to Trotters," *Chicago Tribune*, March 1, 1949, sec. 3, 1. The *New York Times* presented only the score of these two games without any article. When the Chicago Stags folded, the *Chicago Tribune* reciprocated by not providing much coverage of games at Madison Square Garden.

71. "Clifton, Negro Ace, Goes to Knickerbocker Five," *NYT*, May 25, 1950, 51.

72. "New York Quintet Bows," *NYT*, April 12, 1948, 29.

73. The Knicks played in a division that had just one former NBL team in Syracuse, New York.

74. "Pro Rules Sought for College Fives," *NYT*, March 18, 1955, 37.

75. Jeremiah Tax, "New Pros," *SI*, Nov. 12, 1956, C5; Jeremiah Tax, "This Vintage Year," *SI*, Nov. 4, 1957, 38.

76. James Enright, "NBA Casts Bait for Stars in NIBL," *TSN*, March 2, 1960, sec. 2, 6.

77. Tom Meany, "Cage Circuit Next to Farm?" *TSN*, Dec. 29, 1948, sec. 2, 8.

78. Star center Bob Kurland was one such player. After playing for the AAU's Phillips 66ers (also known as the Oilers), he went on to work for Phillips Petroleum company and rose to senior marketing executive in that company.

79. U.S. House, *Organized Professional Team Sports*, 2873.

80. Ben Gould, "Med Student Vandeweghe Doctors Knicks in Clutch," *TSN*, Jan. 11, 1950, sec. 2, 5; Salzberg, *From Set Shot to Slam Dunk*, 161; George Puscas, "Yardley Missile Master on Court or Off," *TSN*, Feb. 5, 1958, sec. 2, 3; "Knicks Draft Bunt and Seven Others," *NYT*, April 27, 1952, sec. V, 3.

81. Mort Leve, "Many Cage Stars in Industry Loop," *TSN*, Feb. 4, 1953, sec. 2, 1. For a description of the AAU basketball teams' blurring of the line between professional

and amateur, see Dan Parker, "The Truth about 'Pros' in 'Amateur' Basketball," *Sport*, Jan. 1949, 8–11 and 95–99. Clyde Lovellette stated, "I spent no little time weighing the pros' offer. It was $20,000 a year for three years on one side of the scale measured against the security of a probable lifetime position with Phillips, where basketball is only a sideline" ("Pro Basketball Is Not for Me," *Sport*, Feb. 1953, 30–31 and 84).

82. Jeremiah Tax, "Roundball Bounces Back," *SI*, Oct. 27, 1958, 59. Some observers decried professional basketball's and football's attitude to collegiate athletics. "The college people who rail at baseball's campus raids are well aware that professional football and basketball keep hands off varsity athletes until after graduation for purely selfish reasons. It is a parasitical practice that absolves them from baseball's heavy talent-development costs. Pro football and basketball get the finished college product at no expense. The bachelor's degree, if any, is incidental" (Joseph Sheehan, "Sports for Sports Sake," *NYT*, Jan. 23, 1959, 32). I suspect that many of the pioneering pro players would disagree with Sheehan regarding "incidental" bachelor's degrees, as a good proportion of them thrived in business after retiring from the NBA.

83. Jeremiah Tax, "The Man Who Must Be Different," *SI*, Feb. 3, 1958, 32.

84. Haskell Cohen, "History of the National Basketball Association," in *Official Basketball Guide, 1958–59* (St. Louis, MO: Sporting News, 1958), 7.

85. Salzberg, *From Set Shot to Slam Dunk*, 54 and 69.

86. Ibid., 90–91.

87. Peterson, *Cages to Jump Shots*, 160. Mikan's teammate Dick Triptow recalled that the plan gave Mikan and the other Gears six dollars for each field goal and three dollars for each free throw (Triptow, *Dynasty That Never Was*, 42–43).

88. BAA, "League Minutes," June 6, 1946. The owners initially set a limit of $30,000 but minutes later raised it to $40,000. Lawrence Robinson, "Pro Bids Are Music to Ears of Lavelli," *TSN*, Feb. 16, 1949, sec. 2, 5.

89. Isaacs, *Vintage NBA*, 4. Schayes recalled the league having a $6,000 cap on rookie salaries. He modestly stated, "If I had been with the Knicks, I probably wouldn't have had the opportunity to play as much" (Arnie Burdick, "Set-Shot Schayes—Pros' Dead-Eye Dick," *TSN*, Feb. 17, 1960, sec. 2, 3).

90. "$84,600 in Prize for Pro Quintets," 38; $70,000 Bonus Pool Set," *NYT*, Oct. 29, 1948, 36; "Play-Offs Revised for Pro Quintets," *NYT*, Jan. 22, 1954, 35.

91. Since the northeast region tended to have higher incomes, this ranking was undoubtedly somewhat lower for players performing for the Boston, New York, and Philadelphia teams. U.S. Department of Commerce, *Statistical Abstract of the United States, 1952* (Washington, DC: U.S. Government Printing Office, 1952), 189, 252, 263.

92. Myron Cope, "The Dollar Boom's Impact on Athletes," *Sport*, Oct. 1964, 22–24 and 79–80. Professional wrestlers, too, made far more than the best NBA star during the late 1940s and early 1950s, with Lou Thesz reportedly making $250,000 a season. Even top women professional wrestlers could hope to pull in $30,000 a year (Natie Brown and Tom Davis, "How Wrestling Looks from the Inside," *Sport*, Nov. 1954, 22–23 and 91–93; Jeane Hoffman, "Lady Wrestlers Strike It Rich," *Sport*, June 1951, 36–38).

93. Leo Fischer, "Royals Upset Pro Cage Best," *TSN*, March 21, 1946, 26; "MLB's Minimum Player Salary Rises to $414,000," Associated Press report, ESPN/MLB, http://sports.espn.go.com/mlb/news/story?id=5922336; viewed Feb. 3, 2012.

94. Stan Baumgartner, "Fulks, Relaxed as Rag, Wiping up BAA Again," *TSN*, Jan. 28, 1948, sec. 2, 5.

95. BAA, "League Minutes," Oct. 3, 1946; Jack Barry, "New Stars Shine in Garden," *Boston Garden Arena Sports News* 21, no. 3 (1948–49): 11 and 30. The league increased the team salary limit to $58,000 for the 1948–49 season (BAA, "League Minutes," May 10, 1948).

96. Isaacs, *Vintage NBA*, 61.

97. Koppett, *24 Seconds to Shoot*, 21.

98. Michael Strauss, "Pro Basketball Loop May Grow to Twelve Teams Next Season," *NYT*, Feb. 10, 1948, 29.

99. Triptow, *Dynasty That Never Was*, 119–25; "Franchises Are Approved," *NYT*, June 9, 1947, 28; Peterson, *Cages to Jump Shots*, 162; "Basketball Loop Quits," *NYT*, Nov. 14, 1947, 32.

100. Author Rich Westcott attributes some of the increased field goal accuracy to a change in definition. At some point, league officials decided that a shooter who was fouled during an unsuccessful field goal attempt would not be charged with the attempt (*Mogul*, 268).

101. Leonard Koppett, *The Essence of the Game Is Deception: Thinking about Basketball* (Boston: Sports Illustrated Books, 1973), 26–27. For the importance of the jump shot, see also Larry Klein, "The Toughest Job in Basketball," *Sport*, April 1961, 39; Milton Gross, "Elgin Baylor and Basketball's Big Explosion," *Sport*, April 1961, 28–29 and 94–96.

102. Lapchick quote from Murray Robinson, "Tally-Ho! High-Score Madness," *TSN*, Dec. 18, 1957, sec. 2, 10; Broudy and Yardley quotes from Salzberg, *From Set Shot to Slam Dunk*, 44 and 151. Podoloff's correspondence with the Wilson Sports Company regarding a new basketball is found in the JMOHRC, "NBA Bulletin #4," Oct. 1, 1952.

103. Charles Salzberg, "Basketball Arenas," in *Total Basketball: The Ultimate Basketball Encyclopedia* (Wilmington, DE: Sport Classic Books, 2003), 317.

104. Dick Young, "How Television Tampers with Sports," *Sport*, July 1961, 16–17 and 76–78.

105. JMOHRC, "NBA Bulletin #18," Sept. 29, 1949; "NBA Bulletin #49," Dec. 6, 1949; "NBA Bulletin #66," Feb. 22, 1950.

106. JMOHRC, "NBA Bulletin #33," Oct. 21, 1949; "NBA Bulletin #99," Nov. 4, 1948; see also "NBA Communication #19A," Dec. 3, 1952 for discussion of a new gate-receipt report form.

107. Irv Goodman, "Why They're after Podoloff's Neck," *Sport*, June 1959, 38–39 and 92. Irish had experience watching the NFL during its formative years, as he served as a publicity director (Coenen, *From Sandlots to the Super Bowl*, 93).

Chapter 3. The Merger and Its Aftermath

1. BAA, "League Minutes," June 2, 1947.

2. Michael Strauss, "Pro Basketball Loop May Grow to Twelve Teams Next Season," *NYT*, Feb. 10, 1948, 29.

3. The reader may note that another bush-league aspect of NBL teams was adopting nicknames that reflected the owner's name or primary business.

4. BAA, "League Minutes," Jan. 9, 1947, May 21, 1947, Oct. 10, 1947; "3 Quintets Ready to Change Leagues," *NYT*, May 9, 1948, sec. V, 7; "Leagues Discuss Merger," *NYT*, April 8, 1948, 33. The July 24, 1947, BAA league minutes revealed some animosity toward allowing NBL teams to play in BAA stadiums.

5. BAA, "League Minutes," May 10, 1948; Koppett, *24 Seconds to Shoot*, 35–36; "Four Pro Quintets Jump to New Loop," *NYT*, May 11, 1948, 34.

6. Koppett, *24 Seconds to Shoot*, 28 and 39.

7. "Four Pro Quintets Face Suit on Shift," *NYT*, May 12, 1948, 38; BAA, "League Minutes," May 10, 1948; see also JMOHRC, "BAA Bulletin #107," Sept. 8, 1947.

8. "Basketball Talks Fail," *NYT*, July 2, 1949, 12. The NBA and American Basketball Association (ABA) clash twenty years later featured spirited bidding for players.

9. Bill Roeder, "Merger of Pro Basketball Leagues Hinted," *TSN*, Feb. 18, 1948, sec. 2, 3; see also Tom Briere, "Mighty Mikan, Babe Ruth of Court, Smashes N. L. Basket Scoring Marks," *TSN*, Feb. 18, 1948, sec. 2, 4 for remarks on Mikan's $15,000 salary.

10. BAA, "League Minutes," July 1, 1949, and Aug. 11, 1949.

11. Two of the players had already been drafted: Jones by the Washington Capitols and Beard by the Chicago Stags. The Indianapolis Jets had drafted Groza. I found no information on how the league stripped Washington and Chicago of their draft picks ("Play-offs in BAA to Start Tonight," *NYT*, March 22, 1949, 33).

12. Koppett, *24 Seconds to Shoot*, 42; "Pro Court War Looming," *NYT*, Aug. 18, 1948, 31; Frank Elkins, "Rival Basketball Circuits Merge into One Loop of Eighteen Clubs," *NYT*, Aug. 4, 1949, 29; "Basketball Loop Sets up Divisions," *NYT*, Aug. 12, 1949, 24.

13. Koppett erroneously reported that the Denver Nuggets and the Waterloo Hawks hadn't bothered to complete the previous NBL schedule (Koppett, *24 Seconds to Shoot*, 43; Nelson, *National Basketball League*, 223).

14. Koppett, *24 Seconds to Shoot*, 50.

15. "Stags' Quintet Gets 10 Players in Draft," *NYT*, April 26, 1950, 40.

16. Pluto, *Tall Tales*, 34.

17. "New Circuit Discussed," *NYT*, April 28, 1957, sec. V, 4; "Pro Court Loop Formed," *NYT*, May 18, 1957, 13.

18. Stan Baumgartner, "As Fulks Goes, So Go Warriors, Coach Says," *TSN*, Jan. 25, 1950, sec. 2, 8.

19. JMOHRC, "NBA Bulletin #242," Dec. 6, 1951.

20. Stan Baumgartner, "Cup Overfloweth: Pro Cagers Shaky," *TSN*, Dec. 14, 1949, sec. 2, 1 and 8.

21. Peterson, *Cages to Jump Shots*, 173; Fisher, "Rochester Royals," 30.

22. "Consumer Price Index for All Urban Consumers: All Items," Jan. 1, 1946, to Jan. 1, 2010, research.stlouisfed.org/fred2/data/CPIAUCNS.txt; viewed Feb. 28, 2010.

23. Fisher, "Rochester Royals," 21.

24. BAA, "League Minutes," June 6, 1946; "Sbarbaro in Pro Basketball," *NYT*, Sept. 11, 1946, 11; Koppett, *24 Seconds to 24*, 16 and 48.

25. Koppett, *Essence of the Game*, 232–33.

26. In economic terms, as long as the price is greater than the average variable cost, the Knicks should operate in the short run.

27. One of the hockey arena owners testified about being better off filling his arena with ice shows and boxing instead of hockey (U.S. House, *Organized Professional Team Sports*, 2977).

28. "Bullets' Quintet Sold," *NYT*, April 24, 1951, 39; "Business Group in Drive to Save Bullet Quintet," *NYT*, Nov. 21, 1954, sec. V, 4. The team's twenty-eight wins out of forty-eight games during the 1947–48 season would be its second highest number of wins in a season. The trouble for Baltimore was that the league kept lengthening the season, so the team's win-loss percentage fell rapidly.

29. William J. Flynn, "Bullets Suspend NBA Operations," *NYT*, Nov. 27, 1954, 9.

30. "Capital Promoter to Drop Hockey, Basketball Teams," *NYT*, Dec. 5, 1947, 35.

31. "Move to Sell Clubs Fails," *NYT*, Jan. 9, 1951, 33. The Washington club apparently was losing $3,000 to $4,000 weekly before folding (Ben Gould, "Pro Basket Loop Hit by New Storms," *TSN*, Jan. 17, 1951, sec. 2, 1 and 6). The figure for total net gate receipts in the team's final four home games is from JMOHRC, Box 5, Professional Men, National Basketball Association, "Gate Receipts."

32. Bill Hosokawa, "Player-Owned Nuggets in New Pro Experiment," *TSN*, Feb. 16, 1949, sec. 2, 6.

33. Paul Walk acquired the team from Frank Kautsky, but the league had to loan the Jets $20,000. The team went into receivership in 1949 (BAA, "League Minutes," July 23, 1948, April 21, 1949, and June 20, 1949).

34. Salzberg, "Basketball Arenas," 316; see also Jim Dailey, "The Great Basketball Experiment," *Sport*, Jan. 1950, 60–62 and 86.

35. Angelo Angelopolous, "Groza 'Shot in Arm' for Big League Basketball," *TSN*, Dec. 14, 1949, sec. 2, 3.

36. The team's demise after the 1952–53 season was cloaked in some ambiguity. Podoloff told reporters, "As of this moment the Indianapolis club ceases to function. It is not going to operate again." He then added something to the effect that the team's president might be able to sell the team ("Indianapolis Out of Loop; NBA Bars Spivey," *NYT*, April 24, 1953, 3). See also Dailey, "Great Basketball Experiment," *Sport*, Jan. 1950, 60–62 and 86; JMOHRC, Professional Men, National Basketball Association, "Communication 42C," Jan. 22, 1953; "Communication 45A," Jan. 23, 1953; "Communication 46A," Jan. 28, 1953.

37. "Anderson Five Put Out," *NYT*, April 11, 1950, 38. Podoloff informed the NBA

owners, "I have made an agreement with Mr. Ike Duffey to settle for $20,000.00 his claim against the National Basketball Association for $25,000 in connection with the sale of the Anderson team and franchise with the understanding that the NBA shall retain title to those players whose contracts were the subject of the original sale as have not been signed to contracts by members of the NBA" (JMOHRC, "NBA Bulletin #127," Nov. 27, 1950).

38. "Toledo, Dayton in League," *NYT*, June 5, 1950, 27.

39. "Basketball Loop Votes to Disband," *NYT*, Oct. 24, 1952, 29; "Pro Court Circuit Reorganized Here," *NYT*, Nov. 14, 1952, 26. The league's Jersey City team stoked controversy by signing players Sherman White, Alex Groza, and Ralph Beard, who had been banned by the NBA for their collegiate gambling activities. The Elmira Colonels then signed Bill Spivey. Because these players were banned, no NBA team would consent to playing an exhibition game with an ABL "outlaw" team. Rather than acquire the taint of disrespectability, league president John O'Brien persuaded his fellow owners to disband, although the remaining six members (sans Jersey City and Elmira) attempted to reorganize a week later.

40. "3 Fives Quit NBA; Plan Rival Circuit," *NYT*, April 25, 1950, 37. See also JMOHRC, "NBA Bulletin #163," Feb. 22, 1951, and "NBA Bulletin #174," March 30, 1951, for sales of Chicago and St. Louis players.

41. "Chicago Quintet Is Out," *NYT*, Sept. 26, 1950, 41. See also Goodman, "Why They're after Podoloff's Neck," 38–39 and 92. After the Chicago Stags requested that the NBA buy the team, Podoloff "called the seven league owners who he felt could afford it, and he tapped each of them for $5,000. The final price paid to Chicago was $30,000, so he returned the $5,000 to the owner who could least afford the tap." Podoloff used similar tactics in liquidating the St. Louis Bombers.

42. "Files in Circuit Court," *NYT*, Jan. 9, 1951, 33.

43. Phil Elderkin, "NBA Will Free 'Sweet 16' in Expansion Plan," *TSN*, Jan. 11, 1961, sec. 2, 8.

44. Broeg, "Unwieldy Basket Loop," sec. 2, 1.

45. Harry Sheer, "Zaslofsky Came for a Trial, Stayed as Stag Sharpshoot," *TSN*, Feb. 2, 1949, sec. 2, 6.

46. JMOHRC, "NBA Bulletin #77," May 18, 1950; Peterson, *Cages to Jump Shots*, 173.

47. Isaacs, *Vintage NBA*, 35.

48. Pluto, *Tall Tales*, 106–107; King, "Pros Steal Garden Show," sec. 2, 2.

49. "Pro Basketball Players Obtain Promise Ex-Baltimore Athletes Will Get Back Pay," *NYT*, Jan. 7, 1955, 24.

50. BAA, "League Minutes," June 6, 1946, Oct. 3, 1946, May 21, 1947, Dec. 16, 1947, and May 10, 1948; "Pro Court Rules, Revised," *NYT*, Oct. 30, 1947, 35; "Player Limit Is Reduced, Rule Changed by NBA," *NYT*, June 21, 1950, 37.

51. Jack Durkin, "Boys from Syracuse Win 30 of First 36 Games," *TSN*, Jan. 25, 1950, sec. 2, 5.

52. Al Ruck, "Hitting the Hoop: Old Celtic on Game Today—and Yesterday," *TSN*, Feb. 11, 1948, sec. 2, 8.

53. Stan Baumgartner, "Talent Pileup at Top May Topple NBA," *TSN*, Dec. 24, 1952, sec. 2, 1.

54. New York Knickerbockers program, Nov. 10, 1949, 14.

55. "'Jumping' Ban Widens," *NYT*, Oct. 13, 1947, 34; Peterson, *Cages to Jump Shots*, 153.

56. Bill Carlson, "Pro Basketball's Most Valuable—Mikan or Share?" *TSN*, Jan. 9, 1952, sec. 2, 1.

57. David Surdam, "The Coase Theorem and Player Movement in Major League Baseball," *Journal of Sports Economics* 7 (May 2006): 201–21.

58. "Detroit Five Withdraws," *NYT*, July 10, 1947, 30.

59. Lou Chapman, "Selvy's Point Sprees Put New Life in Milwaukee's Hawks," *TSN*, Jan. 19, 1955, sec. 2, 9.

60. Koppett, *24 Seconds to Shoot*, 54; see also Linn, "Wonderful Wizard," 52–60 (see intro., n. 6); JMOHRC, "NBA Bulletin #174," March 30, 1951.

61. Arthur Daley, "Sports of the *Times*: Another Scandal?" *NYT*, Jan. 12, 1954, 26.

62. Koppett, *Essence of the Game*, 17.

63. Ibid., 209–10 and 214.

64. Charles Rosen, *Scandals of '51* (New York: Holt, Rinehart, and Winston, 1978), 111–12.

65. Isaacs, *Vintage NBA*, xiv; Stephen B. Young, *The History of Professional Basketball, 1946–1979*, master's thesis, Western Illinois University, Macomb, Illinois, 1981, 8; Fletcher H. Gregory, *Professional Basketball Players' Challenges to the Legality of NBA Policies, 1954–1976*, master's thesis, Pennsylvania State University, State College, Pennsylvania, 1985.

66. "Gambling in the Garden," *Time*, Oct. 30, 1944, 81.

67. Warren Moscow, "Sollazzo Indicted in Tax Case; Garden May Drop Basketball," *NYT*, March 1, 1951, 1. At first many colleges indicated that they still would be willing to send their teams to Madison Square Garden (Leonard Koppett, "36 of 40 Visiting Colleges Favor Continuing Play on Garden Floor," *New York Herald Tribune*, Jan. 25, 1952, 22). For a comprehensive look at the 1951 scandals, see Rosen's *Scandals of '51*. Unfortunately, Rosen does not include citations for his otherwise comprehensive and well-written book.

68. Pluto, *Tall Tales*, 21.

69. "Fulks Tells Court of Bribe Attempt," *NYT*, Dec. 11, 1958, 19; Stan Baumgartner, "Pro Sports on Guard, Fulks Case Emphasizes," *TSN*, Dec. 22, 1948, sec. 2, 2.

70. "Fulks Tells Court of Bribe Attempt," 19.

71. "Bribe Defendant Cleared," *NYT*, March 5, 1959, 28; "Cage Star Bribe Offer Cited in Philadelphia," *NYT*, Jan. 13, 1949, 12. Were collegiate athletes employees of their colleges and universities? Universities and colleges certainly hoped not, lest they be liable for Workers' Compensation for injured athletes (Walter Byers, *Unsportsman-*

like Conduct: Exploiting College Athletes [Ann Arbor: University of Michigan Press, 1995], 69).

72. "Referee Is Victim of Fake Telegram," *NYT*, April 4, 1950, 40.

73. Isaacs, *Vintage NBA*, xiv.

74. "3 Basketball Aces on Kentucky Team Admit '49 Fix Here," *NYT*, Oct. 21, 1951, 1; "Basketball Stars Must Sell Stock," *NYT*, Oct. 23, 1951, 26. In a weird parallel, Charles Rosen claims that the CCNY players were promised a franchise of their own in either Brooklyn or Chicago, similar to the Beard-Groza group. The players were arrested for point shaving before they could turn pro and give the NBA another black eye. Unfortunately, this "secret deal" was so secret that I have not encountered any collaborative evidence (Rosen, *Scandals of '51*, 95).

75. Koppett, *24 Second to Shoot*, 63; "Appeals Bribe Sentence," *NYT*, Dec. 13, 1951, 51.

76. "Indianapolis Out of Loop; NBA Bars Spivey," *NYT*, April 24, 1953, 3. The following year, Villanova player Bob Schafer was kidnapped by four men who encouraged him to be "less active" in upcoming games before releasing him ("Basketball Star Kidnapped an Hour," *NYT*, Jan. 11, 1954, 85; Rosen, *Scandals of '51*, 212–13).

77. "Referee Accused in Basketball Fix," *NYT*, Nov. 2, 1951, 18. See also JMOHRC, "NBA Bulletin #226," Nov. 12, 1951.

78. Quote from "Referee Is Named in Basketball Fix," *NYT*, Feb. 19, 1952, 20; "$15,000 Bail Set for Basketball Referee Accused of Fixing Professional Contests," *NYT*, Nov. 3, 1951, 32.

79. "Sollazzo Testifies in Basketball Fix," *NYT*, Feb. 10, 1953, 22; for other evidence against Levy, see "Referee Linked to Fix," *NYT*, Feb. 14, 1953, 18.

80. Rosen, *Scandals of of '51*, 193; for quote, see also 99–102 and 192–93 for fuller description of Levy's actions; "Ex-Referee Guilty in Basketball Bribe," *NYT*, March 28, 1953, 36; "Basketball Fixer Jailed," *NYT*, April 23, 1953, 44; "Sollazzo Guilty Again," *NYT*, May 14, 1953, 16; "Fix Conviction Reversed," *NYT*, March 4, 1954, 27.

81. Koppett, *24 Seconds to Shoot*, 83.

82. First quote from Louis Effrat, "Pro Basketball Drops Molinas, Ex-Columbia Star, for Wagering," *NYT*, Jan. 11, 1954, 1; second and third quotes from Arthur Daley, "Sports of the *Times*: Another Scandal?" *NYT*, Jan. 12, 1954, 26.

83. "Molinas Cleared in Betting Inquiry," *NYT*, March 25, 1954, 42; see also "Molinas to Be Queried," *NYT*, Jan. 12, 24; "Grand Jury Begins Hearing on Molinas," *NYT*, Jan. 13, 1954, 33; "Molinas Defies Inquiry," *NYT*, Jan. 16, 1954, 30.

84. "Basketball Loop Sued by Molinas," *NYT*, June 5, 1958, 41; "Player Sues League," *NYT*, Oct. 1, 1958, 31; "Court Denies Damages to Suspended Player," *NYT*, June 24, 1954, 38; "Hearing for Molinas Weighed," *NYT*, May 22, 1954, 24. See also "Molinas' $3 Million Trust Suit Dismissed," *TSN*, Jan. 18, 1961, sec. 2, 6.

85. Salzberg, *From Set Shot to Slam Dunk*, 166. The playoff game in question was the seventh game of the championship series and was played in Syracuse. Yardley's recollection does not completely jibe with the *New York Times* account of the game. Dolph Schayes had put the Nats up 91–90 with a free throw, but Yardley tied the

game with his own free throw. King made a free throw to put Syracuse back in front 92–91. With seconds remaining, he then stole a Pistons pass, presumably the pass Yardley recalled. Yardley himself had a poor game, with just nine points instead of his seventeen-point average (*NYT*, April 11, 1955, 31). Charles Rosen also described some suspicious activities in the NBA, quoting a bookie reminiscing, "We had to take a total of ten NBA ballgames off the boards that season. The word was around that there was business going on" (Rosen, *Scandals of '51*, 233, see also 193 and 221–24).

86. "Nationals Down Celtic Five, 101–89," *NYT*, Dec. 12, 1955, 41.

87. "Loop President Studies Efforts to 'Fix' Games," *NYT*, Dec. 13, 1955, 57. The college game suffered from another round of gambling incidents in 1960–61 (Jimmy Breslin, "Where the Basketball Scandals Will Lead," *Sport*, Dec. 1961, 34–37 and 91–95). One author suggested a bizarre solution for gambling based on the point spread. He wanted to make the game be in two twenty-minute "quarters." Each quarter's score would determine a "winner." If each team won a quarter, then the teams would play a ten-minute overtime. "If the point spread doesn't go, the game will. It's as simple as that" (Bobby Sand, "A Proposal: Revolutionize Basketball," *Sport*, Feb. 1952, 10–11 and 85). Needless to say, his idea went nowhere.

88. Jimmy Breslin, "The Untold Facts behind the Basketball Scandals," *Sport*, Nov. 1961, 16–19 and 78–80. For the impact on convicted and implicated players' later lives, see Jack Zanger, "The Basketball Fixers—Three Years After," *Sport*, Feb. 1954, 36–38 and 79; Sherman White, "The Basketball Fix Wrecked My Life," *Sport*, July 1951, 14–15 and 76–77. Rosen, *Scandals of '51*, also describes these players' post-basketball lives.

89. David S. Neft and Richard M. Cohen, *The Sports Encyclopedia: Pro Basketball*, 5th ed. (New York: St. Martin's, 1992), 75–77.

90. Isaacs, *Vintage NBA*, 107; Louis Effrat, "Wildcats Toppled by the Utes, 49–45," *NYT*, March 25, 1947, 32; "Knickerbockers Who Open Season Thursday," *NYT*, Nov. 11, 1947, 40; "Knick Five Cuts Squad," *NYT*, Nov. 25, 1947, 39; George Vecsey, "Pioneering Knick Returns to Garden," *NYT*, Aug. 10, 2009, n.p. (http://www.nytimes.com/2009/08/11/sports/basketball/11vecsey.html, viewed Sept. 14, 2010).

91. "Globetrotters Win, 47–44," *NYT*, Jan. 10, 1951, 34; "Basketball Series Announced Here Yesterday," *NYT*, Feb. 7, 1951, 38; "Attendance Mark Set," *NYT*, April 11, 1951, 41; "38,184 See Globetrotters Win," *NYT*, April 30, 1951, 25; "Bans Globetrotter Five," *NYT*, April 30, 1951, sec. V, 4.

92. Cooper had already experienced explicit racism while playing for Duquesne University. His team was scheduled to play the University of Tennessee in McKeesport, Pennsylvania, but the Tennessee school refused to play unless Cooper was barred from the game. Duquesne officials said its coach agreed "not to use Cooper unless he had to, in a close game," but this was not satisfactory to the Tennessee coach ("Negro Star Is Barred," *NYT*, Dec. 24, 1946, 21).

93. "Clifton, Negro Ace, Goes to Knickerbocker Five," *NYT*, May 25, 1950, 43.

94. "Cooper Erases NBA Color Line," Rochester Royals program, 1950–51, 25.

95. Ron Thomas, *They Cleared the Lane: The NBA's Black Pioneers* (Lincoln: University of Nebraska Press, 2002), 129.

96. Fisher, "Rochester Royals," 34 and 36; quote on 36.

97. Nelson, *National Basketball League*, 168.

Chapter 4. Shakedown

1. Fisher, "Rochester Royals," 27; Surdam, *Postwar Yankees*, 85–125; Tom Fitzgerald, "Attendance Decline Has Hockey Owners Worried," *Boston Globe*, Dec. 31, 1950, 21.

2. According to the *New York Times* account of the December 14, 1949, game, 9,500 fans showed up to watch Mikan. This was not a particularly large crowd for a game at Madison Square Garden, but, then, it was played on a Wednesday night (Joseph Sheehan, "Knicks Beat Laker Five with Alert, Aggressive Attack at Garden," *NYT*, Dec. 15, 1949, 54).

3. Schumacher, *Mr. Basketball*, 163. Mikan and the Lakers spoiled the Knicks' 1948–49 home debut by winning before 15,000-plus fans. In the next game between the two teams at the Garden, the Knicks held Mikan to a measly twenty-four points to win the game before 15,500 fans. The third game between the two teams was not so successful, as only 9,184 fans witnessed Mikan break the BAA single-game scoring record by tallying forty-eight points. The Knicks proved no more successful at stopping Mikan in Minneapolis when George broke his scoring record by erupting for fifty-one points against them on March 14, 1949 (Louis Effrat, "Minneapolis Conquers Knicks Five at Garden," *NYT*, Nov. 12, 1948, 34; Joseph Sheehan, "Knicks Upset Strong Minneapolis Quintet with Dazzling Attack at Garden," *NYT*, Dec. 23, 1948, 27; Louis Effrat, "Mikan Sets Garden Scoring Mark as Lakers Rout Knick Five, 101–74," *NYT*, Feb. 23, 1949, 32; "Lakers Down Knick Five," *NYT*, March 14, 1949, 25).

4. This certainly was the attitude of my father, who admired Cousy but groused about the taller Russell and Chamberlain.

5. Koppett, *Essence of the Game*, 198–99; Clif Keane, "Celtics Show 75 P.C. Gain in Attendance—Profit in Playoffs Seen," *Boston Globe*, March 19, 1951, 13.

6. Lou Chapman, "Selvy's Point Sprees Put New Life in Milwaukee's Hawks," *TSN*, Jan. 19, 1955, sec. 2, 9.

7. Koppett, *24 Seconds to Shoot*, 41.

8. Schumacher, *Mr. Basketball*, 121; "Globetrotters Win, 47–44," *NYT*, Jan. 10, 1951, 34; "Basketball Series Announced Here Yesterday," *NYT*, Feb. 7, 1951, 38; "Attendance Mark Set," *NYT*, April 11, 1951, 41; "38,184 See Globetrotters Win," *NYT*, April 30, 1951, 25; Hy Hurwitz, "Red Auerbach Raps Plan to Curb Offenses," *TSN*, Feb. 3, 1954, sec. 2, 1.

9. "Knick Five Loses to Capitols, 70–64," *NYT*, Jan. 1, 1950, 85; Louis Effrat, "Knicks Roll to an 81–59 Victory before Sell-Out Crowd of 18,000," *NYT*, Jan. 2, 1950, 33.

10. "Lakers Halt Globetrotters," *NYT*, Feb. 22, 1950, 35; "Stags Halt Knicks, 85–75," *NYT*, March 15, 1950; "Knicks Topple Pistons," *NYT*, Jan. 9, 1951, 44. The Globetrot-

ters did well touring against a team of college all-stars, including 17,114 at Madison Square Garden (with no NBA game on the bill); 11,379 in Buffalo; 7,932 in Kansas City; 6,500 at Stillwater, Oklahoma; 17,187 in St. Louis, a record crowd for basketball in that city; 12,076 in Detroit; and a gargantuan crowd of 31,684 in Pasadena at the Rose Bowl (Michael Strauss, "Globetrotter Five Triumphs, 65 to 58," *NYT*, April 2, 1951, 33; "Globetrotter Five Bows," *NYT*, April 4, 1951, 39; "Globetrotters Beaten," *NYT*, April 9, 1951, 34; "Globetrotter Five Loses," *NYT*, April 15, 1951, 50; "17,187 See Globetrotters Win," *NYT*, April 16, 1951, 38; "Globe Trotters on Top, 54–42," *NYT*, April 18, 1951, 53; "Attendance Mark Set," NYT, April 11, 1951, 50). A year later the Globetrotters played two games against another college all-star team. Both games were held at Madison Square Garden on March 30, 1952. The arena charged separate admission for each game. More than 35,500 fans paid to see the Globetrotters. Sportswriter Michael Strauss described the crowd as "not the usual blase, late-arriving Garden throngs, either. The fans were out early to see the thirty-minute vaudeville program and basketball passing exhibition by the Negro precisionists from Chicago that preceded the contest. They marveled at the deft ball-handling, pin-point passing and sleight-of-hand tricks all done to jive-music time" (Michael Strauss, "35,548 Fans Watch Antics of Trotters," *NYT*, March 31, 1952, 24).

11. BAA, "League Minutes," Dec. 5, 1946; Broeg, "Cage Pros Plan 2 Doses," sec. 2, 1–2.

12. Nelson, *National Basketball League*, 79–80 and 146; see also BAA, "League Minutes," July 24, 1947, and July 23, 1948.

13. Fisher, "Rochester Royals," 26 and 39.

14. Ibid., 40.

15. Lowell Reidenbaugh, "Kerner Cashing in as Promotion King," *TSN*, March 23, 1960, sec. 1; see also Gilbert Rogin, "'You're Looking at Success,'" *SI*, Oct. 24, 1960, 46, for the 15 percent figure.

16. JMOHRC, "NBA Bulletin #183," May 7, 1951.

17. Myron Cope, " The Big Z and His Misfiring Pistons," *SI*, Dec. 18, 1967, 28.

18. JMOHRC, "NBA Bulletin #46," Nov. 29, 1949.

19. "East All-Star Pros Win," *NYT*, March 3, 1951, 11; JMOHRC, "NBA Bulletin #169," March 5, 1951; "NBA Communication #43," Jan. 22, 1953.

20. "Stokes Fund Aided," *NYT*, Oct. 22, 1958, 42. Today Stokes is remembered, if at all, for his tragic injury and debilitation after a fall in a game triggered encephalopathy. His teammate Jack Twyman stepped in and became his legal guardian for the remaining years of his life, eventually organizing a fund-raising game. Although football's Gale Sayers and Brian Piccolo have their made-for-television movie classic, the movie detailing the story of Stokes and Twyman did not achieve the same popularity. It remains one of the NBA's most intriguing "what ifs"—Stokes teaming with Wayne Embry, Jack Twyman, and Oscar Robertson (and, later, Jerry Lucas). See also Earl Lawson, "The Tragedy of Maurice Stokes," *Sport*, Feb. 1959, 18–19 and 88–89.

21. For an in-depth look at this famous game, Chamberlain, and the effect on

America's perception of the NBA, see Gary Pomerantz, *Wilt, 1962: The Night of 100 Points and the Dawn of a New Era* (New York: Crown Publishers, 2005).

22. Lowell Reidenbaugh, "'NBA Major Loop—But,' Says Eckman," *TSN*, Dec. 19, 1956, sec. 2, 1.

23. Broeg, "Unwieldy Basket Loop," sec. 2, 2; JMOHRC, "BAA Bulletin #70," April 4, 1948.

24. Bill Mokray, "NBA Travel-Log Jumps to 265,862 Miles," *TSN*, Jan. 8, 1958, sec. 2, 1–2; Bill Mokray, "299,368 Miles Logged by NBA Clubs in '59–60," *TSN*, sec. 2, 2.

25. JMOHRC, "NBA Bulletin #116," Jan. 3, 1949.

26. Mokray, "NBA Travel-Log Jumps," sec. 2, 2; Westcott, *Mogul*, 9; BAA, "League Minutes," Oct. 3, 1946, and Oct. 3, 1947; Marvin Miller, *A Whole Different Ball Game: The Sport and Business of Baseball* (New York: Birch Lane Press Book, 1991), 163. Information at the Naismith Memorial Basketball Hall of Fame confirms the four dollar and five dollar figures (JMOHRC, "NBA Bulletin #88," March 26, 1947; Box 2, "Basketball Association of America Playoff Plan, Season—1948–1949").

27. U.S. House, *Organized Professional Team Sports*, 2934–35.

28. Many of the prime passenger trains at the time had famous names.

29. Isaacs, *Vintage NBA*, 113; Koppett, *Essence of the Game*, 191–93. Today's stars, if they found themselves in such a predicament, could at least rely on their "posses" or entourages to tote their bags. In the past, only coaches, team officials, and players traveled together, so players had to carry their own luggage. In the Koppett version the proprietor of the Green Parrot would fix breakfast for the players before their departure by private automobiles to Fort Wayne.

30. Mokray, "NBA Travel-Log Jumps," sec. 2, 2.

31. "Hawk Quintet Leases Plane," *NYT*, Oct. 22, 1958, 42; "Laker Team Safe in Plane Mishap," *NYT*, Jan. 19, 1960, 43; see also Carroll, Iowa's commemoration of the near-crash's fiftieth anniversary in "Airplane Crash Remembered," *Des Moines Register*, Jan. 17, 2010, 2-C. The basketball players' experience happened almost a year after the "day the music died" (Feb. 3, 1959), as Don McLean famously wrote in "American Pie." According to sportswriter Al Silverman, there was a bizarre twist to the story, as the "first outsider to greet the plane was the town's undertaker. He explained apologetically that he had not come seeking business" (Al Silverman, "What Happens If a Ball Club's Plane Goes Down?" *Sport*, June 1960, 28–29 and 72–73).

32. Koppett, *Essence of the Game*, 184–90; Murray, "Trip for Ten Tall Men," 52–55 and 59 (see intro., n. 2); see also Irv Goodman, "Cousy, Sharman, Russell & Co.," *Sport*, March 1958, 52–62. When Pistons owner Fred Zollner purchased a plane for his team's use, he thoughtfully refurbished the plane with extra-large bathrooms (Murray Olderman, "Pro Basketball's Fun at Fort Wayne," *Sport*, April 1955, 16–19 and 64–66).

33. JMOHRC, "NBA Bulletin #6," Oct. 9, 1952.

34. JMOHRC, "NBA Communication #47," Jan. 30, 1953; "NBA Bulletin #84," March 13, 1947; "NBA Bulletin #79," Sept. 9, 1948; "NBA Bulletin #99," Nov. 4, 1948.

35. Koppett, *24 Seconds to Shoot*, 37 and 49–50.

36. "Pro Basketball Teams to Play 72 Games Each," *NYT*, April 26, 1953, sec. V, 9.

37. Joe King, "Irish Suggests a Cut in NBA's 72-Game Card," *TSN*, Feb. 6, 1957, sec. 2, 3.

38. Westcott, *Mogul*, 143–46 and 178; Reidenbaugh, "'NBA Major Loop," sec. 2, 1.

39. Bob Vetrone, "Gottlieb Denies Control of NBA Card," *TSN*, Dec. 18, 1957, sec. 2, 1–2.

40. Mokray, "NBA Travel-Log Jumps," sec. 2, 2.

41. Lowell Reidenbaugh, "Kerner Urges Two-Game NBA Series," *TSN*, Jan. 14, 1959, sec. 2, 2.

42. Ibid., 1–2.

43. An article published in December 1952 showed that of 2,218 games played in the NBA, the home team won 66.4 percent of the time (Bill Mokray, "Cage Quints Average Only .333 on Road," *TSN*, Dec. 31, 1952, sec. 2, 7). For Major League Baseball home/road win-loss information, see www.Baseball-reference.com/leagues, viewed March 6, 2010.

44. Koppett, *Essence of the Game*, 87; Bob Wolf, "Home Floor Gives Basket Teams 3 to 1 Edge in Victory, Big Ten Records Show," *TSN*, Feb. 8, 1950, sec. 2, 4.

45. Isaacs, *Vintage NBA*, 121.

46. On at least one occasion, two teams actually played each other twice in the same day. The Milwaukee Hawks played two games with the Baltimore Bullets on March 8, 1954 ("National Basketball Association Boxscores," *NYT*, March 9, 1954, 31).

47. Salzberg, *From Set Shot to Slam Dunk*, 118–19.

48. Tobias J. Moskowitz and L. Jon Wertheim discuss the subtle forces acting upon referees; they find, for instance, that in a scramble between a star player and a non-star player for a loose ball, the latter gets whistled more frequently for a loose ball foul. They attribute an unwillingness by referees to affect the outcome by calling fouls on star players who are in danger of fouling out of the game. Their data appears to be of modern vintage and may not be applicable to the 1950s, nor does it address the issue of the home-court advantage (Tobias J. Moskowitz and L. Jon Wertheim, *Scorecasting The Hidden Influences behind How Sports Are Played and Games Are Won* [New York: Crown Archetype, 2011], 20–21).

49. Salzberg, *From Set Shot to Slam Dunk*, 183–204. Al Cervi was a constant critic of the referees. The *Boston Globe* ran a couple of articles where he blasted the referees: "Twenty-two times in 26 games we've had [Max Tabacci] and there's always trouble. The officials in this league aren't schooled. They don't know what they're doing out there. I've never seen such an exhibition and I've been in this game ever since I can remember" (Clif Keane, "Cervi Blames Officials, Auerbach Blames Cervi—Officials Blame Both Teams!" *Boston Globe*, Dec. 27, 1950, 8; see also Harold Kaese, "Officiating, Not Rules, Needs Improving—Cervi," *Boston Globe*, Dec. 27, 1950, 8).

50. "Pro Court Player Banned," *NYT*, Dec. 23, 1948, 28.

51. Bob Burnes, "BAA Fails to Back Refs, Gibbs Asserts," *TSN*, Jan. 19, 1949, sec. 2,

8; see also "Anonymous," "Confessions of a Basketball Referee," *Sport*, March 1958, 12–15 and 86.

52. Lester Bromberg, "What's Wrong with Cage Officiating," *TSN*, Feb. 16, 1949, sec. 2, 3; Milton Gross, "Speaking Out: Life Continues Tough for Pro Cage Officials," *TSN*, Feb. 6, 1952, sec. 2, 8; Dan Parker, "They Whistle While They Work," *Colliers*, Dec. 17, 1949, 20–21, 67, and 69.

53. "Nucatola Leaves NBA's Staff in Controversy over Officiating," *NYT*, Jan. 28, 1954; see also "Harrison Fined $600," *NYT*, March 30, 1954, 33; John Nucatola, "The Trouble with Pro Basketball," *Sport*, Jan. 1955, 30–31 and 66–69.

54. Lowell Reidenbaugh, "NBA Refs Expected to Seek Contracts," *TSN*, Feb. 26, 1958, sec. 2, 1; Fred Byrod, "Like to Travel? Take a Whirl as Pro Cage Ref," *TSN*, Feb. 3, 1960, sec. 2, 4; Lowell Reidenbaugh, "NBA Shuns Coast Expansion, Eyes Entry in Chicago," *TSN*, Feb. 4, 1959, sec. 2, 2.

55. Dick Young, "Star Macauley Lofty in Value as Coach, Too," *TSN*, March 4, 1959, sec. 2, 6; see also Koppett, *24 Seconds to Shoot*, 54. In a similar incident, Podoloff persuaded Boston owner Walter Brown not to strip the ailing Anderson Packers club of its better players (Harold Rosenthal, "Podoloff Lashes Back at Critic of Deal Okays," *TSN*, Feb. 11, 1959, sec. 2, 4). Podoloff later testified before a congressional committee that the league constitution stipulated how players from a defunct team would be assigned to surviving teams, instituted, in part, because of Irish's attempt to buy the St. Louis Bombers (U.S. House, *Organized Professional Team Sports*, 2863). For the Brouthers case in baseball, see U.S. House, *Organized Baseball: Report of the Subcommittee on Study of Monopoly Power of the Committee on the Judiciary Pursuant to H. Res. 95. Documents and Reports.* House Report no. 2002, 6. 82nd Cong., 1st sess. (Washington, DC: U.S. Government Printing Office, 1952), 31.

56. Salzberg, "Basketball Arenas," 317.

57. Isaacs, *Vintage NBA*, 5 and 80; quote is on 80.

58. Ben Gould, "Knicks Trying Trick of Teaching Felix Ball-Holding Knack," *TSN*, Nov. 24, 1954, sec. 2, 6; Koppett, *24 Seconds to Shoot*, 55.

59. Lowell Reidenbaugh, "Kill Territorial Draft in NBA—Kerner," *TSN*, Jan. 18, 1956, sec. 2, 2.

60. Jack Barry, "Owner of Champ Celtics Wants to Assist Also-Rans," *TSN*, Feb. 24, 1960, sec. 2, 1; Stan Baumgartner, "Talent Pileup at Top May Topple NBA," *TSN*, Dec. 24, 1952, sec. 2, 2. The NBA owners approved a one-year change to the reverse-order draft in May 1964. The teams with the worst records in their respective divisions would each get two picks before the draft resumed its normal order. One team would get the first and fourth pick, while the other would get the second and third picks ("N.B.A. Acts to Aid Last-Place Fives," *NYT*, May 27, 1964, 34).

61. Ed Linn, "Is the N.B.A. Big League?" *Sport*, Jan. 1957, 10–11 and 82–85.

62. "Knick-Syracuse Game Tonight Played with 12-Foot Foul Lanes," New York Knickerbockers program, Oct. 28, 1950, 11; "Wider Foul Lanes Urged," *NYT*, Feb. 6, 1951, 38; Arthur Daley, "Sports of the *Times*: Let's Not," *NYT*, Feb. 1, 1951, 34.

63. Mikan quote in Connie Kirchberg, *Hoop Lore: A History of the National Basketball Association* (Jefferson, NC: McFarland, 2007), 69; Bob Vetrone, "Foul-Lane Widening Please Cage Pros, Fans," *TSN*, Jan. 16, 1952, sec. 2, 2.

64. Schumacher, *Mr. Basketball*, 228; "Lakers in Front, 65 to 63," *NYT*, March 8, 1954, 34. Schumacher claims this was an exhibition game, but the *New York Times* article merely referred to it as an "experimental game." According to *Times* issues between May 5 and May 10, the game counted in the standings. Stew Thornley claims it was both an experimental and an official game and reported the best quote emanating from the game. Five-foot ten-inch guard Slater Martin said, "I advocate a six-foot basket. It would make a Mikan out of me" (Stew Thornley, "Minneapolis Lakers: Game with 12-Foot Baskets," http://stewthornley.net/mplslakers_12foot .html, viewed March 20, 2010). The Milwaukee Hawks not only had to play this strange game, but they also had to play two games—a real doubleheader—with the Baltimore Bullets the next day.

65. Bill Carlson, "Cervi Calls for Curb on Skyscrapers," *TSN*, Dec. 16, 1953, sec. 2, 2; "Height Limit Proposed for Men in Basketball," *NYT*, Aug. 11, 1958, 27. With respect to the maximum-height rule, one can imagine a big red line painted on a gym wall with the statement, "Must stand below this line in order to play, and no fair slouching."

66. Yardley quote in Pluto, *Tall Tales*, 55; Salzberg, *From Set Shot to Slam Dunk*, 175–76. Of course, hockey continued to have its share of rough play, as witnessed in the *Sporting News* headline "Goriest Year for Ice Game" (Geoffrey Fisher, "Goriest Year for Ice Game," *TSN*, Jan. 25, 1950, sec. 2, 8). See also John Wong's *Lords of the Rinks* for a discussion on dealing with violence in hockey (John Chi-Kit Wong, *Lords of the Rinks: The Emergence of the National Hockey League, 1875–1936* [Toronto: University of Toronto Press, 2005], 62).

67. Wayne Embry, *The Inside Game: Race, Power, and Politics in the NBA* (Akron, OH: University of Akron Press, 2004), 97–98. Schumacher relates a similar story regarding veterans roughing up young Dolph Schayes (Schumacher, *Mr. Basketball*, 160). Schayes describes how he and fellow veterans tested their rookie teammates: "The first thing we do against a rookie on rebounds is to belt him. It's the same principle as throwing at a batter's head in baseball. The purpose is not to hurt the man. We want to see how he responds to a challenge. If he doesn't hit back, you needn't bother to learn his name. He won't be around long" (Stanley Franks, "Battles under the Boards," *Saturday Evening Post*, Feb. 4, 1961, 34–35 and 64–66). Even as physically dominant a player as Maurice Stokes got tested (Irv Goodman, "Royal Rookie," *Sport*, March 1956, 36–39 and 69–71). I presume some unlucky Baltimore Bullets veteran got to "test" Wes Unseld when he was a rookie. As Mr. T. would say, "I pity the fool."

68. Louis Effrat, "Garden Threatens to Drop Pro Basketball Games if Rough Play Continues," *NYT*, Jan. 9, 1951, 33; Hal Freeman, "Pro Cage Games Hurt by Trading of Fouls—Irish," *TSN*, Jan. 13, 1954, sec. 2, 8.

69. Everett B. Morris, "Professional Basketball—What Is Its Future?" in New York Knickerbockers program, Feb. 23, 1954, 3.

70. Arthur Daley, "Sports of the *Times*: Blowing the Whistle," *NYT*, April 21, 1954, 38.

71. BAA, "League Minutes," Oct. 3, 1947; "Pro Court Rules Revised," *NYT*, Oct. 30, 1947, 35.

72. Quote in Michael Strauss, "Owner of Warriors Stunned by Loss of His Star," *NYT*, March 26, 1960, 16; Jeremiah Tax, "Chamberlain's Big Mistake," *SI*, April 4, 1960, 58.

73. "Cousy Belittles Charges by Wilt," *NYT*, March 27, 1960, sec. V, 4; "Cousy Gives Celtics' Views," *NYT*, March 26, 1960, 16.

74. Lincoln Werden, "Coaching Barred by Chamberlain," *NYT*, March 28, 1960, 37.

75. "Scoring Ace Drops Retirement Plan," *NYT*, Aug. 11, 1960, 21. A skeptic might think the whole brouhaha was a negotiating ploy. In his next season Chamberlain attempted even more free throws than before en route to his record-breaking scoring season of 1961–62, when he attempted a record 1,363 free throws. He led the league in free-throw attempts nine times. He also led the league in minutes played eight of his first nine seasons, only missing several games during the 1964–65 season. Of course, he is renowned for having never fouled out of a game. See Dolph Schayes's opinion on Wilt's retirement in "NBA Players Talk Back: Wilt Chamberlain as We Knew Him," *Sport*, Aug. 1960, 18–19 and 66–68.

76. "Lakers in Front, 65 to 63," *NYT*, March 8, 1954, 34; Ed Pollock, "Playing the Game: A Remedy for Foul Line Parades," *TSN*, Jan. 23, 1952, sec. 2, 8.

77. "Cage Officials Seated," *NYT*, March 11, 1952, 31.

78. "N.C.A.A. Basketball Proposals Approve Conference Tourneys," *NYT*, Nov. 14, 1952, 26.

79. Joseph Sheehan, "Six Rule Changes Are Proposed by Nation's Basketball Coaches," *NYT*, March 25, 1948, 38.

Chapter 5. Stability

1. Kerner claimed that he was $165,000 in the hole (Rogin, "'You're Looking at Success,'" 45; see ch. 4, n. 15).

2. Pluto, *Tall Tales*, 146. The same story is related in Brock, "NBA Attendance," 322, and Rogin, "'You're Looking at Success,'" 46. For younger readers, the Four Freshmen was a singing group and not a college basketball recruiting class.

3. Rogin, "'You're Looking at Success,'" 46.

4. Lowell Reidenbaugh, "Hawks Burying St. Louis 'Sport Graveyard' Tab," *TSN*, Jan. 16, 1957, sec. 2, 2; Lowell Reidenbaugh, "Hawks' Owner Kerner a One-Sport Man," *TSN*, Jan. 15, 1958, sec. 2, 4.

5. Gerald Astor, "Halfway Point in Pro Basketball," *SI*, Jan. 24, 1955, 46. The writer also cited the new twenty-four-second rule as boosting attendance.

6. Tax, "This Vintage Year," 38.

7. Jeremiah Tax, "A Blessed Event," *SI*, Feb. 25, 1957, 37–38.

8. Bill Mokray, "NBA All-Star Clash Tribute to Vision of Walter Brown," *TSN*, Jan. 9, 1957, sec. 2, 9.

9. Jeremiah Tax, "Short, Sweet Series for Slick Celtics," *SI*, April 20, 1959, 67.

10. Fisher, "Rochester Royals," 32.

11. U.S. House, *Organized Professional Team Sports*, 2934.

12. Rogin, "'You're Looking at Success,'" 46.

13. Certainly fans could purchase concessions, as several team programs listed prices. During the 1940s cups of soda often went for a dime, and a hot dog cost fifteen cents in Boston; soda and hot dogs were fifteen and twenty cents respectively in Chicago. The Washington Capitols listed similar concession prices in their 1946–47 program. Despite the postwar hike in prices throughout the economy, the Boston Garden concessionaire had not raised the prices for sodas and hot dogs three seasons later. By the late 1950s, concession prices appear to have risen. The Rochester Royals sold soft drinks for ten and twenty cents, but red hots were selling for twenty-five cents (*Boston Garden Arena News*, 1947–48, 30; *Chicago Stadium Review*, Jan. 28, 1949, n.p.; JMOHRC, Professional Men, Basketball Association of America, "Washington Capitols, 1946–47"; *Boston Garden Arena News*, Nov. 23, 1950, 20; Rochester Royals program, 1959–60, 9).

14. JMOHRC, "NBA Bulletin #132," April 14, 1949.

15. Broudy quote in Salzberg, *From Set Shot to Slam Dunk*, 36; Jack Barry, "Pro Basketball's Future Promising," *Boston Garden Arena Sports News* 20, no. 5 (1947–48): 9; see U.S. House, *Organized Professional Team Sports*, 2857.

16. U.S. House, *Organized Professional Team Sports*, 2869 and 2954; see also JMOHRC, "BAA Bulletin #84," March 17, 1947. The owners were certainly imbued with territorial imperatives reminiscent of European powers carving up Africa in the nineteenth century. You can imagine them saying, "Toronto desires Texas, Oklahoma and Kentucky for exclusive negotiating rights." The St. Louis Bombers wanted to choose from the states of Missouri, Oklahoma, and Iowa, as well as the Universities of Illinois, Kansas, and Kentucky. At least the Chicago officials had a sense of satire that enlivened BAA Bulletin #84: "Chicago basketball club requests following territory. All territory bounded on north by Canada, on south by Mexico, on east by Massachusetts, on west by Hawaii. However will accept following: Illinois except extreme southerly portion, Indiana, Minnesota, Kentucky, part of Oklahoma, Wisconsin, Iowa, Texas, California, Oregon, Washington, Utah, Colorado."

17. Alex Sachare, ed., *The Official NBA Basketball Encyclopedia*, 2nd ed. (New York: Villard Books, 1994), 325–32.

18. William J. Briordy, "Gola Is Drafted by Warrior Five," *NYT*, April 14, 1955, 39.

19. "NBA Territorial Pick," Wikipedia, http://en.wikipedia.org/wiki/NBA_territorial_pick; viewed Jan. 28, 2010.

20. Tax, "This Vintage Year," 51.

21. Briordy, "Gola Is Drafted by Warrior Five," 39.

22. Reidenbaugh, "Kill Territorial Draft in NBA," sec. 2, 1.

23. Lowell Reidenbaugh, "NBA Territorial Draft 'Failure,' Says Auerbach," *TSN*, Jan. 23, 1957, sec. 2, 2.

24. Joe King, "'NBA Needs Territorial Draft,'—Irish, *TSN*, Jan. 30, 1957, sec. 2, 1. Irish's provincialism seems ironic, given his chronic battles against small-city teams.

25. "Pistons Top Lakers, 19–18," *NYT*, Nov. 23, 1950, 58; Holtzman quote in Isaacs, *Vintage NBA*, 83. An article in the *Boston Globe* stated that the previous combined low score was 38 ("Fort Wayne Upsets Lakers 19 to 18!" *Boston Globe*, Nov. 23, 1950, 56). The *Boston Globe* confirmed Holzman's recollection: "Two of the overtime sessions tonight were scoreless as both teams concentrated on freezing the ball for one shot" ("Indianapolis Victor, 75–73, in Six-Overtime N.B.A. Tilt," *Boston Globe*, Jan. 7, 1951, 48). George Beahon wrote a lengthier description of the Rochester-Indianapolis game: "The customers, who complained, were burned up at the unchallenged freeze. Possibly 200 walked out, but there was little booing" (George Beahon, "Freezing Tactics Helped Establish Six Overtime Period N.B.A. Record," *Boston Globe*, Jan. 8, 1951, 4).

26. Murray Janoff, "Pro Moguls Constantly Trying to Better Game," New York Knickerbockers program, Nov. 11, 1954, 3; "Play-Offs Revised for Pro Quintets," *NYT*, Jan. 22, 1954, 35.

27. Dick Young, "The Solution—Make Them Shoot!" New York Knickerbockers program, Dec. 25, 1953, 3.

28. Stan Baumgartner, "Pro Cage League Rule Changes to Speed Up Attack," *TSN*, Oct. 28, 1953, sec. 2, 2; Stan Baumgartner, "Gottlieb Plan Cuts Fouling, Speeds Play," *TSN*, Feb. 13, 1952, sec. 2, 1.

29. Leonard Koppett, *24 Seconds to Shoot*, 87. The *New York Times'* description of the game, in the March 21, 1954, issue, called it a "foul-filled contest" with ninety-five fouls called. Nine players fouled out.

30. "Basketball Loop Changes 2 Rules," *NYT*, April 24, 1954, 23; Bill Roeder, "NBA 24-Second Rule Scores with Fans," *TSN*, Nov. 17, 1954, sec. 2, 3.

31. Jack Barry, "Macauley Called Time-Limit Turn," *TSN*, Jan. 18, 1956, sec. 2, 8.

32. Bob Sexton, "The Father of the 24-Second Rule," 6; see also H. Cohen, "History of the NBA," 5; Lowell Reidenbaugh, "Keep Hands off NBA Code—Auerbach," *TSN*, Dec. 21, 1955, sec. 2, 1.

33. Harold Rosenthal, "Hoop Pros High in Popularity under Podoloff," *TSN*, Jan. 15, 1958, sec. 2, 2.

34. Hal Lebovitz, "'Offense Killing Game'—Saperstein," *TSN*, Jan. 27, 1954, sec. 2, 2.

35. James Enright, "30-Second Rule—Big Pain to Coach," *TSN*, Jan. 20, 1960, sec. 2, 8. When Saperstein launched the short-lived American Basketball League, he chided the NBA for its reliance upon tall players. "Look, over 80 per cent of the adult male population of the U.S. is under six feet tall. Yet the whole NBA last year had only one player under six feet, Slater Martin. Do you blame the public for not buying NBA basketball with its seven-foot skyscrapers and ridiculously high scores?" To back his beliefs, he implemented new rules designed to help the "little man" compete,

including a three-point shot from twenty-one feet or more, widening the base of the key area, and allowing liberal use of hands on defense and bodily contact (Jack McDonald, "New Cage Loop to Tailor Rules for Little Guys," *TSN*, Feb. 1, 1961, sec. 2, 6).

36. Koppett, *24 Seconds to Shoot*, 99.

37. JMOHRC, Professional Men, National Basketball Association, "Attendance."

38. Jack Barry, "Vet Pros Urge Three Points for 30-Foot Shot," *TSN*, Jan. 25, 1961, sec. 2, 1–2; "Grenert Suggests 20-Foot Goals Count Three Points," *TSN*, Jan. 13, 1954, sec. 2, 8.

39. Jeremiah Tax, "Free-Scoring Farce," *SI*, Feb. 4, 1957, 42; Jeremiah Tax, "Who Said the Big Men Were Taking Over?" *SI*, April 28, 1958, 44–45.

40. Podoloff quote in Joe King, "How High Is Up? Top-Point Knicks NBA Also-Rans," *TSN*, Feb. 5, 1958, sec. 2, 2; see also Murray Robinson, "Tally-Ho! High-Score Madness," *TSN*, Dec. 18, 1957, sec. 2, 10.

41. Dick Young, "High-Point Tilts Help Basketball," *TSN*, March 16, 1960, sec. 2, 4. College basketball was not immune to the pitfalls of stalling. Even modern-day fans can recall Pete Carril's Princeton (New Jersey) Tigers slowing down the game in order to minimize the number of possessions and heightening the effects of variance on a game's outcome or the Villanova Wildcats defeating the Georgetown Hoyas in the 1985 NCAA Championship Game.

42. Jimmy Jemail, "Jimmy Jemail's Hotbox: Do You Favor the 24-Second Rule for College Basketball?" *SI*, Jan. 31, 1955, 2; Hugo Autz, "Coaches 3 to 1 for Ball Control on Court," *TSN*, Jan. 24, 1951, sec. 2, 2; Joe King, "'College Time Limit Near'—Lapchick," *TSN*, Feb. 19, 1958, sec. 2, 1.

43. Ken Loeffler, "'Time to Revive Zone,' Loeffler Tells NBA," *TSN*, Feb. 12, 1958, sec. 2, 3. His argument seems rather dubious. College coaches were already chasing talent, whether offensive or defensive.

44. David Surdam, *Postwar Yankees*, 126–62; Surdam, *Wins, Losses, and Empty Seats: How Baseball Outlasted the Great Depression* (Lincoln: University of Nebraska Press, 2011), 208–13.

45. Isaacs, *Vintage NBA*, 109.

46. "The News of Radio," *NYT*, May 19, 1948, 54; "Knicks' 18 Garden League Games This Season Will Be Televised," New York Knickerbockers program, Oct. 28, 1950, 11.

47. "Baltimore Five to Halt Telecasting of Contests," *NYT*, Dec. 23, 1948, 27.

48. Isaacs, *Vintage NBA*, 114.

49. "Sports Study Shows TV Helps in Long Run," *TSN*, Feb. 8, 1950, 23; "Pros and Antis Scan TV's Effect on Gate," *TSN*, Oct. 18, 1950, 2; Jordan, "Long-Range Effect of Television."

50. Peterson, *Cages to Jump Shots*, 173–74. A letter from a television executive to Podoloff outlined the terms: "For the rights to televise twenty games during the regular season, we propose to secure for the league the sum of $30,000." An additional

$10,000 was promised for playoff games (JMOHRC, "NBA Bulletin #33a," Oct. 21, 1949).

51. Pluto, *Tall Tales*, 23.

52. *Basketball's Best: 1953–54*, 26; Koppett, *24 Seconds to Shoot*, 23.

53. Joe King, "16,478 Fans Cheer as All-Star Thriller Gives NBA Big Lift," *TSN*, Feb. 3, 1954, sec. 2, 6; Pluto, *Tall Tales*, 28. *Basketball's Best: 1953–54*, 26, states DuMont was broadcasting the games during 1953–54. Ted Brock, writing in *Total Basketball*, claims there were no NBA games on television until 1954, but he echoes the rest of the DuMont and NBC contract information cited above (Brock, "NBA Attendance," 322).

54. U.S. House, *Organized Professional Team Sports*, 2883–84.

55. Harold Rosenthal, "Nation-Wide NBA Dream of Podoloff," *TSN*, Feb. 1, 1956, sec. 2, 1; see also Rosenthal, "Hoop Pros High in Popularity," sec. 2, 2. Podoloff's is an amusing statement, given that the author, not quite 5'6″ tall, could easily "post up" the NBA president. While some readers might scoff that Podoloff was thinking nationally and not globally, he left a league that would be solid enough on which to erect an international brand for David Stern and subsequent presidents.

56. Harold Rosenthal, "Podoloff Slams Lid on Pro Cage Farm Club Talk," *TSN*, Jan. 8, 1958, sec. 2, 8. Clearly the idea that a player such as LeBron James could take an hour of prime-time television on July 8, 2010, to tease the audience watching ESPN as to his choice of team would have astounded NBA participants of the 1950s.

57. Harold Rosenthal, "TV Brightens Cage Pros' Gate Picture," *TSN*, Jan. 23, 1957, sec. 2, 1.

58. Clif Keane, "Tip-Off Tidbits," *TSN*, Dec. 25, 1957, sec. 2, 10; Arthur Daley, "Sports of *The Times*: Mutiny on the Bounty," *NYT*, Jan. 23, 1964, 40; "N.B.A. Acts to Aid Last-Place Fives," *NYT*, May 27, 1964, 34.

59. Tax, "Roundball Bounces Back," 31.

60. Joe King, "Irish Seeks More TV $$ for NBA, NHL," *TSN*, Feb. 12, 1958, sec. 2, 1.

61. Joseph M. Sheehan, "Garden Figures Indicate a Halt in Downward Attendance Trend," *NYT*, Jan. 14, 1955, 25.

62. Haskell Cohen, "Review of the 1958–59 Season," in *Official Basketball Guide, 1959–60* (St. Louis, MO: Sporting News, 1959), 7.

63. I can recall being a child racing home from church, after a stop at McDonalds, and watching the NBA *Game of the Week*. Ned Irish must have been happy, because his Knicks never seemed to be participating. The games appeared to be permutations of Los Angeles, Philadelphia, or Boston, with Baylor, West, Chamberlain, and Russell. Were New York, Cincinnati, and Detroit even in the league?

64. A "prisoners' dilemma" occurs when participants in a strategic situation exercise their best strategy but end up collectively worse off by doing so.

65. *Basketball's Best: 1958–59*, 48; *Basketball's Best: 1959–60*, n.p; *Basketball's Best: 1961–62*, n.p.; Bill Mokray, *1961–1962 Official NBA Guide* (St. Louis, MO: Sporting News, 1961), 3–5; Mokray, *1962–1963 Official NBA Guide*, 3–5.

66. Fisher, "Rochester Royals," 42.

67. Dick Young, "How Television Tampers with Sports," *Sport*, July 1961, 16–17 and 76–78.

Chapter 6. Moving to Major League Status

1. *Basketball's Best: 1961–62*, 31; John Thorn, Pete Palmer, and Michael Gershman, eds., *Total Baseball*, 7th ed. (Kingston, NY: Total Sports Publishing, 2001), 76.

2. Haskell Cohen, "Review of the 1959–60 Season," in *Official Basketball Guide, 1960–61* (St. Louis, MO: Sporting News, 1960), 7.

3. Tax, "Who Said the Big Men Were Taking Over?" 45; Haskell Cohen, "Review of the 1958–59 Season," in *Official Basketball Guide, 1959–60* (St. Louis, MO: Sporting News, 1959), 7.

4. Lowell Reidenbaugh, "Top NBA Rivals Set Traps for Favored Celtics, Hawks," *TSN*, Oct. 19, 1960, sec. 2, 7; Phil Elderkin, "Lakers Winning New Friends in 1st L.A. Season," *TSN*, Dec. 21, 1960, sec. 2, 8.

5. "Royals Check Doormat Role, Shake Up NBA," *TSN*, Nov. 2, 1960, sec. 2, 8; Phil Elderkin, "Lakers Winning New Friends in 1st L.A. Season," *TSN*, Dec. 21, 1960, sec. 2, 8. The Dodgers debuted in Los Angeles with a three-game series with the San Francisco Giants. The series drew 167,000 paying patrons. The Giants' visiting share alone was almost $46,000 (Dick Young, "N.L. Finding Rich Gravy in L.A. Bowl," *TSN*, April 30, 1958, 1).

6. Jim Enright, "Wilt Lures Fans to Trotter Games," *TSN*, Dec. 3, 1958, sec. 2, 8; Art Morrow, "Tall Stilt Roars—Box Office Bucks Soar," *TSN*, Feb. 3, 1960, sec. 2, 1; Tax, "Chamberlain's Big Mistake," 58.

7. Lowell Reidenbaugh, "Bill Russell Just Finding Range, Says Red," *TSN*, Jan. 30, 1957, sec. 2, 2.

8. "Royals See Rosy Future in Big O and Bigger Gates, *TSN*, Oct. 26, 1960, sec. 2, 6.

9. William Leggett, "The New Kid on the Block Takes on the Champ," *SI*, Nov. 14, 1960, 24–25.

10. Prospective buyers of teams in smaller cities would consider the potential for moving the team to a larger, more-profitable location in making an offer.

11. Quirk and Fort, *Pay Dirt*, 57.

12. Pluto, *Tall Tales*, 208; "Warrior Quintet Is Sold," *NYT*, April 26, 1952, 29; Westcott, *Mogul*, 172.

13. JMOHRC, "NBA Bulletin #213A," Oct. 9, 1951; Quirk and Fort (*Pay Dirt*, 447) claim it was 1949.

14. "Royals Sold to Man Who Hopes to Return Quintet to Rochester," *NYT*, March 27, 1958, 46; "Cincinnati Group Buys Royals' Five," *NYT*, April 8, 1958, 39.

15. "Bid to Lakers Weighed," *NYT*, Feb. 24, 1957, sec. 6, 22; "Marty Marion Buys Lakers for $150,000," *NYT*, Feb. 27, 1957, 30.

16. "Gola, Ending Holdout, Signs with Warriors," *NYT*, Oct. 8, 1955, 15; "Celtics

Sign Russell," *NYT*, Dec. 20, 1956, 41; see also King, "Pros Steal Garden Show," sec. 2, 2; Goodman, "Cousy, Sharman, Russell & Co.," 52–62; Murray Olderman, "Elgin Baylor: One-Man Franchise," *Sport*, April 1959, 24–26 and 80–81.

17. Koppett, *24 Seconds to Shoot*, 100; Fisher, "Rochester Royals, 32.

18. First two quotes from Pluto, *Tall Tales*, 147; third quote from Lowell Reidenbaugh, "Cool Clyde Helping Hawks Set Hot Pace," *TSN*, Dec. 17, 1958, sec. 2, 6. Then again, Kerner was impulsive about firing coaches. After firing Alex Hannum, who had just led the team to a league championship, Kerner sought out Ed Macauley, who had been popular with St. Louis fans, offering him more than $100,000 for a five-year contract (Lowell Reidenbaugh, "Grand Guy Ed Calls Time on 100-G Offer," *TSN*, Jan. 21, 1959, sec. 2, 4; Dick Young, "Star Macauley Lofty in Value as Coach, Too," *TSN*, March 4, 1959, sec. 2, 6). Macauley lasted two seasons.

19. Joseph Sheehan, "Stilt Too Big to Play with Pennies," *NYT*, June 5, 1958, 41; Irv Goodman, "Wilt vs. the NBA," *Sport*, April 1959, 20–21 and 84–86. By the late 1960s, facing legal challenges, the league would rewrite the rule and allow some players with remaining college eligibility to enter the NBA draft.

20. Art Morrow, "Tall Stilt Roars—Box Office Bucks Soar," *TSN*, Feb. 3, 1960, sec. 2, 2.

21. Ralph Ray, "Steamed-Up Stilt Shows Refs How to Use Whistle," *TSN*, Feb. 24, 1960, sec. 2, 2.

22. "Wilt Scores 28 Points, *NYT*, April 3, 1960, sec. 5, 4; "Chamberlain Joins Globetrotters for Chicago Game on Saturday," *NYT*, March 31, 1960, 44; "Scoring Ace Drops Retirement Plan," *NYT*, Aug. 11, 1960, 21; James Enright, "Trotters May Bill Stilt Second Year," *TSN*, Jan. 21, 1959, sec. 2, 10. Years later, when reminiscing with Terry Pluto, Chamberlain recalled that Gottlieb offered him $25,000 to sign after his junior season at the University of Kansas. The Globetrotters offered $50,000 plus a bonus plan, while a spin-off of the Globetrotters, the Harlem Magicians, offered $100,000. Supposedly Marques Haynes and Goose Tatum told him they'd give him a cashier's check for that amount. Gottlieb lured Chamberlain away from the Globetrotters for a $65,000 salary. While Gottlieb trumpeted that Chamberlain was the best-paid player in basketball, he actually paid the player more than was publicized. "We kept it quiet to eliminate jealousy or any other problems," he said (Pluto, *Tall Tales*, 216). Apparently Gottlieb's pursuit of Chamberlain alienated him from longtime friend Abe Saperstein (see Westcott, *Mogul*, 243).

23. "Celtics' Star Shares Gate in Record Pact," *NYT*, Sept. 15, 1959, 49; Jim Heffernan, "Warriors Riding High on Wilt the Stilt," *TSN*, Nov. 18, 1959, sec. 2, 7.

24. Sandy Grady, "Resurgence in Cincinnati," *Sport*, March 1961, 18–19 and 67–70; Barry Gottehrer, "Will Oscar Robertson Play in the NBA?" *Sport*, June 1960, 47; Jeremiah Tax, "Bunyan Strides Again," *SI*, April 6, 1959, 18.

25. Bill Furlong, "Walt Bellamy vs. the NBA," *Sport*, Feb. 1963, 35–37 and 68–69.

26. The BAA's "League Minutes" showed that there was remarkable parity in the

team payrolls of the four incoming NBL teams. The teams' payrolls ranged from the Indianapolis Kautskys' $61,505 (nine players) to the Rochester Royals' $67,000 (ten players). The Minneapolis Lakers paid $64,000 to nine players, while the Fort Wayne Pistons paid $62,000 for eleven players (BAA, "League Minutes," May 10, 1948).

27. Surdam, *Postwar Yankees*, 67–72.

28. George Beahon, "Payroll Too High in NBA—Gottlieb," *TSN*, Dec. 2, 1953, sec. 2, 8; U.S. House, *Organized Professional Team Sports*, 2048–52.

29. U.S. House, *Organized Professional Team Sports*, 2873 and 2877.

30. "Sues to Break Contract," *NYT*, Dec. 13, 1946, 32; "Gears Five Ousts Banks," *NYT*, Dec. 14, 1946, 20; "Mikan Sued by Gears," *NYT*, Jan. 18, 1947, 17; Schumacher, *Mr. Basketball*, 76–77; "Mikan Returns to Gears," *NYT*, Jan. 29, 1947, 33; "Mikan Suit Called Test Case for Pros," *NYT*, Jan. 21, 1947, 19; Maurice Shevlin, "Mikan Retires after Gears Lose, 44 to 41," *Chicago Tribune*, Dec. 12, 1946, sec. 4, 59; Maurice Shevlin, "Mikan Sues to Break 5 Year Gear Contract," *Chicago Tribune*, Dec. 13, 1946, sec. 3, 39; "Mikan Sues to End Contract with Gears," *Chicago Daily News*, Dec. 12, 1946. For a former teammate, Richard Triptow's perspective on Mikan's retirement, see Triptow, *Dynasty That Never Was*, 72–75 and 78.

31. Salzberg, *From Set Shot to Slam Dunk*, 93–94.

32. "Court Players Organized," *NYT*, Jan. 19, 1955, 32; Hy Hurwitz, "Cousy Seeks to Form Cage Players' Group," *TSN*, Jan. 19, 1955, sec. 2, 9; "Cousy and Pollard Selected Spokesmen for NBA Players," *TSN*, Jan. 26, 1955, sec. 2, 6; Bob Cousy, "Pro Basketball Needs a Bill of Rights," *Sport*, April 1956, 12–13 and 68–69. Zollner apparently maintained quite amicable relations with workers at his piston-manufacturing plants. Myron Cope wrote: "Zollner is able to march through his plant and know that practically every soul there loves working for him. The pay is tops and the shop is air-conditioned. Twice union organizers have forced recognition elections, and twice they have been walloped. In the 35-year history of the Fort Wayne plant, not one salesman has resigned or been fired" (Cope, "Big Z and His Misfiring Pistons," 27).

33. Ben Gould, "NBA Rigs Zone Defense against Union," *TSN*, Feb. 2, 1955, sec. 2, 1–2.

34. "NBA Players File Demands: Seek a Limit on Exhibitions," *TSN*, Feb. 1, 1956, sec. 2, 7.

35. "Podoloff's Plea Heads Off Union," *NYT*, Jan. 16, 1957, 37; "Pros Weigh Labor Tie," *NYT*, Dec. 27, 1956, 31. As with any new idea, some folks were against it. Like many old-time baseball players, former barnstorming pro Art Spector denied that the players needed a union, citing the "irreparable damage" a union could wreak: "Just imagine a picket line of basketball players around the Garden, carrying placards claiming the management is unfair. If that ever happens, all the good will, all the work everybody has done in the past ten years will go right down the drain" (Tim Morgan, "Union Could Kill NBA, Spector Says," *TSN*, Jan. 30, 1957, sec. 2, 6).

36. Jack Barry, "Cousy Will Quit as Player Prexy—If," *TSN*, Jan. 15, 1958, sec. 2, 1.

37. U.S. House, *Organized Professional Team Sports*, 2897–99, and 2904.

38. Ibid., 2877.

39. Ibid., 2899.

40. Clif Keane, "Tip-Off Tidbits," *TSN*, Dec. 25, 1957, sec. 2, 10; Surdam, *Postwar Yankees*, 220 and 229; Reidenbaugh, "NBA Shuns Coast Expansion," sec. 2, 2; U.S. House, Committee on Education and the Workforce, Subcommittee on Employer-Employee Relations, *Pension Fairness for NBA Pioneers*, 105th Congress, 2nd sess. (Washington, D.C.: U.S. Government Printing Office, 1998).

41. Dan Parker, "The Hockey Rebellion," *SI*, Oct. 28, 1957, 19–20.

42. Arthur Daley, "Sports of *The Times*: Mutiny on the Bounty," *NYT*, Jan. 23, 1964, 40.

43. "NBA Players Threaten Strike in Dispute over Pension Plan," *NYT*, Jan. 15, 1964, 34; Koppett, *Essence of the Game*, 236. Podoloff had been grilled by some congressmen in 1957 on a rule in the standard player contract that forbade striking before a nationally televised game, proving how prescient the owners were in inserting the clause, not that it prevented the threatened 1964 strike (U.S. House, *Organized Professional Team Sports*, 2890).

44. Since the coin flip might have induced weaker teams to play less than their best during the waning stages of the season, the league introduced the lottery system. The lottery system created a more continuous set of odds. Rather than have two teams with a fifty-fifty chance each of getting the top pick, by imbuing more teams with some chance of getting the top pick the league hoped to diminish the incentive for teams to throw in the towel in order to secure a better draft position. The most infamous episode occurred with the 1985 draft. The New York Knicks had one of the lowest odds of winning the lottery but somehow ended up getting the big prize. They immediately drafted Patrick Ewing and had a slightly worse record the next season.

45. As it was, the Bucks returned most of the same players who finished last in 1968–69, adding only Bobby Dandridge with Abdul-Jabbar to the starting lineup. Bird joined a veteran Boston team, supplanting Bob McAdoo. The Celtics' other main addition that season was Nate Archibald. Duncan joined a San Antonio Spurs team that had suffered serious injuries to stars David Robinson and Sean Elliott. With those two veterans healthy and with Duncan replacing Dominique Wilkins, the Spurs reverted back to contending status.

46. "Mikan of Lakers Quits Basketball," *NYT*, Sept. 25, 1954, 20; see also "Mikan Appointed to Lakers' Post," *NYT*, Oct. 6, 1954, 34.

47. Pluto, *Tall Tales*, 121–25; William J. Briordy, "Celtics Acquire Rights to Russell and Jones of San Francisco Five," *NYT*, May 1, 1956, 39.

48. Pluto, *Tall Tales*, 122.

49. Rosenthal, "Podoloff Lashes Back," sec. 2, 4.

50. Lowell Reidenbaugh, "Piontek and Foust Give Hefty Hawks Beefed-Up Bench," *TSN*, Feb. 10, 1960, sec. 2, 2; Rogin, "'You're Looking at Success,'" 48; see ch. 4, n. 15.

51. Reidenbaugh, "Kerner Cashing In," sec. 2, 2.

52. Arthur Daley, "Sports of the *Times*: Just as Expected," *NYT*, Dec. 20, 1956, 41.

53. Arthur Daley, "Education of a Basketball Rookie," *NYT*, Feb. 24, 1957, sec. 6, 22; Goodman, "Cousy, Sharman, Russell & Co.," 52–62.

54. Jeremiah Tax, "Here Comes the Big Fellow at Last," *SI*, Oct. 26, 1959, 16; Goodman, "Wilt vs. the NBA," 20–21 and 84–86.

55. Both quotes from Pluto, *Tall Tales*, 214, and Ted Brock, "NBA Attendance," 323; U.S. House, *Organized Professional Team Sports*, 2860; "Chamberlain Heads List of 81 in Pro Basketball Draft," *NYT*, April 1, 1959, 49; Pluto, *Tall Tales*, 216.

56. Jeffrey Glick, "Professional Sports Franchise Movements and the Sherman Act: When and Where Teams Should Be Able to Move," *Santa Clara Law Review* 23 (Winter 1983): 80.

57. David Q. Voigt, *American Baseball: From Postwar Expansion to the Electronic Age* (Norman: University of Oklahoma Press, 1970), 129.

58. Surdam, "Tale of Two Gate-Sharing Plans," 931–46.

59. "Basketball Franchise Shifted," *NYT*, Aug. 21, 1946, 21.

60. "Denver Five Joins Pros," *NYT*, Aug. 22, 1948, sec. V, 8.

61. "St. Louis Five Approved," *NYT*, May 12, 1955, 38; "NBA Gets Ultimatum from Washington Five," *NYT*, May 14, 1955, 17.

62. "Fort Wayne Five Shifted," *NYT*, Feb. 15, 1957, 27; King, "'NBA Needs Territorial Draft,'" sec. 2, 1; Tax, "Blessed Event," 38.

63. Cope, "Big Z and His Misfiring Pistons," 28.

64. Tommy Devine, "'Pistons Won't Quit Detroit'—Zollner," *TSN*, Jan. 29, 1958, sec. 2, 1; Tommy Devine, "17 Repeaters in NBA All-Star Classic," *TSN*, Jan. 21, 1959, sec. 2, 1; Bob Latshaw, "Tycoon Zollner Packed Power in Pistons," *TSN*, Jan. 21, 1959, sec. 2, 3.

65. "Royals' Quintet Shifts Franchise to Cincinnati," *NYT*, April 4, 1957, 45.

66. Fisher, "Rochester Royals," 41.

67. Jack McDonald, "Pro Cage Game 2 Years Away from West Coast," *Basketball's Best: 1958–59*, 30.

68. Quirk and Fort, *Pay Dirt*, 453, but there is no confirmation in *NYT*; "Lakers List Baylor No. 1 Choice in Draft," *NYT*, April 23, 1958, 47; "Baylor Becomes Pro with Minneapolis Five," *NYT*, June 15, 1958, S14; Tax, "Bunyan Strides Again," 18.

69. Jack McDonald, "Big Coast Crowd Spurs Lakers to Consider Shift," *TSN*, Jan. 21, 1959, sec. 2, 6.

70. Muray Olderman, "Elgin Baylor: One-Man Franchise," *Sport*, April 1959, 24–26 and 80–81.

71. Tax, "Bunyan Strides Again," 18; Tax, "Short, Sweet Series for Slick Celtics," 68.

72. Pluto, *Tall Tales*, 180.

73. Voigt, *American Baseball*, 129; Koppett, *24 Seconds to Shoot*, 134; Pluto, *Tall Tales*, 180. Koppett detailed the other owners' disdain of Irish's pursuit of self-interest: "The basketball writers had written a parody on the song 'Seven-and-a-Half-Cents,' from the musical 'Pajama Game,' that went: 'Seven votes to one vote. Every time a ballot's cast; Seven votes to one vote, That's the score today'" (Koppett, *24 Seconds to Shoot*, 134).

74. "Suitable Dates Must Be Provided," *NYT*, April 28, 1960, 48.

75. Ibid.

76. Pluto, *Tall Tales*, 182.

77. Ibid.

78. Bob Hunter, "Westward-Ho Lakers Strike Gold in L.A.," *TSN*, Jan. 28, 1961, sec. 2, 1–2.

79. Phil Elderkin, "Lakers Winning New Friends in 1st L.A. Season," *TSN*, sec. 2, 8.

80. "$850,000 Offered by San Francisco," *NYT*, May 3, 1962, 41; "Warriors Appear a Certainty to Transfer to San Francisco," *NYT*, April 12, 1962, 45; Robert Teague, "NBA Bars $850,000 Deal to Shift Warriors to West Coast," *NYT*, May 5, 1962, 23; William J. Briordy, "Warriors Shifted to Coast," *NYT*, May 24, 1962, 46.

81. "Four Cities Seek Basketball League Franchises," *NYT*, Dec. 21, 1954, 37.

82. Surdam, *Postwar Yankees*, 83–84; Bill Veeck, *The Hustler's Handbook* (New York: Putnam, 1965), 330.

83. Leonard Lewin, "Plenty of Good Players for NBA Expansion," New York Knickerbockers program, Dec. 26, 1955, 3.

84. Tax, "Blessed Event," 37. Another proposal was to admit two expansion teams. The incumbent teams could protect just six of their ten active players. The two expansion teams could choose among the thirty-two available players (King, "'NBA Needs Territorial Draft,'" sec. 2, 1).

85. King, "'NBA Needs Territorial Draft,'" sec. 2, 1.

86. U.S. House, *Organized Professional Team Sports*, 2867–68.

87. Quote from "Washington Bid Fails," *NYT*, April 29, 1956, sec. 5, 2; "New Pro Five Sought," *NYT*, March 10, 1956, 12; "Anti-Trust Suit Upheld," *NYT*, Dec. 13, 1956, 52.

88. "Question of Pro Basketball Expansion to Coast Put Off Till 1959 by NBA," *NYT*, May 8, 1958, 39.

89. Jerry Holtzman, "Saperstein Sees NBA Expansion to Coast in '59," *TSN*, Jan. 7, 1959, sec. 2, 8.

90. First Podoloff quote in Reidenbaugh, "NBA Shuns Coast Expansion," sec. 2, 1–2; second Podoloff quote in "NBA Moguls Consider Expansion," *TSN*, Jan. 21, 1959, sec. 2, 6. Ben Kerner preferred a second league of new clubs instead of expanding the NBA. He worried that a new club's struggles would be a drag on the established teams (James Enright, "Kerner Wants 2 Pro Cage Loops," *TSN*, Dec. 14, 1960, sec. 2, 8).

91. "National Basketball Association Admits Chicago as Ninth Team in League," *NYT*, Sept. 17, 1959, 53; Koppett, *24 Seconds to Shoot*, 143.

92. Lowell Reidenbaugh, "NBA Set to Reap Rich Rookie Harvest," *TSN*, Feb. 24, 1960, sec. 2, 1; "Pro Court League Wants 15 Teams," *NYT*, Nov. 3, 1959, 40; see also Phil Elderkin, "NBA Will Free 'Sweet 16' in Expansion Plan," *TSN*, Jan. 11, 1961, sec. 2, 8.

93. Koppett, *24 Seconds to Shoot*, 143–44.

94. Phil Elderkin, "Chi's Packers Spend 500 Gs to Finish Last," *TSN*, Dec. 27, 1961, sec. 2, 10.

95. "Pro Court League Wants 15 Teams," *NYT*, Nov. 3, 1959, 40; Maurice Podoloff, "Signs Point to Record Season," in *Official Basketball Guide, 1960–61*, 1960, 5. Adding an element of confusion was another press announcement reported in the *New York Times* that Chicago and Pittsburgh received franchises for the 1961–62 season ("Pittsburgh Gets Permit for Team," *NYT*, Oct. 8, 1960, 21).

96. Salzberg, *From Set Shot to Slam Dunk*, 233; Thomas, *They Cleared the Lane*, 251–55.

97. "Baylor, NBA Star, Balks at Hotel Ban," *NYT*, Jan. 17, 1959, 1 and 7.

98. Halsey Hall, "Baylor Built up His Game 'Playing Someone Better,'" *TSN*, Feb. 18, 1959, sec. 4, 4.

99. "Charleston Mayor Regrets Race Case," *NYT*, Jan. 19, 1959, 15.

100. Hall, "Baylor Built up His Game," sec. 4, 4.

101. Joseph Nichols, "Basketball Unit Will Discuss Bias, *NYT*, Jan. 18, 1959, 52.

102. Damon Stetson, "NBA Acts to Bar Racial Incidents," *NYT*, Jan. 23, 1959, 15.

103. JMOHRC, "NBA Bulletin #96," Sept. 18, 1950.

104. John Devaney, "Pro Basketball's Hidden Fear," *Sport*, Feb. 1966, 32–33, 89-90, and 92.

Appendix A. Estimating Factors Affecting Net Gate Receipts

1. Jeffrey M. Wooldridge, *Introductory Econometrics: A Modern Approach*, 4th ed. (Mason, OH: South-Western, Cengage Learning, 2009), 457.

Selected Bibliography

Official League Records

Association for Professional Basketball Research. "Basketball Association of America League Minutes, 1946–49." APBR.org/baaminutes.html.

Basketball Association of America. Bulletins and other materials. Housed at Joseph M. O'Brien Historical Resource Center, Naismith Memorial Basketball Hall of Fame.

National Basketball Association. Bulletins and other materials. Housed at Joseph M. O'Brien Historical Resource Center, Naismith Memorial Basketball Hall of Fame.

Books, Theses, Journals, and Other Articles

Auerbach, Red, and John Feinstein. *Let Me Tell You a Story: A Lifetime in the Game.* New York: Little, Brown, 2004.

Barry, Jack. "Pro Basketball's Future Promising." *Boston Garden Arena Sports News* 20, no. 5 (1947–48): 9 and 11.

———. "New Stars Shine in Garden." *Boston Garden Arena Sports News* 21, no. 3 (1948–49): 9, 11, and 30–31.

Bjarkman, Peter C. *The Encyclopedia of Pro Basketball Team Histories.* New York: Carroll and Graf, 1994.

Brock, Ted. "NBA Attendance." *Total Basketball,* 321–26.

Byers, Walter. *Unsportsmanlike Conduct: Exploiting College Athletes.* Ann Arbor: University of Michigan Press, 1995.

Carter, Craig, and Rob Reheuser, eds. *The Sporting News Official NBA Guide, 2002–2003 Edition.* St. Louis, Mo.: Sporting News, 2002.

Coase, Ronald. "The Problem of Social Cost." *Journal of Law and Economics* 3 (1960): 1–44.

Coenen, Craig R. *From Sandlots to the Super Bowl: The National Football League.* Knoxville: University of Tennessee Press, 2005.

Cohen, Haskell. "History of the National Basketball Association." In *Official Basketball Guide, 1958–59.* St. Louis, Mo.: Sporting News, 1958. 5 and 7.

———. "Review of 1958–59 Season." In *Official Basketball Guide, 1959–60.* St. Louis, Mo.: Sporting News, 1959. 7.

———. "Review of the 1959–60 Season." In *Official Basketball Guide, 1960–61.* St. Louis, Mo.: Sporting News, 1960. 7.

Cole, Lewis. *A Loose Game: The Sport and Business of Basketball.* Indianapolis: Bobbs-Merrill, 1978.

Dodd, Donald. *Historical Statistics of the States of the United States: Two Centuries of the Census, 1790–1990.* Westport, Conn.: Greenwood Press, 1993.

Durslag, Melvin. "Short Finds Rich Pickings in Los Angeles." *Syracuse Basketball Magazine* (1962–63): 3.

Embry, Wayne. *The Inside Game: Race, Power, and Politics in the NBA.* Akron, Ohio: University of Akron Press, 2004.

Figone, Albert J. "Gambling and College Basketball: The Scandal of 1951." *Journal of Sport History* 16 (1989): 44–61.

Fisher, Donald M. 1993. "The Rochester Royals and the Transformation of Professional Basketball, 1945–57." *International Journal of the History of Sport* 10 (1993): 20–48.

Fort, Rodney D. *Sports Economics*, 2nd ed. Upper Saddle River, N.J.: Pearson Education, 2006.

"Gambling in the Garden." *Time* 44, no. 18 (1944): 81.

Gems, Gerald R. "Blocked Shot: The Development of Basketball in the African-American Community of Chicago." *Journal of Sport History* 22 (1995): 135–48.

Glick, Jeffrey. "Professional Sports Franchise Movements and the Sherman Act: When and Where Teams Should Be Able to Move." *Santa Clara Law Review* 23 (Winter 1983): 55–94.

Golenpaul, Dan, ed. *Information Please Almanac: Atlas and Yearbook, 1966.* New York: Simon and Schuster, 1965.

Gregory, Fletcher H. *Professional Basketball Players' Challenges to the Legality of NBA Policies, 1954–1976.* Master's thesis. Pennsylvania State University, State College, 1985.

Grundman, Adolph H. *The Golden Age of Amateur Basketball: The AAU Tournament, 1921–1968.* Lincoln: University of Nebraska Press, 2004.

Hollander, Zander, ed. *The Modern Encyclopedia of Basketball*, 2nd ed. Garden City, N.Y.: Dolphin Books, 1979.

Isaacs, Neil. *Vintage NBA: The Pioneer Era, 1946–1956.* Indianapolis: Masters Press, 1996.

Janoff, Murray. "Pro Moguls Constantly Trying to Better Game." In New York Knickerbockers program. November 11, 1954. 3.

Johnson, Lloyd, and Miles Wolff, eds. *The Encyclopedia of Minor League Baseball.* Durham, N.C.: Baseball America, 1993.

Jordan, Jerry N. *The Long-Range Effect of Television and Other Factors on Sports Attendance.* Master's thesis, University of Pennsylvania, Philadelphia, 1950.

Kieran, John, ed. *Information Please Almanac 1952.* New York: Macmillan, 1951.

Kirchberg, Connie. *Hoop Lore: A History of the National Basketball Association.* Jefferson, N.C.: McFarland, 2007.

"Knicks' 18 Garden League Games This Season Will be Televised." In New York Knickerbockers program. October 28, 1950. 11.

"Knicks-Syracuse Game Tonight Played with 12-Foot Foul Lanes." In New York Knickerbockers program. October 28, 1950. 11.

Koppett, Leonard. *The Essence of the Game Is Deception: Thinking about Basketball.* Boston: Sports Illustrated Books, 1973.

———. *24 Seconds to Shoot.* 1968. Kingston, NY: Total Sports Illustrated Classics, 1999.

Lewin, Leonard. "Plenty of Good Players for NBA Expansion." In New York Knickerbockers program. December 26, 1955. 3.

Maher, Tod, and Bob Gill. *The Pro Football Encyclopedia: The Complete and Definitive Record of Professional Football.* New York: Macmillan, 1997.

McDonald, Jack. "Pro Cage Game 2 Years away from West Coast." In *Basketball's Best: A Pictorial Review of the 1958–59 NBA.* Coral Gables, FL: Bruce Hale Publications, 1958. 30.

Miller, Marvin. *A Whole Different Ball Game: The Sport and Business of Baseball.* New York: Birch Lane Press Book, 1991.

Mokray, Bill, ed. *1961 Official NBA Guide.* St. Louis, Mo.: Sporting News, 1961.

———. *1962–63 Official NBA Guide.* St. Louis, Mo.: Sporting News, 1962.

Morris, Everett B. "Professional Basketball—What Is Its Future?" In New York Knickerbockers program. February 23, 1954. 3.

Moskowitz, Tobias J., and L. Jon Wertheim. *Scorecasting: The Hidden Influences behind How Sports Are Played and Games Are Won.* New York: Crown Archetype, 2011.

Neal-Lunsford, Jeff. "Sport in the Land of Television: The Use of Sport in Network Prime-Time Schedules, 1946–50." *Journal of Sport History* 19 (1992): 56–76.

Neft, David S., and Richard M. Cohen. *The Sports Encyclopedia: Pro Basketball,* 5th ed. New York: St. Martin's, 1992.

Nelson, Murry. *The National Basketball League: A History, 1935–1949.* Jefferson, N.C.: McFarland, 2009.

Peterson, Robert W. *Cages to Jump Shots: Pro Basketball's Early Years.* New York: Oxford University Press, 1990.

Pluto, Terry. *Tall Tales: The Glory Years of the NBA.* New York: Simon and Schuster, 1992.

Podoloff, Maurice. "Signs Point to Record Season." In Mokray, *Official Basketball Guide, 1960–61.* 5.

Pomerantz, Gary. *Wilt, 1962: The Night of 100 Points and the Dawn of a New Era.* New York: Crown Publishers, 2005.

Quirk, James, and Rodney D. Fort. *Pay Dirt: The Business of Professional Team Sports.* Princeton, N.J.: Princeton University Press, 1992.

Rosen, Charles. *Scandals of '51.* New York: Holt, Rinehart, and Winston, 1978.

Rottenberg, Simon. "The Baseball Players' Labor Market." *Journal of Political Economy* 64 (1956): 242–58.

Sachare, Alex, ed. *The Official NBA Basketball Encyclopedia,* 2nd ed. New York: Villard Books, 1994.

Salzberg, Charles. *From Set Shot to Slam Dunk: The Glory Days of Basketball in the Words of Those Played It.* 1987. Lincoln: University of Nebraska Press, 1998.

———. "Basketball Arenas." *Total Basketball,* 311–20.

Schumacher, Michael. *Mr. Basketball: George Mikan, The Minneapolis Lakers, and the Birth of the NBA.* New York: Bloomsbury USA, 2007.

Sexton, Bob. "The Father of the 24-Second Rule, Danny Biasone . . . Emigrant Boy to President of the World Champions." In *Basketball's Best: A Pictorial Review of the 1955–56 NBA.* Coral Gables, FL: Bruce Hale Publications, 1995. 6.

Surdam, David. "The American 'Not-So-Socialist' League in the Postwar Era: The Limitations of Gate Sharing in Reducing Revenue Disparity in Baseball." *Journal of Sports Economics* 3 (August 2002): 264–90.

———. "The Coase Theorem and Player Movement in Major League Baseball." *Journal of Sports Economics* 7 (May 2006): 201–21.

———. "A Tale of Two Gate-Sharing Plans: The National Football League and the National League, 1952–1956." *Southern Economic Journal* 73 (April 2007): 931–46.

———. *The Postwar Yankees: Baseball's Golden Age Revisited.* Lincoln: University of Nebraska Press, 2008.

———. "What Brings Fans to the Ball Park? Evidence from New York Yankees' and Philadelphia Phillies' Financial Records." *Journal of Economics* 35 (2009): 35–48.

———. *Wins, Losses, and Empty Seats: Baseball during the Depression.* Lincoln: University of Nebraska Press, 2011.

Thomas, Ron. *They Cleared the Lane: The NBA's Black Pioneers.* Lincoln: University of Nebraska Press, 2002.

Thorn, John, Pete Palmer, and Michael Gershman, eds. *Total Baseball: The Official Encyclopedia of Major League Baseball,* 7th ed. (Kingston, N.Y.: Total Sports Publishing, 2001).

Total Basketball: The Ultimate Basketball Encyclopedia. Wilmington, Del.: Sport Classic Books, 2003.

Triptow, Richard F. *The Dynasty That Never Was: Chicago's First Professional Basketball Champions—The American Gears.* n.p.: Richard F. Triptow, 1996.

U.S. Department of Commerce. *Statistical Abstract of the United States, 1952.* Washington, D.C.: U.S. Government Printing Office, 1952.

———. *Census of Population,* Vol. 1. *Characteristics of Population.* Pt. A, Number of Inhabitants. Washington, D.C.: U.S. Government Printing Office, 1961.

———. Bureau of the Census. *Historical Statistics of the United States: Colonial Times to 1970.* Washington, D.C.: U.S. Government Printing Office, 1975.

U.S. House. *Organized Baseball: Hearings before the Subcommittee on Study of Monopoly Power of the Committee on the Judiciary.* Serial no. 1. Pt. 6. 82nd Cong., 1st sess. Washington, D.C.: U.S. Government Printing Office, 1952.

———. *Organized Baseball: Report of the Subcommittee on Study of Monopoly Power of the Committee on the Judiciary Pursuant to H. Res. 95. Documents and Reports.* House Report no. 2002, 6. 82nd Cong., 1st sess. Washington, D.C.: U.S. Government Printing Office, 1952.

———. Antitrust Subcommittee, Committee on the Judiciary. *Organized Professional Team Sports: Hearings before the Antitrust Subcommittee of the Committee on the Judiciary.* Serial no. 8. 85th Congress. Washington, D.C.: U.S. Government Printing Office, 1957.

———. Antitrust Subcommittee, Committee on the Judiciary. *A Bill to Allow the Merger of Two or More Professional Basketball Leagues.* 92nd Congress. Washington, D.C.: U.S. Government Printing Office, 1972.

———. Committee on Education and the Workforce. Subcommittee on Employer-Employee Relations. *Pension Fairness for NBA Pioneers.* 105th Congress, 2nd sess. Washington, D.C.: U.S. Government Printing Office, 1998.

Veeck, Bill. *The Hustler's Handbook.* New York: Putnam, 1965.

Voigt, David Q. *American Baseball: From Postwar Expansion to the Electronic Age.* Norman: University of Oklahoma Press, 1970.

Westcott, Rich. *The Mogul: Eddie Gottlieb, Philadelphia Sports Legend and Pro Basketball Pioneer.* Philadelphia: Temple University Press, 2008.

Wong, John Chi-Kit. *Lord of the Rinks: The Emergence of the National Hockey League, 1875–1936.* Toronto: University of Toronto Press, 2005.

Wooldridge, Jeffrey M. *Introductory Econometrics: A Modern Approach,* 4th ed. Mason, Ohio: South-Western, Cengage Learning, 2009.

Young, Dick. "The Solution—Make Them Shoot!" In New York Knickerbockers program. December 25, 1953. 3.

Young, Stephen B. *The History of Professional Basketball, 1946–1979.* Master's thesis. Western Illinois University, Macomb, 1981.

Index

Abdul-Jabbar, Kareem, 54, 72, 105, 117, 146, 227n45
African American coaches, 162
African American players, 82, 108, 124–25; and attendance, 135, 163; and competitive balance, 69, 145, 150; and discrimination, 17–18, 83, 84, 162–63, 212n92; and salaries, 46. *See also* integration
Alcindor, Lew. *See* Abdul-Jabbar, Kareem
Allen, Forrest ("Phog"), 76, 105
All-NBA Teams, 182–83
All-Star games, 26, 84, 91–92, 130, 144
Amateur Athletic Union (AAU), 129, 197n6; and player salaries, 45, 46, 158, 166, 204n78, 204n81; and quality of play, 39, 42
American Basketball Association (ABA), 35, 54, 59, 152, 167
American Basketball League (ABL), 23, 43, 49, 65, 78, 162, 167, 209n39; founding of, by Abe Saperstein, 59, 221n35
American Professional Football Association (APFA), 21
Anderson Packers, 38, 63, 70, 71, 217n55; and merger of the BAA and NBL, 57–58, 64–65, 208n37
antitrust exemptions, 5, 85–86; and congressional hearings (1957), 7, 113–14, 129, 159
arenas. *See* facilities
Arizin, Paul, 117
attendance, 59–60, 174, 179, 181, 190, 201n37; and All-Star games, 91–92; and base-

ball, 28, 37, 87, 89, 133, 224n5; and the Boston Celtics, 26, 61, 88, 112, 149, 163; and city size, 89, 153, 165; and debut of the BAA, 24; and doubleheaders, 29, 68, 87, 89–90; and the Harlem Globetrotters, 89, 134, 213n10; and integration, 135, 163; at Madison Square Garden, 28, 29, 30, 56, 61, 88, 89, 181, 202n39, 213n2; and marquee players, 87–88; and the National Basketball League (NBL), 30–31, 90; and the National Hockey League (NHL), 29, 87, 201n29, 201n35; and the New York Knicks, 28, 29, 30, 60, 61, 133, 181, 201n37; and promotions, 90–91; and revenue, 27–31, 60, 91, 112, 179; rising, 133–35, 163; and the Rochester Royals, 30–31, 61, 90, 153; and the shot clock, 123; and television, 112, 128, 129–30
Auerbach, Arnold ("Red"), 42, 118; and the Boston Celtics, 26, 73, 88, 147, 148, 149, 150; and the Washington Capitols, 34, 40, 41

Baechtold, Jim, 123
ball imperfections, 51–52
Baltimore Bullets, 49, 58, 59, 84, 93, 124, 208n28; and attendance, 127–28; and championship titles, 43, 63; folding of the, 58, 63, 67, 73, 123, 159
Baltimore Wizards, 161
Barksdale, Don, 39, 84

DAVID GEORGE SURDAM is an associate professor of economics at the University of Northern Iowa and the author of *Wins, Losses, and Empty Seats: How Baseball Outlasted the Great Depression.*

The University of Illinois Press
is a founding member of the
Association of American University Presses.

Composed in 10.5/13 Minion Pro Regular
with Century Gothic display
by Celia Shapland
at the University of Illinois Press
Manufactured by Thomson-Shore, Inc.

University of Illinois Press
1325 South Oak Street
Champaign, IL 61820-6903
www.press.uillinois.edu